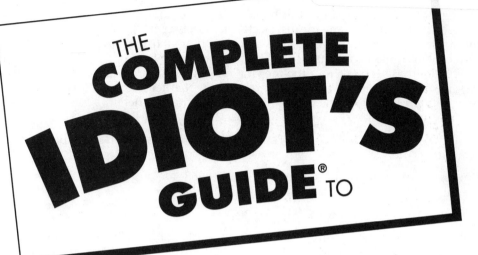

THE
COMPLETE
IDIOT'S
GUIDE® TO

Sports History & Trivia

by Mike McGovern

ALPHA

A Pearson Education Company

Copyright © 2002 by Mike McGovern

THE COMPLETE IDIOT'S GUIDE TO and Design are registered trademarks of Pearson Education, Inc.

International Standard Book Number: 0-02-863963-4
Library of Congress Catalog Card Number: 2001093556

04   03   02   8   7   6   5   4   3   2   1

Interpretation of the printing code: The rightmost number of the first series of numbers is the year of the book's printing; the rightmost number of the second series of numbers is the number of the book's printing. For example, a printing code of 02-1 shows that the first printing occurred in 2002.

Printed in the United States of America

Publisher
Marie Butler-Knight

Product Manager
Phil Kitchel

Managing Editor
Jennifer Chisholm

Acquisitions Editor
Randy Ladenheim-Gil

Development Editor
Michael Thomas

Production Editor
Billy Fields

Copy Editor
Amy Borrelli

Illustrator
Jody P. Schaeffer

Cover Designers
Mike Freeland
Kevin Spear

Book Designers
Scott Cook and Amy Adams of DesignLab

Indexer
Tonya Heard

Layout/Proofreading
Angela Calvert
John Etchison
Kimberly Tucker

Contents at a Glance

Appendixes

Contents

Foreword

Sports trivia. Like jumbo shrimp, it's an oxymoron. I mean, to a true sports fan there is *no* tidbit of information too trivial, too insignificant not to get excited about. There is no gray area not worth debating, especially when it comes with conflicting stories, such as the question of who really invented baseball, one of the many topics Mike McGovern adroitly covers in this book. In short, there is nothing "trivial" about it.

At ESPN, we are subjected to literally thousands of facts, statistics, and anecdotes each night. Working there is like being in a sports bar on steroids. From my desk alone, I can see twelve TVs, have access to thirty more, and at any one time we will have two dozen different events on in eight different sports, from four different continents! Rooms full of press guides, almanacs, yearbooks, record books ... safe to say there is *lots* of information on every sport imaginable. Yet it never seems to get boring, and most times it is far more than that. It is entertaining, frequently enlightening, and often literally delightful.

Like a child opening a present, when we "open" some meaty sports trivia fact, we are excited by what we will find. Will we be surprised? Disappointed? Will we say, "Oh yeah, I *knew* that!" reaffirming our knowledge of the games we love, or will we add some new nugget of information that makes our involvement with the sport that much more enjoyable?

Through sports trivia, we weave with that invisible thread the continuity that makes sports great. The stories and riddles that are inherent in sports trivia unite us, giving so many of us who may have little else in common some shared memories. It brings different segments of society together, it serves as a bond from one generation to the next, and on top of that, it provides great fodder for a debate at the local pub, or as a way to pass the hours on a long road trip.

All that from something called "trivia." Seems anything but, doesn't it? As such, you need to leave something this important in expert hands—and you have here in Mike McGovern's. He takes you down an enlightening and entertaining path as you discover things you didn't know, corrects some things you thought you *did* know, and makes the journey one of great fun every step of the way.

You know, there are nights when I can't remember a friend's phone number. And yet I *do* remember that Charlie Silvera was the bullpen catcher for many of the Yankees championship teams in the '40s and '50s; or that the reason Chuck Mercein has his hands up in the air in the famous Ice Bowl photograph—where Bart Starr sneaks in behind Jerry Kramer's and Ken Bowman's blocks to win the 1967 NFL championship game—is *not* to signal "touchdown," but so the officials wouldn't think he illegally helped push Starr across the goal line. And I think, "Wouldn't I be better served if I could somehow let that go, and make room in my head for the more practical day-to-day stuff?"

Then I read a book like this, and I am reminded how tragic that would be.

Bob Valvano
ESPN Radio

Bob Valvano joined ESPN Radio as the host of the V Show (Late GameNight) in 1998. Prior to that he served as analyst for University of Louisville basketball telecasts and sideline reporter for television coverage of University of Louisville football games. He coached basketball for 19 seasons before entering broadcasting full time. He successfully rebuilt four different college programs, setting all-time records for wins in a season at three different colleges—Kutztown University, Catholic University, and St. Mary's College. His last season on the sidelines saw him guide Bellarmine College to its 10th winningest season, and a No. 25 power rating in Division II. Valvano lettered in soccer, basketball, and golf at Virginia Wesleyan College, and was named All-Conference 1st team and soccer MVP.

Introduction

It's not exactly a news flash to say that sports have become a major part of many people's lives.

Fans live and die with their favorite teams; they paint their faces in the colors of their favorite teams; they spend big bucks to outfit themselves from head to toe in the clothing of their favorite teams.

ESPN, the all-sports television network—not to mention the "worldwide leader" in sports—is one of the most recognizable brand names in the world. And there's not just one ESPN; there's ESPN2, ESPNews, and ESPN Classic. There is even a TV network dedicated solely to golf.

Certain sporting events go way beyond sports; they're happenings. The Super Bowl might as well be declared a national holiday. The Olympics, Winter and Summer, entice fans to watch sports they've never heard of. And Tiger Woods has transformed even routine golf tournaments into major events.

This book will help give you a broad overview of many different sports, in case you're not quite up to speed on all of them. It will also satisfy your craving for more sports history and trivia if you just can't get enough.

What You'll Find in This Book

The Complete Idiot's Guide to Sports History and Trivia is divided into seven sections.

Part 1, "America's First Great Sport," explains the origins of baseball, and takes a look at some of the game's greatest players and most significant occurrences.

This section also explains the impact of the Negro Leagues and of Jackie Robinson, the first African American to break the color barrier in Major League Baseball.

Part 2, "Football: America's New Pastime," details the tremendous growth of football, from its early days when it was played only in college to the pro leagues that predated the National Football League to the game today.

You'll learn about early icons such as Jim Thorpe and Bronko Nagurski; great college coaches such as Joe Paterno and Paul "Bear" Bryant; and outstanding players such as Johnny Unitas and Jerry Rice. We'll also relive some of the most memorable Super Bowl moments.

In **Part 3, "Hoop Dreams,"** you'll find out that basketball really was invented using a peach basket as the goal.

The game has come a long way since its earliest days, and we'll check out the players, coaches, and events that helped shape basketball.

In **Part 4, "Going It Alone: Golf, Tennis, and Boxing,"** individual sports take center stage. Golf and tennis are each steeped in tradition; boxing, on the other hand, has a tradition that in recent years has left a lot to be desired.

But all three sports boast terrific champions—Jack Nicklaus and Tiger Woods in golf, Rod Laver and Billie Jean King in tennis, Muhammad Ali and Sugar Ray Leonard in boxing. We'll learn about them and many more.

Hockey and soccer are the focus of **Part 5, "Frozen Ponds, Big Kicks."** We'll look at the development of the National Hockey League, from the "Original Six" teams to the 30 that are in the league today, as well as the stars who paved the way.

For many people in the United States, Pele is the only soccer player they know. You'll learn about his impact on the game, and the impact made by the victorious U.S. Women's World Cup team.

In **Part 6, "The Olympic Spirit,"** we explore the Summer and Winter Games. We'll look at the origins of the Olympics and the athletes that have become household names—Jesse Owens, Mark Spitz, Olga Korbut, Peggy Fleming, Bonnie Blair, Jean-Claude Killy, and many more.

The final section, **Part 7, "Speed Thrills,"** explains the different types of auto racing—Indy car, NASCAR, drag racing, and Formula One. You'll find out about some of the most accomplished drivers of all time—Indy car's Mario Andretti, NASCAR's Richard Petty, drag racing's John Force, and Formula One's Alain Prost, to name a few.

The last chapter in each part contains a quiz of 20 questions and answers. You also get some concluding facts and figures and quotable quotes.

Extras

In addition to the book's seven parts, you'll find four types of sidebars that provide little bits of information that might come in handy.

The Fundamentals

These boxes contain definitions of terms to help you better understand the basics and lingo of each sport.

Sports Strategies

These tips supply factual information that add to your knowledge about a subject or a person.

The Inside Skinny

These entries provide some behind-the-scenes information.

Two-Minute Warning

These tidbits will help correct mistaken impressions you might have had about athletes and their sports.

Acknowledgments

Thanks go to Randy Ladenheim-Gil, Mike Thomas, and Billy Fields at Pearson Education, and copy editor Amy Borrelli, for their advice and patience; to Bert Holtje of James Peter Associates, a wonderful man whose encouragement and guidance were invaluable; to Diane Staskowski, whose photographs provide another reason to buy this book; and to Bob Valvano (whom I knew before he hit the big time), who remains one of the nicest guys you'll ever meet and who graciously agreed to write the foreword.

But the biggest thanks go to my wife, Susan, and our two kids, Sara and Ryan, who couldn't have been more understanding. They made me realize I couldn't be more fortunate.

Trademarks

All terms mentioned in this book that are known to be or are suspected of being trademarks or service marks have been appropriately capitalized. Alpha Books and Pearson Education, Inc. cannot attest to the accuracy of this information. Use of a term in this book should not be regarded as affecting the validity of any trademark or service mark.

Part 1

America's First Great Sport

The first thing that strikes you about baseball's early days is the uncertainty about who invented the game. If you're like most folks, you'd probably say Abner Double-day, but you'll find out otherwise in Chapter 1, "Play Ball!"

You'll also find out that a baseball player was responsible for a landmark event that went way beyond the fun and games of sport. Jackie Robinson's breaking of the major league color barrier was a big story on more than just the sports pages.

Who's the one baseball player that everyone has heard of? That's an easy one. Babe Ruth. In this part, we'll look at the Bambino's career and its impact on the game, along with some other players such as Hank Aaron, Ted Williams, and Mickey Mantle. There are sections on the great pitchers, such as Sandy Koufax and Bob Gibson, and on today's best players, such as Barry Bonds and Mark McGwire. You'll also find out how Mother Nature rocked the 1989 World Series.

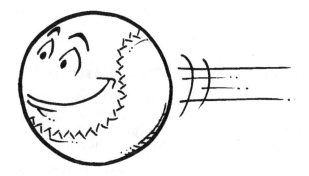

Chapter 1

Play Ball!

In This Chapter

➤ The games people played before baseball

➤ Abner Doubleday: inventor or impostor?

➤ The birth of the pro leagues

➤ The Negro leagues and players

➤ The impact of Jackie Robinson

Baseball was America's first great sport, although ironically, the game was developed in England as an offshoot of cricket. Before we called it baseball, the game had a variety of names and two inventors, one of whom turned out to be the figment of someone's imagination. But none of that kept baseball from becoming hugely popular.

The rules of the game were standardized in 1845 by Alexander Cartwright. He's the person credited with inventing the game we know today. But for a long time, historians gave all the credit to Abner Doubleday. As you'll see later in this chapter, ol' Abner was an impostor. Word has it that he didn't even like outdoor activities. Too bad there weren't domed stadiums in those days.

Regardless of who invented the game, there's no question that it caught on then like *Survivor* has now. There were teams in small towns and big cities. The first pro team was formed soon after the Civil War ended, and the Cincinnati Red Stockings actually paid players, a concept that would catch on.

The Negro leagues were formed out of necessity at about the same time, because African Americans weren't welcome to play on the same team with whites. Some of the game's greatest players played in the Negro leagues—even though it would be years before they were officially recognized.

Sports Strategies

Henry Chadwick was the first newspaper reporter to cover baseball. In an article for *Spalding's Baseball Guide* in 1903, Chadwick, a native of England, wrote that baseball was a descendant of rounders. This piece of information didn't sit well with A.G. Spalding, the publisher, who insisted that baseball was an American invention.

Before There Was Baseball

Stick and ball games are nothing new. Even cavemen are thought to have enjoyed them in between hunting and drawing on the walls of their caves. Baseball as we know it originated from an English game called rounders.

Now, what the heck is rounders, you ask? Well, rounders was played using four posts on a field laid out like a pentagon with one open side. The batter stood 28 feet from the bowler, whose job it was to throw the ball above the knee and below the head of the batter. The object was to hit the ball and get from the first post to the fourth post.

Circling the posts was called a rounder and was worth one point. There were nine players on a team, nine outs in an inning, and two innings in a match.

By the late 1700s, rounders began to be called townball, because the rules changed from town to town. So did the name. The game also was known as bat and ball, or stickball, or base, or baste. But it didn't matter a bit what the game was called. The main thing was that people loved playing it.

The Myth of Abner Doubleday

Imagine that you're sitting in the hot seat on *Who Wants to Be a Millionaire?* and Regis asks, "Who invented baseball?" If Abner Doubleday was your final answer, you'd be accepting condolences from Regis, because you'd be dead wrong.

It's true that the early histories of the game cite Doubleday as the inventor, but that turned out to be a bum steer. Doubleday received credit because of A.G. Spalding, who was a publisher and sporting goods magnate. Spalding, his buttons bursting with nationalistic pride, couldn't bear to believe that baseball was anything other than a completely American game, and he authorized a group of researchers to prove it.

The "proof" came largely in the form of one letter, written by a man named Abner Graves. Graves's letter told a wonderful story of how he grew up in Cooperstown, New York, with Doubleday, who invented baseball in 1839.

That letter was all Spalding needed. He was thrilled to think that Doubleday, who went on to become a major general for the Union in the Civil War, had invented baseball.

But it turned out Graves's story contained a few holes—holes big enough to drive a Chevy Suburban through. First of all, Doubleday had never set foot in Cooperstown, let alone attend school there. In 1839, when he was supposedly inventing baseball in Cooperstown, he was actually attending West Point as a cadet.

There was also no mention of Doubleday inventing baseball in his numerous diaries and writings. And here's the real kicker: Doubleday didn't even like sports. His favorite outdoor activity was topography, making maps of the area surrounding his family home in Auburn, New York.

Poor old Graves, who was in his 80s when he wrote the letter, died shortly afterwards in an insane asylum.

Two-Minute Warning

Abner Graves, whose letter was the basis for crediting Abner Doubleday with inventing baseball, claimed to be a childhood playmate of Doubleday's in Cooperstown, New York. Even though there was no evidence that the letter was true, it was accepted as fact. The verification of Graves's story, if you could call it that, was based largely on a rotting baseball found among his personal effects.

The Real Inventor

Alexander Cartwright, who standardized the rules of the game in 1845, is the person who deserves the credit for inventing baseball as we know it today. Here's what he did:

➤ Reconfigured the field into a diamond shape

➤ Placed the bases 90 feet apart

➤ Renamed the fourth base "home"

➤ Established that three strikes were an out and that three outs constituted a half-inning

Cartwright's contributions to the game didn't become public until 1937, when it was decided that the National Baseball Hall of Fame would be located in Cooperstown. Why? Because it was still the common belief that Doubleday had invented the game there, of course.

But during the planning for the Hall of Fame, Cartwright's grandson, Bruce, decided enough was enough. He wrote to baseball officials and told them about his grandfather. He even produced his grandfather's diaries as further proof.

Bruce Cartwright's case was made airtight when Robert Henderson, a New York City librarian, offered his own research, which showed Cartwright was the inventor.

Even though Doubleday was exposed as an impostor, the Hall of Fame was nevertheless built in Cooperstown. But any doubt as to who invented the game should be erased once you get inside. Alexander Cartwright is enshrined there. Abner Doubleday isn't.

The Professional Leagues Are Born

The first organized baseball league was formed in 1858. The National Association of Base Ball Players (NABBP) was made up of 22 amateur teams from the New York City area. Over the next two years, teams from Pennsylvania and New Jersey were added. After the Civil War, when people presumably had more time and less stress, membership in the league grew to more than 300 teams in 1867.

The NABBP was against professionalism, even though—wink, wink—many players were secretly paid or given jobs by sponsors. But the NABBP wasn't against charging admission to games. Once the players realized someone was making money off them, it was only a matter of time before they decided that they wanted in on the action.

That time came in 1869 when the Cincinnati Red Stockings became the first professional team. Two brothers, Harry and George Wright, recruited the best players in the United States and took them on a tour. The Red Stockings trampled the competition. They won 56 straight games, tied a game, and then won 27 more in a row. They finally lost to the Brooklyn Athletics in 1870.

The Fundamentals

The **National League,** formed in 1876, was made up of eight teams: Chicago, St. Louis, Cincinnati, Louisville, Boston, Hartford, New York, and Philadelphia. Not surprisingly, the National League is referred to as the Senior Circuit.

From then on, paying players became the rule, not the exception. The amateur leagues couldn't compete—who'd want to play for free when there were dollars to be pocketed?—so most of them disappeared.

The first pro league, the National Association, was formed in 1871 with nine teams, but it lasted only a few seasons. The fans stayed away because they didn't like the gambling that took place, and they also didn't like the fact that liquor was sold at the games. Coors and Budweiser are thankful that's not the case today.

The National Association was replaced by the *National League,* which has been in operation ever since. The reason it survived early on was simple: Businessmen ran the National League, not the players.

The National League was able to withstand challenges from the Union Association in 1884 and the Players League in 1890. Both wannabe leagues went belly-up after one season.

That was not the case with the American League, which began play in 1901. The AL prospered by raiding the National League of its best players. The NL owners ended up turning on each other, and it took a three-man commission to restore order.

Maybe those three guys should've left their peacemaking formula for the generations to follow, because the two leagues have been able to coexist ever since.

Mixing It Up

If you remember your American history lessons, you're aware that the professional baseball we've been talking about until now was exclusively a white man's game. The United States was a segregated nation—and baseball would continue to be segregated until 1947.

But just because African Americans weren't allowed to play with whites, didn't mean they didn't play. Some of the best players in baseball history were black. It's just that it took awhile for most white folks to notice. And the real shame is that it took decades before black players got the chance to showcase their talents in the National and American leagues.

The first officially recorded appearance of a black baseball team occurred in 1867. The occasion was the "championship of the colored clubs," and it featured the Uniques of Brooklyn, who played host to the Excelsiors of Philadelphia. The Excelsiors won (yep, you heard it correctly) 37–24.

The first black professional team was formed in 1885. The Cuban Giants, which originated on Long Island, New York, played mostly exhibition games, and from 1889 through 1891, represented three successive cities in three different leagues.

It wasn't until 1920 that Andrew "Rube" Foster, who would come to be known as the father of black baseball, founded the Negro National League. Financial problems plagued the Negro National League and other black leagues that popped up from time to time. All of them eventually folded.

In 1933, a new Negro National League was formed, and four years later, the Negro American League began. The two leagues existed until 1948, the year after the color barrier in Major League Baseball was broken by Jackie Robinson.

The Inside Skinny

The Negro leagues played much shorter seasons than the white major league teams did. When the Negro league season was over, the players went on barnstorming tours on which they played exhibition games, often involving some of the best players from the National and American leagues. The Kansas City Monarchs barnstormed without a league affiliation from 1931 through 1936, and they did so with a portable lighting system that allowed night games to be played.

Unfortunately, the stars of the Negro leagues were unknown and unappreciated by most of the white baseball fans of the day. Their exploits went unnoticed and their accomplishments unheralded.

The Fundamentals

Batting average is calculated by dividing the number of hits by the number of times at bat. These days, anything above .270 is considered good. Hitting above .300 makes a player a rich man. Not since Ted Williams did it in 1941 has a player hit .400.

Sports Strategies

When the Homestead Grays folded in 1948, Buck Leonard was making $1,000 a month, plus $2-a-day meal money. It was reported that he was the third-highest paid player in the Negro leagues, behind Satchel Paige and Josh Gibson. That's a far cry from what he was making in 1934, his first year with the Grays, when he took home $125 a month and got 60¢ a day for meals.

Even though the game became integrated in 1947, it took another 15 years before the Hall of Fame opened its doors to Negro league players.

Lethal Weapons

They were a pitcher's worst nightmare. Josh Gibson, a catcher, was known as the black Babe Ruth. His teammate on the Homestead Grays, first baseman Walter "Buck" Leonard, was often called the Lou Gehrig of the Negro leagues. Talk about a 1-2 combination!

Leonard had Popeye arms and powerfully built legs. He was a great fielder and a dangerous hitter. He spent his entire 17-year career with the legendary Homestead Grays, and he was a prime reason for their success—nine straight league titles, from 1937 through 1945, and another in 1948. Leonard had a *batting average* of .300 or better 10 times and .400 or better three times.

A year after he retired from the Grays in 1951, Leonard received an offer from the St. Louis Browns of the American League. He was 44, however, and realized that his best days were behind him. He declined the opportunity.

Gibson was a Paul Bunyan–like character with larger-than-life accomplishments. The Negro National League Baseball Museum credits him with hitting 972 home runs in an 18-year career. (For comparison, Hank Aaron, the all-time leader, hit 755 in a 22-year career.) To save you the trouble of doing the math, that computes to an average of 54 home runs a season. The Baseball Hall of Fame claims the number is somewhat lower, "almost 800." Still, you'd definitely want him in your lineup. (It's also been said that he hit 84 home runs in one season. Eat your heart out, Mark McGwire.)

Regardless of the disparity in statistics, which weren't nearly as precise in those days, there is no doubt that Gibson was a home run machine. Judy Johnson, another of Gibson's teammates who is also a Hall of Famer, said, "If Josh Gibson had been in the big leagues in his prime, Babe Ruth and Hank Aaron would still be chasing him for the home run record."

Can you imagine the salaries Leonard and Gibson could command in today's over-inflated market? It boggles the mind.

Gibson was no slouch when it came to hitting for average, either. His lifetime batting average in the Negro National League was .391 and he won the league batting title in 1943 with the Homestead Grays, hitting .521. Plus, the guy was renowned as perhaps the best catcher in baseball. Not just Negro League Baseball, but all of baseball.

Unfortunately, Gibson never made it to the major leagues, even though it was rumored that the Pittsburgh Pirates and the Washington Senators considered making him offers. Neither did. He didn't even see Jackie Robinson break the color barrier. Gibson died of a cerebral hemorrhage on Jan. 20, 1947, one month after his 35th birthday and less than three months before Robinson made history.

Speed Demon

His first name was James, but everyone knew him as Cool Papa Bell, the fastest man ever to play in the Negro leagues.

Bell's blinding speed led to some legendary stories. Okay, okay. So, many of them are exaggerated. They're still worth telling:

➤ Bell was once timed circling the bases in 12 seconds.

➤ He could go from first to third on a bunt.

➤ He could steal two bases on one pitch.

➤ He could turn off the light in his room and be in bed before the room was dark.

➤ He once was declared out when he was hit by his own batted ball as he slid into second base.

Now, that's fast!

What's true about Bell is that he once stole 175 bases in a 200-game season. His speed also made him an excellent center fielder. He played from 1922 through 1946 and had a lifetime batting average of .341. After his retirement, Bell served as a coach for the Kansas City Monarchs and helped prepare Jackie Robinson for the major leagues.

The Total Package

How's this for a measure of greatness? Oscar Charleston, considered by many to be the best all-around player in the history of the Negro leagues, was said to be Ty Cobb, Tris Speaker, and Babe Ruth all rolled into one. How would you like to be his agent in today's market?

There wasn't anything Charleston couldn't do and do well. He could hit for power and hit for average, he could run, he could field, and he could throw. He also was a student of the game, which helped him become one of the most successful managers in the Negro leagues after his playing career ended.

Charleston's batting average was almost always over .300—and usually much higher than that, rarely dipping below .350. The Hoosier Comet, as he was known, hit over .400 three times, including a career high .445 in 1925. John McGraw, the legendary manager of the New York Giants who knew a thing or two about ballplayers, called Charleston the greatest player he had ever seen.

Unfortunately, Charleston retired in 1944 and missed the integration of baseball by three years.

Making His Pitch

If Satchel Paige were a pitcher in today's game, he'd be a superstar athlete with his own TV show, his mug on magazine covers, and commercial endorsements for everything from Wheaties to Nike. Paige had it all—talent, personality, charisma, and showmanship. These attributes made him arguably the biggest star to come out of the Negro leagues.

Paige, whose first name was Leroy, got his nickname because when he was a kid he carried bags—or satchels—at the train station in Mobile, Alabama. Satchel ran into some trouble at age 12, when he got caught stealing some toys and was sent off to the Industrial School for Negro Children. It was at that school that he learned to play baseball, and was first recognized as exceptional. By the time he was 18, Paige was pitching for the Birmingham Black Barons in the Negro leagues.

And what a pitcher he was! Paige was known for a blazing fastball, which he threw with pinpoint control. He called his fastball the "small ball" and by the time it reached the batter, Paige likened it to a "fish egg."

Regardless of what his pitch was called, it was darn near impossible to hit. Paige dominated the Negro leagues for most of the 1930s and '40s. Exact records weren't kept in the Negro leagues, but it's estimated that he pitched in about 2,500 games, winning more than 2,000.

Paige, who began his Negro league career in 1926, had two of his best seasons with the Pittsburgh Crawfords. His combined record in 1932 and 1933 was 63 wins and 11 losses.

The Inside Skinny

Satchel Paige threw 250 shutouts and 55 no-hitters during his Negro league career. And unlike today's starting pitchers, who work every fourth or fifth day, Paige once started 29 games in one month and during some year-round seasons appeared in as many as 200.

But all was not well. Paige left the Crawfords a year later over a contract dispute and formed the Satchel Paige All-Stars. The team crisscrossed the United States on a barnstorming tour and played all comers. Not one to be shy about promoting himself, Paige billed himself as "the world's greatest pitcher—guaranteed to strike out the first nine men."

Paige and his team faced the best players in the major leagues, and won praise from the likes of Hall of Famers Joe DiMaggio, Charlie Gehringer, Jimmie Foxx, Rogers Hornsby, and Hack Wilson.

But Paige didn't become an icon just because he could throw the ball. He was famous—to black and white fans—because of his quick wit, his great sense of humor, and his ability to work a crowd. The stories about Paige are probably a mixture of fact and fiction, but they're entertaining nonetheless. You decide which is real and which is fantasy:

➤ Paige would instruct his outfielders to sit behind the pitcher's mound, while he went on to strike out the side with the tying run on base.

➤ He would intentionally walk the bases loaded so he could pitch to Josh Gibson, "the black Babe Ruth."

➤ He could throw 20 consecutive pitches over, not the plate, but a chewing gum wrapper being used as the plate.

Paige's legend preceded him to every game, which is why he transcended Negro League Baseball.

Many people, Paige included, thought he would be the player to break the color barrier in Major League Baseball instead of Jackie Robinson. It wasn't until 1948 that Paige made it to the major leagues. He was signed by the Cleveland Indians at age 42 and was the oldest rookie ever to play in the majors.

Despite his "advanced" age, Paige still could pack 'em in. A total of more than 200,000 fans watched his first three starts for the Indians. He finished his rookie season with a 6–1 record and a 2.48 earned run average, helping Cleveland to the American League pennant and the World Series championship.

Paige spent one more season with the Indians, went back to barnstorming for two seasons, and then put in three seasons with the St. Louis Browns. He retired in 1954—or so it seemed. In 1965, Paige pitched one game for the Kansas City Athletics. He was 59 years old, which makes him the oldest man ever to pitch in a major league game.

The Big Breakthrough

More than 50 years after Jackie Robinson broke baseball's color barrier and became the first African American ever to play in the major leagues, he remains one of the most socially significant athletes of all time.

Robinson was raised by his mother in a poor neighborhood in Pasadena, California. While many of his friends got into trouble, Robinson kept himself on the straight and narrow by focusing on sports.

Besides Baseball

Robinson is best remembered for his baseball career, but his athletic ability was much broader. He was a four-sport letterman at John Muir Technical School, then started his college career at Pasadena Junior College in 1937. Robinson could do it all. He led the football team to 11 straight wins, set a national long jump record, and helped his baseball team to the Southern California Junior College title.

Jackie Robinson broke the color barrier in Major League Baseball.

Photo: Icon Sports Media

Robinson accepted a scholarship to UCLA and picked up right where he left off. He became the first UCLA athlete to letter in four sports (baseball, football, basketball, and track).

In basketball, he led the Pacific Coast Conference in scoring as a junior and senior. In football, he led the nation in 1939 in yards per carry (12) and in average punt return yardage (20). But that wasn't all. Robinson also won swimming championships, reached the semifinals of the national Negro league tennis tournament, and won the 1940 NCAA long jump title.

Financial hardship forced Robinson to leave UCLA before earning his degree. He eventually enlisted in the U.S. Army and attained the rank of second lieutenant. After his honorable discharge in 1944, Robinson joined the Kansas City Monarchs of the Negro American League.

A Noble Experiment

At about the same time Robinson returned to playing baseball, there was a guy named Branch Rickey about to conduct what he called his "noble experiment." Rickey, the president of the Brooklyn Dodgers, wanted to integrate the major leagues, and he knew he needed the right player to pull it off.

Integrating the leagues was a risky proposition indeed, but Rickey thought that Robinson just might be the right man for the job. While he had confidence in Robinson, Rickey knew that integrating the league wouldn't be easy, and he told Robinson that in no uncertain terms.

Sports Strategies

Before joining the Brooklyn Dodgers organization, Jackie Robinson played 47 games as a member of the Kansas City Monarchs of the Negro American League. He hit .387, with 14 doubles, 4 triples, 5 home runs, and 13 stolen bases.

"We're tackling something big here, Jackie," Rickey told Robinson. "If we fail, no one will try it again for 20 years. I know you're a good ballplayer. What I don't know is whether you have the guts."

Robinson, who also realized the difficulties he would face, wondered if Rickey was looking for "a Negro who is afraid to fight back." Rickey, however, was looking for just the opposite. "Robinson," answered Rickey, "I'm looking for a ballplayer with guts enough not to fight back."

Robinson, who spent the 1946 season playing with the Montreal Royals, a Dodger minor league team, made history on April 15, 1947 at age 28. But he didn't make many friends. Robinson was called names, he was thrown at by pitchers and spiked by base runners, and he was subjected to death threats.

In spite of all that, he displayed enough guts not to fight back. Robinson was the model of decorum. He conducted himself with grace and dignity, and he let his play do the talking.

Proving the Point

Robinson's play spoke volumes. He hit .297, with 175 hits, 125 runs, 12 home runs, 48 runs batted in, and a league-leading 29 stolen bases. He was named the National League Rookie of the Year for 1947. Two years later, Robinson was named the National League Most Valuable Player. He led the league in hitting (.342) and had 203 hits, 16 home runs, 124 RBIs, and 37 stolen bases.

Robinson was the complete player: He could hit, run, and throw. Plus, his daring on the base paths was considerably more than what fans in those days were used to seeing. But what was most important, for him and the black athletes who followed him, was that he more than lived up to Rickey's faith in him.

Said Robinson's teammate and friend, Pee Wee Reese: "I don't know any other ballplayer who could have done what he did. To be able to hit with everybody yelling at him. He had to block all that out. To do what he did has got to be the most tremendous thing I've ever seen in sports."

Two-Minute Warning

Jackie Robinson wasn't just a star in the sports world. He appeared on the covers of *Time* and *Life* magazines; he played himself in *The Jackie Robinson Story*, a 1950 film; and he finished second to Bing Crosby as the nation's Most Admired Man in a 1947 Associated Press poll.

Robinson retired after the 1956 season. In his 10 seasons, he helped the Dodgers win six National League pennants and the 1955 World Series. He had a lifetime batting average of .311, with 1,518 hits, 137 home runs, 734 RBIs, and 197 stolen bases. You can only imagine how much better his statistics would have been had the prime years of his career not been taken from him due to the color barrier.

Jackie Robinson was rewarded with induction into the Baseball Hall of Fame in 1962, his first year of eligibility. Ten years later, the 25th anniversary of his major league debut, Robinson threw the ceremonial first pitch of the World Series between the Oakland A's and the Cincinnati Reds. Nine days later, he died of a massive heart attack.

During a yearlong celebration to commemorate the 50th anniversary of his breakthrough, Major League Baseball retired his uniform number 42, meaning no other player on any major league team can ever wear it.

The Least You Need to Know

➤ Baseball, as we know it today, is a variation of an English game called rounders.

➤ Contrary to popular notion, Abner Doubleday did not invent the game of baseball. Alexander Cartwright is credited with having invented it.

➤ The Cincinnati Red Stockings were the first professional team.

➤ The Negro leagues produced some of the greatest players in the game.

➤ Jackie Robinson broke the color barrier in Major League Baseball on April 15, 1947.

Baseball's Standard

Now that you've learned a little bit about baseball's roots and we've cleared up the confusion over who the heck invented the game, let's look at some of the sport's greatest players.

None was greater than Babe Ruth, who continues to be an enduring icon even though his heyday occurred in the 1920s. Come to think of it, the Bambino was one of the main reasons the '20s were roaring!

The Sultan of Swat

When you think about the greatest athletes of all time, George Herman "Babe" Ruth has to be near the top of a very short list—right up there with Michael Jordan and Muhammad Ali.

The Babe could do it all. He was best known for hitting home runs. He hit them a country mile and he hit them often. But he began his career as—are you ready for this?—a pitcher with the Boston Red Sox.

That's right, for a time Babe Ruth was the best left-handed pitcher in baseball. From 1915 through 1917, he won 65 games. In 1918, he helped the Red Sox to the World Series championship as a pitcher, a first baseman, and an outfielder. Like I said, the Babe could do it all.

Ruth was moved to the outfield in 1919 and to New York in 1920, when he became a New York Yankee. He was sold to the Yankees by Boston owner Harry Frazee, who needed cash.

Bad move. Very bad move. Frazee should've sold his car, his house, or the clothes off his back. Anything but Babe Ruth.

The Red Sox have been paying ever since. The World Series title they won in 1918 was their last. Since Ruth joined the team, the Yankees have gone on to become, well, the Yankees—one of the most storied franchises in all of sports.

In Ruth's first year with the Yankees, he led the American League with 54 home runs. No other player hit more than 19 that season.

But Babe was just warming up. The following year he hit 59 home runs and by the end of his third full season, he was the all-time home run leader in the major leagues with 137. It had taken the previous leader, Roger Connor, 18 years to get to 136.

But the best of the Babe could be summed up with two numbers—60 and 714. He hit 60 home runs in 1927, a single-season record that stood until 1961, and he hit 714 in his career, a mark that stood until 1974.

Talk about greatness standing the test of time!

Power to Spare

Every time Hank Aaron, Willie Mays, Frank Robinson, and Mickey Mantle came to the plate, the crowd began buzzing, because there was the chance—a pretty good chance—that the baseball might leave the park.

And it did, a total of 2,537 times.

Two-Minute Warning

Babe Ruth may have put on a few pounds and had that roly-poly look about him as he got older. But when he was young, he was fit, trim, and well-conditioned. He had good speed and could run, throw, field, and hit. Unfortunately, his indulgent lifestyle caught up with him.

The Inside Skinny

Babe Ruth's ability to hit baseballs out of ballparks made him hugely popular. In 1920, the Yankees became the first team to reach the one million mark in attendance. Two years later, the Yankees moved into a brand spanking new stadium. Its official name was Yankee Stadium, but it was known as the House That Ruth Built.

Hammerin' Hank

Hank Aaron broke one of the most cherished records in all of sports when he hit the 715th home run of his career on April 8, 1974, to break Babe Ruth's record.

Now, you'd think Aaron would've been thrilled with his accomplishment. After all, breaking a record that stood for nearly 40 years and had been held by the Bambino was worth breaking out the party hats and noisemakers. Unfortunately, Aaron felt more relief than euphoria, because he had been inundated with racially motivated hate mail and death threats that came from bigots unhappy that an African American was about to nudge Ruth from the record books.

Aaron went on to hit 755 home runs in his 23-year career—No. 1 all time.

Aaron, an outfielder, wasn't just a guy who could hit home runs. No sirree. He also holds major league records for total bases (6,856), extra-base hits (1,477), and runs batted in (2,297). He had a lifetime batting average of .305 and he also could run, field, and throw.

No wonder that in 1982, Aaron came within nine votes out of 415 cast of becoming the first player unanimously elected to the Baseball Hall of Fame.

Two-Minute Warning

Legend has it that Babe Ruth once visited a sick child in the hospital, promising him a home run the next day—and hit three. Legend also has it that Ruth pointed to the center-field bleachers in the 1932 World Series, one pitch before he homered to that exact spot. Believe it ... or not.

The Say-Hey Kid

Baseball people are always talking about five-tool players, and they don't mean players toting a hammer, screwdriver, saw, pliers, and wrench. A five-tool player can hit for average, hit for power, run, field, and throw. There were none better at all five than Willie Mays, a center fielder for the New York, then San Francisco, Giants.

Mays was supremely talented and played the game with the enthusiasm and exuberance of a kid. He always seemed to be having the time of his life.

Sports Strategies

Hank Aaron's 755 career home runs were hit off 310 different pitchers. Don Drysdale of the Los Angeles Dodgers was the most victimized, surrendering 17 of Aaron's home runs.

Willie Mays of the San Francisco Giants was one of the game's greatest all-around players.

Photo: Icon Sports Media

Willie Mays is third all time in home runs (660) and 10th all time in hits (3,283). He won two National League Most Valuable Player Awards, and he earned 12 straight *Gold Glove* Awards for being the best fielder at his position.

But in spite of all his accolades and honors, when you think about Willie Mays, you can't help but think of "The Catch." In the first game of the 1954 World Series against the Cleveland Indians in the Polo Grounds, Indians batter Vic Wertz hit a fly ball to the deepest part of center field. Mays ran the ball down, caught it over his shoulder and with his back to home plate, then whirled and threw to the infield to keep the base runners from advancing.

It has to be seen to be believed. Thank goodness for that old newsreel footage!

Sports Strategies

Willie Mays's love for the game—or at least for the ball—began at a very early age. Before he was able to walk, his father, Willie Sr., would roll a ball back and forth with him. Willie Jr. loved it so much that he would cry when his dad stopped.

The Mick

To this day, Mickey Mantle is credited with hitting two of the longest home runs in the history of baseball. The balls might as well have been shot from a bazooka for as far as they traveled.

In 1953, he hit a home run in Griffith Stadium in Washington that sailed over a sign atop the bleachers and into a yard across the street. We can only hope no one was plopped in a lawn chair, enjoying the sunshine. Total estimated distance: 565 feet.

The other tape-measure home run was a near miss, but a colossal feat just the same. In 1956, Mantle came within 18 inches of hitting the first ball out of Yankee Stadium.

Mantle hit 536 home runs in his career and won three American League Most Valuable Player Awards. But as talented as he was, you can't help but wonder what might've been had he not been so injury-prone and so fond of carousing with his teammates.

Still, the Mick was a bona fide hero and his death in 1995, from liver cancer, left millions grieving his loss.

Feat ... Repeat

When you think of the great players in Major League Baseball history, some names automatically pop into your head—Ruth, Gehrig, Mays, Mantle, Cobb, Williams, DiMaggio. Unless you put your thinking cap on, Frank Robinson probably wouldn't come to mind. But the power-hitting outfielder belongs on that best-ever list.

How could you possibly not include him? He is the only player to win Most Valuable Player Awards in the National League (1961) and the American League (1966). He won the *Triple Crown* in 1966, when he led the American League in batting, home runs, and runs batted in. He also was the first player to hit 200 home runs in each league and the first to hit home runs for each league in the All-Star Game.

Robinson's awards and accolades are a matter of record, but what you won't find in the record book is that he not only could hit, he often *got* hit. Robinson is one of the most-hit players in baseball history, because he stood so close to the plate. And pity those pitchers who threw inside to back him off the plate. Whenever Robinson was hit or knocked down, it only made him more determined to make that pitcher pay.

And they did. Robinson had a .294 lifetime batting average, and hit 586 career home runs to rank fourth all time.

The Fundamentals

The **Gold Glove** is awarded annually to the best-fielding player at each position. The winners are determined by a vote of the Major League coaches and managers.

The Fundamentals

The **Triple Crown** is one of baseball's rarest accomplishments. To win the Triple Crown, a player must lead the league in batting average, home runs, and runs batted in. Nobody has won the Triple Crown since Carl Yastrzemski in 1967.

19

Two-Minute Warning

Mickey Mantle is best remembered as being a soft-spoken country boy from a small town in Oklahoma. But when he first joined the Yankees in 1952, he had a bit of a temper. Once, after he struck out, he went into the dugout and took a swing at the water cooler. Said his manager, Casey Stengel, "That water cooler ain't striking you out, son."

Two-Minute Warning

Despite spending his entire career with the Boston Red Sox and putting up eye-popping numbers, Ted Williams and the Boston fans did not have what you'd call a loving relationship. It got so bad that in Williams's final game, in 1960, he homered in his final at bat, but refused to tip his hat to the crowd.

Oh, one more thing about Frank Robinson: He was the first African-American manager in baseball history with Cleveland in 1975, and he managed in both leagues.

Hit Men

The ability to hit a baseball coming at you at 90-plus miles an hour isn't the easiest thing in the world to do. It takes a combination of strength, anticipation, good reflexes, and, in the case of Ted Williams, x-ray eyes. Well, maybe not x-ray eyes, but close.

Teddy Ballgame

Ted Williams of the Boston Red Sox had powerful forearms, strong wrists, and eyes like a hawk. The combination of attributes helped make him one of the best hitters ever. There was nothing this guy couldn't hit. Witness his six American League batting titles, his two Triple Crowns, his two Most Valuable Player Awards, and his 521 career home runs.

Williams's arms and wrists enabled him to wait until the very last instant to swing, and his eyes helped him see the ball with remarkable clarity. As legend has it, Williams was able to distinguish the seams and read the writing on the baseball—as it was speeding toward him. Doctors from the Navy examined him and determined his eyes were one in a hundred thousand. His vision was an eye-popping 20/10.

Williams, nicknamed Teddy Ballgame and the Splendid Splinter, was the last player to hit .400 in a season, which is one of the game's magical milestones.

In 1941, Williams entered the last day of the season with his batting average at exactly .400. His manager, Joe Cronin, gave Williams the option of not playing in the doubleheader, to protect his average. Williams not only played, he got four hits in the first game and two more in the second. He finished the season hitting .406.

The Georgia Peach

Ty Cobb's nickname was the Georgia Peach, which conjures up the notion of a sweetheart of a guy. You know, a real prince.

Well, nothing could be further from the truth. Besides being one of the most accomplished hitters and base stealers in baseball history, Cobb was also mean-spirited and downright nasty. Even his own teammates weren't crazy about him.

Cobb, who spent most of his career with the Detroit Tigers, routinely taunted the opposition and battled with fans. Legend has it that he wore razor-sharp spikes to intentionally injure players when he slid into bases.

So Cobb wouldn't have been mistaken for Mr. Congeniality, but there is no denying his talent. He won 12 batting titles, including nine straight, and his .367 lifetime batting average is the best ever.

Cobb retired in 1928 with 4,191 hits, a record that stood until 1985, when Pete Rose surpassed it.

Sports Strategies

Ty Cobb was a terrific base stealer. Maybe it was due to those lethal spikes. But whatever the reason, he led the American League in stolen bases six times; swiped 892 in his career, good for fourth all time; and he stole home 54 times.

The Yankee Clipper

Joe DiMaggio of the New York Yankees was a Hall of Fame baseball player, and he was as big a hero as any sport has ever produced. How's that for a daily double?

DiMaggio was a combination of talent, grace, elegance, charisma, and mystique. Fans revered the Yankee Clipper like no other player.

From May 15 to July 17, 1941, DiMaggio played in 56 games and got a hit in every one. The odds of accomplishing such a feat are incalculable. No one's ever come close to matching his 56-game hitting streak, which remains one of the game's most significant records.

DiMaggio was also half of one of the entertainment world's most significant marriages. On January 14, 1954, the wildly popular baseball player married Marilyn Monroe, a wildly popular actress. Can you imagine the hubbub a similar union would create today? *Entertainment Tonight* would be on call 24/7.

Sports Strategies

Joe DiMaggio's talent translated into championships for the Yankees. He played 13 seasons, all with the Yanks, and helped them win 10 American League pennants and nine World Series titles.

21

Unfortunately, the marriage lasted only nine months. But so devoted was DiMaggio to his ex-wife that he placed flowers on her grave three times a week for 20 years.

The Fundamentals

A **shutout** is a game in which a pitcher pitches a complete game and doesn't allow any runs.

The Fundamentals

The **Cy Young Award** is voted on by the Baseball Writers Association of America and is given to the best pitcher in each league. It is named for Cy Young, the all-time leader in career wins with 511.

Earned run average is the average number of earned runs scored on a pitcher per nine innings. It is calculated by taking the number of earned runs scored on the pitcher, divided by the total number of innings pitched and multiplied by nine. An ERA of less than 4.00 is considered good; an ERA of less than 3.00 is considered outstanding.

Charlie Hustle

Pete Rose came by his Charlie Hustle nickname honestly. He didn't do anything halfway. He ran full-speed to first base even after a walk. He slid into bases head-first instead of feet first. And God help anybody in his way, because Rose would run him over.

Once, Rose steamrolled catcher Ray Fosse of the Cleveland Indians, knocking him into the middle of next week, in order to score the winning run. Did he do it in a playoff game? In a World Series game? No on both counts. He did it in the All-Star Game, where that kind of aggressiveness is unheard of. But that was Pete Rose—all intensity, all the time.

Rose's most memorable on-field accomplishment occurred on September 11, 1985 at Riverfront Stadium in Cincinnati, when he got a single off San Diego's Eric Show and broke Ty Cobb's record of 4,191 hits.

Unfortunately, Rose might be best remembered for an off-the-field activity—gambling—that has cost him a spot in the Hall of Fame. (Check out Chapter 3, "The Good, the Bad, and the Ugly," for more.)

Call to Arms

Sandy Koufax wasn't around for very long; Walter Johnson seemingly was around forever. As for Bob Gibson, opposing hitters wish he wouldn't have been around at all.

They all had one thing in common, though: They were among the best ever to throw a baseball.

Reluctant Hero

For a guy who didn't like the limelight and shunned celebrity, Sandy Koufax sure made life tough on himself.

The Los Angeles Dodgers' left-hander was the premier pitcher in baseball from 1961 through 1966. For those six seasons, he was virtually unhittable. Koufax won 129 games, led the National league in *earned run average* five straight years, and won three *Cy Young awards* as the best pitcher in baseball. He led the league in *shutouts* three times and in strikeouts four times.

Said Willie Stargell, a Hall of Famer for the Pittsburgh Pirates, "Trying to hit him was like trying to drink coffee with a fork."

Koufax retired in 1966 because of an arm injury. Five years later he became the youngest inductee into the Baseball Hall of Fame.

He Gave a Hoot

You've probably heard the expression, "If looks could kill ...." Well, if you were faced with stepping into the batter's box and trying to get a hit off Bob "Hoot" Gibson, you just might wish you were dead.

Gibson had a menacing scowl and an arm just as frightening. He was one of the most dominating, overpowering pitchers in baseball history. He thought home plate was his personal possession, and woe to the batter who thought otherwise.

The season Gibson enjoyed—but no hitters did— in 1968 was something to behold. He won 22 games, struck out 268, and registered a 1.12 earned run average in leading the St. Louis Cardinals to the World Series. Included in those 22 victories were 13 shutouts, five consecutively, and a 92-inning span during which he gave up only two earned runs.

It was easier to hit the lottery than it was Bob Gibson.

Two-Minute Warning

Bob Gibson's intensity against the opposition was legendary. But he didn't always endear himself to his teammates, either. One time, his catcher, Tim McCarver, went to the mound to calm Gibson down. Gibson admonished McCarver, saying, "The only thing you know about pitching is how hard it is to hit."

The Big Train

Walter "The Big Train" Johnson grew up as a farm boy in Kansas, so it figured that once he became a pitcher for the Washington Senators, he'd be a workhorse. Johnson spent 21 years in the big leagues and won 417 games, second all time to Cy Young.

To save you the trouble of doing the math, that's an average of 20 wins a year. Metronomes aren't that consistent. And 110 of those wins—or about one in four— were shutouts.

There was nothing too complicated about the secret to Johnson's success. As Ty Cobb put it, "Just speed, raw speed, blinding speed, too much speed." The Big Train, named by legendary sportswriter Grantland Rice, because Johnson's size and fastball reminded him of an express train, could throw it and throw it hard. Hitters usually found themselves swinging and missing. Johnson struck out 3,508 batters in his career and led the American League in strikeouts 12 times.

Today's Best

So here's the question: Do the superstars of today measure up to the superstars of yesterday?

Guaranteed, these guys could.

The Inside Skinny

In September 1908, Walter Johnson did the impossible. He started three consecutive games against the New York Yankees and won all three by shutouts. He added two victories over the Philadelphia Athletics Sept. 10 and 11, giving him five wins in eight days.

The Sons Also Rise

You want to know why Barry Bonds of the San Francisco Giants and Ken Griffey Jr. of the Cincinnati Reds are so talented? It's in the genes.

Their fathers, Bobby Bonds and Ken Griffey Sr., enjoyed outstanding careers of their own. But the kids have put up numbers far better than their old men.

Barry Bonds has hit more than 500 home runs and won three National League Most Valuable Player Awards. Ken Griffey Jr. has hit more than 440 home runs (in three fewer seasons than Bonds), has won one American League Most Valuable Player Award, and was named to the All-Century Team.

Should *their* sons make it to the majors, just imagine the tough acts they'll have to follow in upholding the family tradition.

Big Mac

Do you believe in magic? You do if you got caught up in Mark McGwire's 1998 season, when he broke Roger Maris's single-season home run mark of 61.

McGwire, a first baseman for the St. Louis Cardinals, didn't just break the record, he smashed it to smithereens, hitting 70 home runs and winning a season-long duel with Sammy Sosa of the Chicago Cubs, who finished with 66. The battle between McGuire and Sosa got the attention of even the most casual baseball fans, those who wouldn't know home plate from a dinner plate.

McGwire hit No. 60 on September 5, tied Maris with No. 61 on September 7, and hit the record-breaker September 8 against Steve Trachsel of the Cubs.

Big Mac finished the season in a rush, hitting five home runs in a three-day span in late September.

And just to prove his 1998 season was no fluke, McGwire followed it up with 65 home runs in 1999.

Three-Peat

Pedro Martinez looks like a guy who would get sand kicked in his face on the beach. You know, the 97-pound weakling type. But whoever said looks can be deceiving must've had Martinez in mind, because the Boston Red Sox right-hander is one of the hardest-throwing pitchers in the game today.

Imagine trying to hit a white marble fired from a gun and you have some idea of what it's like trying to hit one of Martinez's pitches.

He is only the third pitcher to win the Cy Young Award in both leagues, winning it in 1997 with the Montreal Expos (National League) and in 1999 and 2000 with the Boston Red Sox. But he was never better than in 1999, when he won the pitching Triple Crown. Martinez led the league in victories (23), earned run average (2.07), and strikeouts (313).

Sports Strategies

The drama of the 1998 and 1999 seasons was missing in 2000. Mark McGwire suffered a variety of injuries during the season, including a knee injury, that limited him to pinch-hitting duties. He managed 32 home runs.

The Least You Need to Know

➤ Babe Ruth, a player of mythic proportions, continues to be one of the sport's great icons.

➤ Henry Aaron broke Babe Ruth's career home run record, but was vilified by many on racial grounds.

➤ Sandy Koufax disliked the fame and celebrity that went along with being one of the game's premier pitchers.

➤ Ty Cobb was called the Georgia Peach, but he was anything but a sweetheart.

➤ Barry Bonds and Ken Griffey Jr. have successfully followed in their fathers' footsteps.

The Good, the Bad, and the Ugly

Baseball has had moments over the years when things haven't been all that rosy. Truth be told, some of the scandals have been downright messy, because they've involved gambling, which is a four-letter word where sports is concerned. Mother Nature has also taken its toll on the game during the 1989 World Series, when an earthquake rocked the Bay Area.

But not all of baseball's off-the-field activities have been bad news. Take Curt Flood, an outfielder for the St. Louis Cardinals. His willingness to stand up and fight for what he considered his rights—not only as a player, but as a human being— eventually changed the game forever.

The Black Sox Scandal

From 1917 through 1919, the Chicago White Sox were the finest team in baseball. They were then what the New York Yankees are today—the best team that money could buy. The White Sox had many of the game's most talented players on their roster—Eddie Collins, "Shoeless" Joe Jackson, Eddie Cicotte, and Buck Weaver. But they also had a real cheapskate for an owner.

How cheap was Charles Comiskey? So cheap that in order to save a few bucks, he cut back on how often the players' uniforms were washed. Which was probably quite noticeable during the dog days of August.

So it shouldn't surprise you that even though Comiskey had the best team in baseball, he paid the players much less than the going rate. Only one player, Hall of Fame second baseman Eddie Collins, was paid what he was worth. His annual salary of $14,500 was more than double any other player's on the team.

Well, as you can imagine, the White Sox players not named Collins weren't exactly thrilled with the payroll situation. They resented Comiskey for paying them so little, and they really resented Collins for getting paid so much.

Comiskey, open-minded fellow that he was, wouldn't even discuss salaries with the players. So Chick Gandil, the White Sox first baseman, decided to take matters into his own hands. He hatched a plan to throw the World Series.

Talk about living dangerously.

Gandil began rounding up players in mid-August, when the White Sox were far ahead in the standings and a lock to reach the World Series. He found seven players to go along with his scheme—pitchers Eddie Cicotte and Lefty Williams, shortstop Swede Risberg, third baseman Buck Weaver, utility infielder Fred McMullen, center fielder Happy Felsch, and left fielder Joe Jackson.

The Fix Is On

Chick Gandil had the players, but the other part of the plan was money. He needed someone to bankroll the operation and make it worth the schemers' while. The going rate to fix a World Series in 1919 turned out to be $100,000, most of which was provided by Arnold Rothstein, a big-time gambler from New York City.

Eddie Cicotte, the starting pitcher for the White Sox in Game 1 of the World Series against the Cincinnati Reds, got his payoff up front. His $10,000 was left under his pillow in his hotel room the night before the opener.

Two-Minute Warning

The betting scandal involving the Chicago White Sox that darn near ruined baseball in 1919 has been referred to as the Black Sox Scandal. But originally, the term "Black Sox" referred to the team's filthy socks.

The Inside Skinny

Eddie Cicotte was the first player approached by Chick Gandil, most likely because he was the bitterest toward Charles Comiskey, the White Sox owner. At the beginning of the season, Comiskey had promised to pay Cicotte $10,000 if he won 30 games in 1919. When Cicotte reached 29 wins, he was benched so that he couldn't reach his goal.

If there were any doubts about whether Cicotte would do his part, they disappeared quickly. He hit the leadoff batter with his second pitch. Holding up a sign with the word "FIX" printed on it couldn't have been a better signal of Cicotte's intentions. The White Sox lost the opener 9–1.

Lefty Williams was the losing pitcher in Game 2, which was also tanked by the White Sox, even though no money changed hands before the game. After the game, Gandil was given $10,000. He expected to receive $40,000. The players, who were so disgruntled with Comiskey, now found themselves feeling pretty much the same about the gamblers who seemed to be selling them short.

The White Sox won Game 3, and before Game 4, Gandil was given $20,000, which was split equally among Risberg, Felsch, Williams, and Jackson. The Reds won—or should I say, the White Sox lost—the next two games.

Another $20,000 was due the White Sox players before Game 6. It never materialized, which made them really ornery. Ornery enough, in fact, to win Games 6 and 7 and cut the Reds' lead to four games to three (in a best-of-nine series).

By this time, the gamblers were getting a tad annoyed. Actually, they were worried that the White Sox would win and the money they bet on the Reds would be nothing but a memory.

So Rothstein had a thug make Lefty Williams, the Game 8 starting pitcher, an offer he couldn't refuse. Williams was told that if he got through the first inning, something might happen to him and maybe even to his wife. Just in case you're wondering, that "something" would not be pleasant.

Williams took the mound scared to death and eager to prove he would play along. He gave up four hits and was back in the safe haven of his dugout after just one-third of an inning. The Reds won the game 10–5 and the Series, five games to three.

Sports Strategies

For three seasons, Major League Baseball experimented with a best-of-nine World Series. It started in 1919 and ended after the 1921 Series. In the 15 World Series before and every one after, the format was the traditional best of seven.

Paying the Price

Rumors that the World Series was fixed were rampant. Newspapers ran stories about the alleged fix, and Comiskey offered a $20,000 reward to anyone offering information about the shenanigans. Of course, Comiskey later lowered his offer to $10,000, but he never had the slightest intention of parting with a dime.

"Shoeless" Joe Jackson, meanwhile, was suffering severe pangs of guilt. He received $5,000 for his role in the fix, but that role was practically nonexistent. Jackson hit .375 in the Series to lead both teams.

Jackson wanted to get advice from Comiskey about whether to keep his $5,000, but Comiskey refused to see him. Later, Jackson sent him a letter, telling him the games might've been fixed, but Comiskey never acknowledged it.

The matter came before a Cook County grand jury in September 1920. Cicotte and Jackson 'fessed up and told the grand jury of their roles. Gandil, the guy who plotted it all, insisted he knew nothing. The grand jury indicted all eight players for conspiracy to defraud the public, but all eight walked. Their acquittal in court was not the end of the story, however.

The unfortunate eight still had to deal with Judge Kenesaw Mountain Landis, the first commissioner of baseball. Landis had so much power he might as well have been king.

Landis didn't care a whit about what the courts did, he meted out the toughest punishment of all: He banned all eight players from organized baseball for life. Said Landis:

Two-Minute Warning

When "Shoeless" Joe Jackson left the Cook County courtroom after being indicted, legend has it that a tearful little boy said, "Say it ain't so, Joe." According to Jackson, the incident never happened; it was concocted by Charley Owens of the *Chicago Daily News.*

"Regardless of the verdict of juries, no player who throws a ballgame, no player that undertakes or promises to throw a ballgame, no player that sits in conference with a bunch of crooked players and gamblers where the ways and means of throwing a game are discussed and does not promptly tell his club about it, will ever play professional baseball."

Buck Weaver didn't receive one red cent from the fix, because other than the initial meeting, he hadn't participated in it. No matter. Landis held him accountable for attending the meeting and keeping his mouth shut.

Weaver's silence cost him dearly. The game paid, too. Public confidence was badly shaken and took years to be restored.

Flood-ing the Market

If today's Major League Baseball players don't know who Curt Flood is, they should be ashamed of themselves. Do not pass GO; do not collect $200.

Players should thank their lucky stars for Flood, because were it not for him and his courageous resolve, chances are they'd be a lot poorer. Flood did the unthinkable in 1969: He challenged baseball's *reserve clause,* which bound a player to his team forever.

The reserve clause had been part of the standard player's contract for nearly a century. But when the Cardinals agreed to trade Flood to the Philadelphia Phillies following the 1969 season, he figured enough was enough.

Flood, one of the best center fielders of his time, had spent 12 years with the Cardinals. He liked St. Louis and he operated several businesses in the area. So he decided, on the whole, that he would rather not be in Philadelphia.

But with the reserve clause firmly entrenched, he had just one option: a lawsuit challenging its legality. Climbing a mountain in a pair of sandals would not have been any more of an uphill battle than Flood faced.

Flood knew full well that he might lose in court. He also knew that he might lose his job and the $100,000 annual salary that went with it. But the principle was more important than his paycheck, so he went forward.

After two years, the case reached the U.S. Supreme Court in 1972, and the court found in favor of baseball, allowing the game to retain the reserve clause. By the time the decision was handed down, Flood, who sat out the 1970 season and then played in 13 games with the Washington Senators in 1971, was out of baseball.

But his fight was not in vain. In 1975, two pitchers—Andy Messersmith of the Los Angeles Dodgers and Dave McNally of the Montreal Expos—challenged the reserve clause and were declared free agents by a federal arbitrator.

What Curt Flood did was to set the wheels of change in motion by standing up for what he believed were his rights as an American. Said Donald Fehr, executive director of the Players' Association, baseball's players union: "This was a person who risked his career, who risked alienation from baseball, all in an effort to say that the circumstances surrounding baseball players were wrong and immoral."

Curt Flood died of cancer in 1997. To show its gratitude, the Players' Association paid Flood's medical bills for the last year of his life. Given all he had done, it was the least the union could do.

The Fundamentals

The **reserve clause** was written into the standard player's contract in 1887. It mandated that a player remain with his team for his entire career, unless the team decided to trade him, release him, or sell his contract to another team.

The Inside Skinny

Shortly after Curt Flood lost his case in the Supreme Court, he left the United States. In 1975, when Peter Seitz, a federal arbitrator, declared two players free agents and validated Flood's stand, Flood was running a tavern in Majorca, Spain.

The Day the Earth Moved

The 1989 World Series was a battle of the Bay Area. The San Francisco Giants and the Oakland Athletics squared off for neighborhood bragging rights. And after the first two games, Oakland was doing all the bragging, winning 5–0 and 5–1.

The scene shifted to San Francisco's Candlestick Park on October 15, 1989, where 60,000 fans were on hand, hoping to see the momentum shift. Instead, it was the earth that shifted.

Just prior to the start of the game, an earthquake that registered 7.1 on the Richter scale struck the Bay Area. The stadium shuddered, the electricity went out, and the television feed disappeared. Suddenly, the World Series wasn't the big story anymore. The earthquake was the worst in San Francisco since 1906.

A section of the San Francisco–Oakland Bay Bridge collapsed, and the city was without power for the first time since the 1906 quake. It took until Oct. 20 to restore the electricity.

Sports Strategies

The Oakland Athletics won the 1989 World Series in a four-game sweep. They were so dominant that they never trailed in any game.

Fires raged throughout the city, including a conflagration at the Marina. The damage in San Francisco alone totaled more than $3 billion.

Obviously, no one was too concerned about baseball. Fay Vincent, the commissioner of baseball, postponed what he called a "modest little sporting event" for at least a week, while the Bay Area tried to return to normal. When it became clear that seven days weren't enough, resumption of the World Series was delayed for another three days.

When the games resumed October 27, the 10-day postponement and the length of time between games, 12 days, were the longest in history. The earthquake also was the first event other than bad weather to result in postponement of a World Series game.

A Thorny Rose

Pete Rose should be the leading character in an unqualified success story. Here's a guy who was born in Cincinnati and eventually became a star player for the Cincinnati Reds. He wasn't a particularly gifted athlete, but that didn't hold him back a bit. Through hard work and bulldog determination, he became one of the great players in baseball history.

Pete Rose, Major League Baseball's all-time hits leader, had his career tarnished by a betting scandal.

Photo: Icon Sports Media

He helped the Reds to two World Series championships and four National League pennants. Later in his career, he was the key ingredient in the Philadelphia Phillies' winning the first World Series championship in their history. He is Major League Baseball's all-time leader in hits with 4,256, and he was the ultimate team player. He was much more interested in winning than in individual accolades.

The Pete Rose story would make for a great movie. Unfortunately, there's more to the story, and it doesn't have a happy ending.

Rose's interest in winning was not confined to the baseball diamond. Rose liked to gamble. He bet on other sports, he bet at the racetrack, he bet on just about anything. And he didn't always win. In fact, during the 1980s he was said to have lost huge amounts of money. But when it was alleged that he bet on baseball games, including games that involved the team he managed, the Cincinnati Reds—well, that was the last straw.

Bart Giamatti, the commissioner of baseball, appointed John Dowd, a former Justice Department lawyer, to investigate the charges. What Dowd discovered wasn't pretty. The Dowd Report claimed that Rose bet on 52 Cincinnati games in 1987. His minimum wager was $10,000 a day. Dowd's findings, by the way, filled 225 pages, as well as seven volumes of additional evidence. If nothing else, he was thorough.

The Inside Skinny

Pete Rose got himself into trouble for more than gambling. In 1988, he was suspended for 30 games for bumping umpire Dave Pallone during an argument. It was the longest suspension in 41 years, since Brooklyn Dodgers manager Leo Durocher was suspended for the entire 1947 season.

Dowd claims to have betting slips in Rose's handwriting, telephone records, records from bookmakers, and 113 witnesses.

Rather than face the music and admit to betting on baseball, Rose agreed to a permanent ban from the game, on August 24, 1989, which would keep him out of the Hall of Fame. In return, Major League Baseball did not issue a finding that he bet on baseball games.

Rose has refused to show even the least bit of remorse, nor has he accepted responsibility for his actions. Instead, he has steadfastly maintained that he did nothing wrong. (What's that they say? Denial isn't just a river in Egypt?)

One more note on Rose: While he didn't serve any jail time for his gambling escapades, he was jailed in 1990 for income tax evasion. He was fined $50,000 and served five months in a minimum-security prison and three more months in a halfway house for failing to report $345,967 in memorabilia income to the IRS.

The Least You Need to Know

➤ The Black Sox Scandal involved eight members of the Chicago White Sox who threw the 1919 World Series. The fix nearly ruined the future of the game.

➤ The stand taken by Curt Flood, against Major League Baseball's reserve clause, eventually changed the game forever.

➤ The 1989 World Series between the Oakland Athletics and San Francisco Giants is best remembered for the earthquake that caused it to be delayed for 10 days.

➤ Pete Rose, who should be one of baseball's most heroic figures, is one of the game's most tragic, because he allegedly bet on baseball and is under a lifetime suspension that keeps him out of the Hall of Fame.

Chapter 4

Game Time

In This Chapter

➤ Trivia quiz

➤ Making the grade

➤ Tidbits, facts, and figures

➤ Quotable quotes

➤ Memorable Fall Classics

This is the chapter that will tell you how much you know. In addition to giving you some trivia with which to amaze your friends, and maybe even win a few friendly wagers, it'll provide you with some pithy quotes from some of baseball's most celebrated athletes.

And what would any chapter on baseball be without a look back on several of the greatest World Series of all time?

Twenty Questions

Okay, class—I mean, readers—it's quiz time. At the end of each of this book's seven parts, I'll ask you 20 trivia questions guaranteed to give your brain a workout.

Now, don't worry about the questions you can't answer. You won't have to scurry off to the library and start leafing through reference books. The answers will be provided in the section following the questions. Just try not to peek right away.

So put your thinking caps on and get ready to test your mettle on these baseball questions. Good luck!

1. Who was the youngest player ever to appear in a Major League Baseball game?
2. Which two players have hit three home runs in a World Series game?
3. Who is the only pitcher to throw a no-hitter in a World Series game?
4. Which team has appeared in the most World Series?
5. Which team has won the most World Series?
6. Who is the only World Series Most Valuable Player to play for the losing team?
7. Who is the only player to hit two grand slams in the same inning?
8. Who hit the most grand slams in one season?
9. Who won the most home run titles in the National League?
10. Who won the most home run titles in the American League?
11. Joe DiMaggio of the New York Yankees has the longest hitting streak in baseball, 56 straight games. Who has the second-longest streak?
12. What pitcher is the all-time major league leader in strikeouts?

The Fundamentals

The **designated hitter** rule was adopted by the American League in 1973 in an effort to generate more offense. Instead of the pitcher batting, another player would bat, but would not play in the field. The rule began as a three-year experiment and continues to this day.

13. Who are the only three players to be members of the 40/40 club (40 home runs, 40 stolen bases in one season)?
14. Who is the only player to be named Most Outstanding Player of the College World Series and inducted into the Baseball Hall of Fame?
15. Who is the last player to hit four home runs in one game?
16. Who was the first *designated hitter*?
17. Which brother combination has the most home runs to its credit?
18. Who won the first Cy Young Award?
19. How many times in Major League Baseball history has an unassisted triple play been made?
20. Who won the most batting titles in major league history?

Twenty Answers

Hopefully, that wasn't too taxing. And hopefully, you didn't ~~s~~
swers. Let's see how you did.

1. In 1944, Joe Nuxhall, a pitcher for the Cincinnati Reds
   tender age of 15. He pitched in one game and didn't r
   1952.

2. Babe Ruth of the New York Yankees, in 1926 and 1928, and Reggie Jackson of
   the New York Yankees, in 1977. Jackson's three home runs, against the Los
   Angeles Dodgers, were particularly noteworthy, because they came on three consecutive pitches from three different pitchers (Burt Hooten, Elias Sosa, and
   Charlie Hough).

3. Don Larsen of the New York Yankees threw a *no-hitter* and went one better by
   also throwing a *perfect game*. He faced the minimum 27 batters in Game 5 of the
   1956 World Series against the Brooklyn Dodgers. He used a paltry 97 pitches—
   less than 10 an inning—in the only no-hitter and perfect game in World Series
   history.

4. The New York Yankees have appeared in 37 World Series, far and away the most
   of any team. The Brooklyn/Los Angeles Dodgers are second with 18; the New
   York/San Francisco Giants are third with 16.

5. Well, this one should be easy. The Yankees' 26 world championships is 20 more
   than the Dodgers, who are second with six.

6. In 1960, Bobby Richardson, second baseman
   for the New York Yankees, was named the
   MVP, even though the Pittsburgh Pirates won
   the Series.

7. Fernando Tatis of the St. Louis Cardinals. He
   hit two grand slams in the third inning
   against the Los Angeles Dodgers on April 23,
   1999. His eight runs batted in the inning are
   a major league record.

8. Don Mattingly of the New York Yankees hit
   six grand slams in 1987.

9. Mike Schmidt, third baseman for the
   Philadelphia Phillies, won the National
   League home run title eight times, one more
   than Ralph Kiner of the New York Giants.

The Fundamentals

In a **no-hitter,** batters can
reach base on errors, walks,
catcher's interference, and being
hit by a pitch, none of which are
counted as hits. In a **perfect
game,** nobody reaches base.

...midt, a third ...n, spent his entire ...r league career with ...e Philadelphia Phillies.

Photo: Icon Sports Media

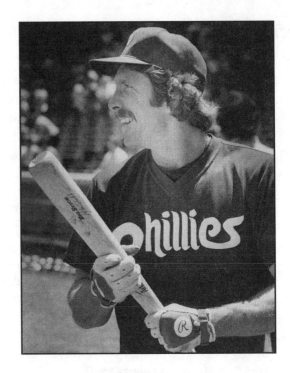

Two-Minute Warning

Mike Schmidt was one of the greatest third basemen in baseball history. He could hit for power and was a terrific fielder. But in spite of his wealth of talent, it took Philadelphia Phillies fans, among the toughest to please in the country, until the end of Schmidt's career to fully appreciate him. Schmidt made everything look effortless. The fans misinterpreted the ease with which he did things with indifference. Too bad.

10. This one you could probably guess. It was Babe Ruth, who won 12 American League home run titles, twice as many as Harmon Killebrew of the Minnesota Twins, who is second on the list.

11. Willie Keeler of Baltimore in 1897 and Pete Rose of the Cincinnati Reds in 1978 each hit in 44 straight games.

12. Pitcher Nolan Ryan is the all-time strikeout leader with 5,714. He averaged 9.55 strikeouts per nine innings.

13. Jose Canseco of the Oakland Athletics had 42 home runs and 40 steals in 1988; Barry Bonds of the San Francisco Giants had 42 home runs and 40 steals in 1996; and Alex Rodriguez of the Seattle Mariners had 42 home runs and 46 steals in 1998.

14. Dave Winfield of the University of Minnesota was named the Most Outstanding Player of the 1973 College World Series. He was inducted into the Hall of Fame in 2001.

15. Mark Whiten of the St. Louis Cardinals is the most recent of 12 players in major league history to homer four times in one game. He did it against the Cincinnati Reds on September 7, 1993. He also had 12 runs batted in the game.

16. Ron Blomberg of the New York Yankees was the first designated hitter, on April 6, 1973. He drew a walk in the first inning with the bases loaded.

17. The Aarons, with Hank doing most of the work. Hank is the all-time career home run leader with 755; Tommie chipped in with 13.

18. Don Newcombe of the Brooklyn Dodgers won the first Cy Young award. He went 27–7 with a 3.06 earned run average in 1956.

19. The unassisted *triple play* is one of the rarest feats in baseball. It's only been accomplished 12 times—only four times since 1927. The last to do it was Oakland Athletics second baseman Randy Velarde on May 29, 2000, against the New York Yankees.

20. Ty Cobb, the Georgia Peach, won the American League batting title 12 times in a 13-season span from 1907–1919. Tris Speaker broke his string in 1916.

The Fundamentals

A **triple play** is one continuing play resulting in three outs. Second baseman Randy Velarde of the Oakland Athletics did it all by himself against the New York Yankees. With runners on first and second, he caught a hard line drive, tagged out Jorge Posada going from first to second, then stepped on second base before Tino Martinez could get back.

Bet You Didn't Know …

➤ In 1901, the first ballpark hot dog was sold at the Polo Grounds in New York City by Harry M. Stevens. No word on whether it was ordered with mustard or ketchup.

➤ In 1909, Shibe Park was built in Philadelphia. It was the first baseball park made of concrete and steel.

➤ Between 1901 and 1906, Jack Taylor, a pitcher with the Cardinals and Cubs, pitched 188 *complete games*. (Bet his arm was tired.)

➤ How's this for a complete game? In 1920, Joe Oeschger of the Boston Braves and Leon Cadore of the Brooklyn Dodgers each went the distance—26 innings—in the longest game in major league history. The game ended 1–1.

The Fundamentals

When a pitcher starts a game and lasts until the outcome is decided, he has thrown a **complete game.**

➤ The longest nine-inning games in major league history lasted four hours, 22 minutes. The Baltimore Orioles beat the New York Yankees 13–9 on September 5, 1997, and the Milwaukee Brewers beat the Chicago White Sox 14–8 on May 11, 2000.

➤ Since you're probably wondering, the shortest nine-inning game in major league history lasted just 51 minutes. (Maybe the players had to catch a train.) It took place on September 28, 1919, when the New York Giants beat the Philadelphia Phillies 6–1.

➤ The first baseball game broadcast on radio took place in 1921. Harold Arlin did the play-by-play on station KDKA in Pittsburgh. By the way, the Pirates beat the Phillies 8–5.

➤ Cincinnati beat Philadelphia 2–1 in the first night game in the major leagues on May 24, 1935.

➤ Paul Schreiber, a right-handed pitcher, sure got plenty of rest between appearances. In 1923 he pitched for the Dodgers. He didn't see action again until 1945 for the New York Yankees.

➤ The first Little League World Series was held in 1947 in Williamsport, Pennsylvania, where it has continued ever since. Only now, it's televised live by ABC Sports.

➤ One of the most famous home runs in major league history came in the third and final game of a playoff for the National League pennant between the Brooklyn Dodgers and New York Giants in 1951. Trailing 4–2 with one out in the ninth, the Giants' Bobby Thomson hit a three-run homer off Ralph Branca to send New York into the World Series.

➤ Two of the great Major League Baseball franchises—the Brooklyn Dodgers and New York Giants—headed west after the 1957 season. The Dodgers took up residence in Los Angeles, and the Giants took their hearts to San Francisco. The broken hearts each team left behind were not easily soothed.

➤ New York City, which lost the Dodgers and Giants, waited only five years to find a replacement. The New York Mets began play in 1962. Also joining the National League in 1962 was the Houston Colt 45s, who would later change their nickname to the Astros.

➤ In 1965, the Houston Astros moved into their new home, the Astrodome, the first indoor baseball stadium. Fittingly, it was billed as the "Eighth Wonder of the World."

➤ Steve Carlton, one of the greatest left-handed pitchers of all time, did the impossible in 1972. Playing for the woeful Philadelphia Phillies, he won a league-leading 27 games, the most ever for a pitcher on a last-place team.

➤ A night baseball game was played at Wrigley Field, home of the Chicago Cubs, for the first time in 1988. That game broke a string of 74 years of day-only games.

➤ Between June 5, 1982, and September 14, 1987, Cal Ripken Jr. of the Baltimore Orioles played 8,243 consecutive innings over a span of 904 games. Talk about work ethic!

➤ George Brett of the Kansas City Royals flirted with the magic mark of .400 throughout the 1980 season. He finished at .390, which was the closest anyone's come to hitting .400 since Ted Williams hit .406 in 1941.

➤ Brooks Robinson of the Baltimore Orioles and Carl Yastrzemski of the Boston Red Sox share the record for loyalty. They played the most years with the same team—23.

Sports Strategies

Cal Ripken Jr. is the all-time leader in consecutive games played with 2,632. He broke Lou Gehrig's record of 2,130 games on September 5, 1995. His streak began May 30, 1982, and ended September 19, 1998.

Say What?

We'll begin this collection of quotable quotes with "Yogi-isms" from Yogi Berra, a former catcher for the New York Yankees who said some of the darndest things anybody's ever said.

➤ On the economy: "A nickel ain't worth a dime anymore."

➤ During an argument with an umpire: "Anybody who can't tell the difference between a ball hitting wood and a ball hitting concrete must be blind."

➤ On his sleeping habits: "I usually take a two-hour nap from one o'clock to four."

➤ Yogi, the manager, on the poor record of his 1984 Yankees team: "I wish I had an answer to that because I'm getting tired of answering that question."

➤ On saving money: "Why buy good luggage? You only use it when you travel."

➤ On why the Yanks lost the 1960 World Series: "We made too many wrong mistakes."

➤ On how many slices he wanted his pizza cut into: "You'd better make it four. I don't think I can eat six."

➤ On the essence of baseball: "Baseball is 90 percent mental. The other half is physical."

Yogi Berra wasn't the only baseball figure worth listening to. Here are some others:

➤ Casey Stengel, former manager of the Yankees and the Mets: "There are three things you can do in a baseball game—you can win, you can lose, or it can rain."

➤ Phil Rizzuto, former Yankees shortstop turned broadcaster, reacting to the news that Pope Paul VI had died: "Well, that kind of puts a damper on even a Yankee win."

➤ Satchel Paige, former Negro league superstar pitcher, on his six rules for a happy life: "1. Avoid fried meats which angry up the blood; 2. If your stomach disputes you, lie down and pacify it with cool thoughts; 3. Keep the juices flowing by jangling around gently as you move; 4. Go very light on vices such as carrying on in society. The social ramble ain't restful; 5. Avoid running at all times; 6. Don't look back, something may be gaining on you."

➤ Tug McGraw, former pitcher for the Phillies and the Mets, on how he planned to spend his $75,000 salary in 1975: "Ninety percent I'll spend on good times, women, and Irish whiskey. The other 10 percent I'll probably waste."

➤ Babe Ruth on reading: "Reading isn't good for a ballplayer. Not good for his eyes. If my eyes went bad even a little bit I couldn't hit home runs. So I gave up reading."

➤ Mickey Lolich, pitcher for the Detroit Tigers, on his physique: "I guess you could say I'm the redemption of the fat man. A guy will be watching me on TV and see that I don't look in any better shape than he is. 'Hey, Maude,' he'll holler. 'Get a load of this guy. And he's a 20-game winner.'"

➤ Reggie Jackson, sixth on the all-time home run list and one of the most outspoken players ever: "The only reason I don't like playing in the World Series is I can't watch myself play."

➤ Jim Bouton, former New York Yankees pitcher and author of *Ball Four:* "I have always thought that baseball was a strange and inefficiently run business, shot through with stupidity, bullheadedness, nepotism, and yes, even dishonesty. The reason baseball calls itself a game, I believe, is that it's too screwed up to be a business."

➤ Mike Schmidt, Philadelphia Phillies Hall of Fame third baseman: "Anytime you think you have the game conquered, the game will turn around and punch you right in the nose."

➤ Billy Martin, former player and major league manager: "When I get through managing, I'm going to open up a kindergarten."

Classic Fall Classics

Every World Series has its moments to remember. Maybe it's a terrific game full of twists and turns, maybe it's a memorable performance by one of the players, or maybe, if you're lucky, it's both. Let's take a look at a few World Series that have produced memories that stood the test of time.

Going, Going, Gone

The Fall Classics in 1960 and 1993 had one thing in common: the drama provided by a series-ending home run.

Miracle by Maz

On paper, the 1960 matchup between the New York Yankees and the Pittsburgh Pirates was a mismatch. But thankfully for the Pirates, the World Series isn't played on paper.

Through the first four games, the Yankees beat the Pirates like a drum, outscoring them 32–12. Only problem for the Yanks was, the Series was tied at two games apiece.

Through six games, the Yanks' domination in runs scored was equally overwhelming at 46–17. The Series remained equal on the scoreboard, too, with each team having won three games.

Which brings us to the seventh game at Forbes Field in Pittsburgh. The Pirates took a 9–7 lead into the ninth, only to see the Yankees tie it.

Ralph Terry pitched the bottom of the ninth for the Yankees—at least what there was of the bottom of the ninth. If you left your seat for another hot dog, you might've missed all the fireworks.

Bill Mazeroski was the first batter in the inning. Regarded as the best defensive second baseman in the history of the game, Maz didn't figure to pose too much of a problem on offense. Or so the Yankees hoped.

Terry's first pitch was a ball. His second pitch was a goner. Mazeroski, inducted into the Baseball Hall of Fame in 2001, homered over the left field wall to give the Pirates a 10–9 victory and a most improbable World Series championship.

The Inside Skinny

The Yankees outscored the Pirates 55–27 and outhit them 91–60 over the seven-game Series. They also won Games 2, 3, and 6 by a combined 35 runs. But those impressive statistics pale in comparison to this one: The Pirates won four of the seven games.

Canadian Club

The Philadelphia Phillies were three outs away from tying the 1993 World Series at three games apiece. They led the Toronto Blue Jays 6–5 in Game 6 at the SkyDome in Toronto.

It was up to Phillies ace reliever Mitch "Wild Thing" Williams to close the deal. You could probably guess that Williams got his Wild Thing nickname not because he was fond of the '60s song of the same name by The Trogs, but because he had a tendency to walk a lot of batters.

True to his nickname, Williams walked the first batter on four pitches, then, after a flyout to left field, gave up a single. So with two runners on, the last guy any pitcher would want to face in that situation came to the plate—Joe Carter, who was known for driving in runs and hitting with power.

The count reached two balls and two strikes. Williams's next pitch reached the left field seats. Carter's three-run homer gave the Blue Jays an 8–6 victory and their second straight World Series championship.

Best Game Ever?

Game 6 of the 1975 World Series between the Boston Red Sox and Cincinnati Reds was postponed for three days, because of torrential rain in Boston. (Who knew Mother Nature wasn't a baseball fan?) The game was finally played October 21, and goodness knows, it was worth the wait. It remains one of the greatest games in World Series history.

Sports Strategies

Bernie Carbo is one of only two players to accomplish the feat of pinch-hitting two home runs in one World Series (he did it in games 3 and 6 of the 1975 Series). The other was Chuck Essigan of the Los Angeles Dodgers in 1959.

The Reds entered the game with a 3–2 Series lead, but Boston bolted to a 3–0 lead in the first inning on a three-run homer by Fred Lynn. By the fifth inning, the Reds had tied it, and by the eighth, they led 6–3.

All the Reds needed to do was get through two more innings—six more outs—to win the World Series championship. But not so fast. The Red Sox rallied to tie it on a three-run pinch-hit homer by Bernie Carbo in the bottom of the eighth.

The Reds escaped a jam in the ninth and the Red Sox did likewise in the 11th. By this time, fans throughout the nation were getting low on fingernails.

But with one out in the bottom of the 12th, Boston catcher Carlton Fisk hit a ball down the left field line—Was it fair? Was it foul?—that bounced off the foul pole for a home run. The Red Sox prevailed 7–6, but their joy was short-lived. The Reds won Game 7.

Miracle Mets

It looked like the 1986 Boston Red Sox were finally going to win a World Series, their first since 1918. All they needed to do was get one more out. Leading the series three games to two, they had taken a 5–3 lead over the New York Mets in the top of the 10th inning of Game 6.

Relief pitcher Calvin Schiraldi got the first two outs of the bottom of the 10th, allowed two singles, then got two strikes on Ray Knight. All he needed was one more strike. The celebrations were about to begin in Beantown.

But a not-so-funny thing happened on the way to the party. Knight looped a single into center, driving in one run and making it 5–4.

Then, disaster struck. (Red Sox fans will probably stop reading at this point.) Pitcher Bob Stanley, who relieved Schiraldi, threw a wild pitch to allow the tying run to score. But the Red Sox still had a chance when New York's Mookie Wilson dribbled a grounder toward first baseman Bill Buckner for what appeared to be the final out. They had no chance when the ball scooted between Buckner's legs and the Mets scored the winning run to even the Series.

New York continued Boston's World Series futility by winning Game 7.

The Least You Need to Know

➤ Joe DiMaggio of the New York Yankees has the longest consecutive-game hitting streak of 56 games.

➤ Babe Ruth and Reggie Jackson are the only two players to hit three home runs in a World Series game.

➤ Ty Cobb led the American League in hitting a record 12 times.

➤ Bill Mazeroski of the Pittsburgh Pirates and Joe Carter of the Toronto Blue Jays each hit a World Series–clinching home run.

➤ Cal Ripken Jr. is the all-time leader in consecutive games played with 2,632.

Part 2

Football: America's New Pastime

Baseball used to be called the national pastime, but in the opinion of many people, those days are gone. Football rules with the American public.

Football in all its varieties—high school football, college football, and especially pro football—has become the *sport in the United States. Fans have thrilled to the sight of Johnny Unitas orchestrating the final minutes of a close game, Lawrence Taylor making a teeth-rattling sack, or Jerry Rice grabbing a pass across the middle.*

And what other sport can lay claim to having its championship game almost regarded as a national holiday?

Chapter 5

Pigskin Preview

In This Chapter

➤ College football's roots

➤ Football on campus

➤ Professors on the sidelines

➤ Heisman Trophy

College football has been around for more than 130 years. But the game as it was played way back when looks nothing like the game today. Would you believe a round ball was used at first? And that no officials were present?

In this chapter, we'll look at how the college game evolved, examine some of the best rivalries in the nation, and focus on four of the best coaches of all time. Let's kick off our chapter on college football!

All-American Game

Football was invented in the good ol' U.S. of A. Oh, there are some similarities to an English game called rugby and to soccer, which is called football throughout the world, but football as we know it today is an American game.

One of the first types of football was played by students at Princeton University in the 1820s. There were no rules, other than for one team to advance the ball past the other.

Then the freshmen and sophomore classes at Harvard got into the act. They played something resembling football on the first Monday of each school year. These games were not for the faint of heart, which is another way of saying they were rough. So rough, in fact, that the annual game was dubbed "Bloody Monday."

By the mid-1860s, after the Civil War had ended, the game became a bit more formalized. Rules were developed at Princeton, while just up the road at Rutgers, students developed their own set of rules.

The two schools made history in November 1869.

The Debut

The first modern football game took place November 6, 1869, between Rutgers and Princeton with about 100 curiosity seekers looking on. (Do I need to mention that it wasn't televised?) The field measured 120 yards long and 75 yards wide, and the ball was round, not egg-shaped.

Those weren't the only differences. Each side used 25 players at a time, and there wasn't an official anywhere to be found. That first football game looked a whole lot more like soccer than it did football. The ball was advanced downfield by kicking it or hitting it with feet, hands, heads, or sides. The object was to get the ball between a set of posts.

Scores were called games, not touchdowns, and it took 10 games to complete the contest. Rutgers won the first encounter 6–4. In a rematch the following week, Princeton, playing on its field and using its rules, beat Rutgers 8–0.

The Inside Skinny

After that second Rutgers-Princeton game, the folks from Princeton demonstrated the art of being gracious winners. They treated their guests to dinner and entertained them with songs and speeches. Perhaps that's how tailgating began.

Over the next 15 or 20 years, the game became more popular and underwent several significant changes, many of which were adopted when the game was played on the professional level:

➤ An egg-shaped rugby ball replaced the round ball

➤ Three officials were used to settle arguments

➤ A crossbar was added to the goalposts, 10 feet high, the same distance as today

➤ The field was reconfigured to almost the same dimensions it is today—120 yards long and 160 feet wide.

➤ The number of players a team could have on the field at one time was reduced from 25 to 15

But the biggest changes didn't occur until the late 1870s, when Walter Camp made his mark.

The Father of American Football

Who knows what direction football might've taken had Walter Camp not come along? But he's responsible for shaping the game into what it is today (which is not to suggest he had anything to do with end-zone dancing or trash-talking).

He never had an official title, but because he was such a leader and so well-respected, his influence, especially as it pertained to rule-making, was significant. It also helped that he played and coached at Yale, which was among the first colleges to play football.

Camp's first claim to fame was as a player for Yale University. He was a disciplined, well-conditioned athlete who was a terrific runner, kicker, and tackler. But as successful as he was on the field, it was his influence off the field that made the biggest impact.

It was Camp's idea to reduce the number of players on the field to 11, to put the ball in play using a scrimmage system, and to develop the concept of downs to determine if a team retained possession.

Camp also was credited with making the game safer. In its early days, football was survival of the fittest. The bigger and tougher you were, the better your chance of success. Strategy and finesse weren't part of the game.

One of the most popular—and most dangerous—plays was the Flying Wedge. A ball carrier would be surrounded by teammates, who often held hands. The only way a defender could penetrate the wedge was to fling himself into the mass of oncoming humanity. Doesn't that sound like a pleasant way to spend a Saturday afternoon?

The Flying Wedge was declared illegal in 1894. In 1906, Camp was instrumental in introducing the forward pass to place more emphasis on skill and less on brute force.

It is not stretching the point to suggest that Walter Camp saved the game.

Two-Minute Warning

All football fans know that to retain possession of the ball, a team needs to gain 10 yards in four plays, or downs. Doing so gets a team a first down and the chance to do it all again. But when Walter Camp came up with the down system, he required teams to make five yards in three downs. The rule wasn't revised until 1912.

Sports Strategies

Walter Camp selected the first college All-America football team in 1889. From 1899 through 1924, his team was considered the official team. That distinction was lost upon Camp's death in 1925. The Walter Camp All-America team is chosen today by the Walter Camp Foundation. It's one of several teams chosen today, including the Associated Press, the Football Writers Association of America and numerous publications.

First Things First

The developments in the game came fast and furious; it seemed there was something new happening all the time. Here's a look at some of the firsts:

➤ In 1877, L. P. Smock, a player for Princeton, designed the first uniform. Judging from the description, there's no chance of it making a comeback. It included a tightly laced canvas jacket, black pants to the knee, stockings, and a jersey with orange trim. Very snappy.

➤ Numbers on the jerseys debuted in 1915, but weren't required until 1937.

➤ In 1903, Harvard built the first concrete stadium designed just for football.

➤ Specific measurements for the football took effect in 1912. The ball became more narrow and pointy starting in 1929.

➤ Goalposts were moved 10 yards back, from the goal line to the back of the end zone, in 1927. The reason? To keep players from running into a goalpost and knocking themselves silly—ooh, that smarts!

➤ Leather helmets were used since the 1890s, but they weren't required until 1939. Plastic helmets made their debut after World War II.

➤ Touchdowns were worth between 1 and 5 points until 1912, when they were worth 6, same as today. Field goals were worth as many as 5 points until 1909, when they were worth 3, same as today.

Sports Strategies

One of the first football rule-making bodies was the Inter-collegiate Football Association, formed in 1873. The IFA eventually gave way to the National Collegiate Athletic Association in 1910. The NCAA, which exists today, oversees all college sports.

College football in its infancy was so far removed from the game that has become such big business today that it's hard to imagine. Let's look at some of the rivalries that have helped make college football such an attraction.

Big Game on Campus

Some of the best rivalries in all of sports are found in college football. And a rivalry isn't just about the game, it's about the pomp and circumstance and pageantry that goes along with it.

The fans get all cranked up; the tailgate parties are a bit fancier (steak instead of hamburgers, perhaps?); and the anticipation is palpable. Add the TV cameras and you have an atmosphere that can't be beat.

These rivalries are among the best of the best.

Army vs. Navy

The Army–Navy game exudes tradition and grandeur. It is a spectacle unlike any other. Neither team figures into the national championship picture anymore, because the schools' No. 1 priority is academics. But the games are as intense as those played at the highest level of the sport.

There was a time when Army and Navy were among the very best teams in America. Twice, in 1944 and 1945, the teams met when they were ranked No. 1 and No. 2. Army was ranked No. 1 each time, and the Cadets won both matchups and went on to win the national championship in each year.

Army leads the series with 48 wins and 46 losses. There have been seven ties. Seventy-five of those 101 games have been held in Philadelphia, which is between West Point, New York, site of Army's campus, and Annapolis, Maryland, where the Naval Academy is located.

The Game

The Army–Navy game may have the tradition of the cadets and the midshipmen, but the Harvard–Yale game gets the prize for the longest tradition. They've been playing "The Game" since 1875.

Any discussion about Harvard–Yale has to include the 1968 game. Yale was ranked 19th in the nation. The Elis had Calvin Hill, a running back who would go on to star for the Dallas Cowboys, and quarterback Brian Dowling, who had a nondescript career in the NFL. He played the 1977 season with the Green Bay Packers and spent several years in the now-defunct World Football League, a short-lived NFL rival.

But Harvard did the unthinkable, scoring 16 points in the final minute to forge a 29–29 tie and ruin Yale's perfect season.

The Iron Bowl

The Alabama vs. Auburn rivalry is a religion in the Deep South, with fans on each side being equally passionate.

The Inside Skinny

The 1893 Army–Navy game was particularly intense—so intense that several fights broke out in the stands. President Grover Cleveland was so outraged at the behavior that he banned the game for several years. But Teddy Roosevelt, an assistant secretary of the Navy, was a catalyst in having the game resume.

The Inside Skinny

Here's a piece of trivia you can impress your friends with: Brian Dowling, the Yale quarterback, was the inspiration for B.D., the character in Doonesbury. Garry Trudeau, the Doonesbury writer, is a 1970 Yale grad.

The Alabama Crimson Tide fans hold most of the bragging rights. Alabama not only leads the rivalry, it's also won more national championships (seven to Auburn's one) and more Southeastern Conference championships (21 to Auburn's 5).

The Tide was coached by Paul "Bear" Bryant, the winningest coach in the history of college football with 323 victories. (More about the Bear later in this chapter.)

The Auburn Tigers, though, can lay claim to the series' most improbable victory. In 1972, Auburn's Bill Newton blocked two punts in the final 5:30 and teammate David Langer returned them both for touchdowns as the Tigers managed a miracle, winning 17–16.

The Big Game

The annual battle between Ohio State and Michigan is arguably the most heated rivalry in major college football. The game always seems to be for the Big Ten championship, with the winner getting the conference's coveted bid to the Rose Bowl.

For years, Michigan's Bo Schembechler and Ohio State's Woody Hayes, both gruff, old-style coaches who weren't crazy about the forward pass, would match wits to see whose team prevailed.

Every Ohio State–Michigan game has been highly anticipated, and most of them live up to the hype. Most … but not all.

Take the game in 1950—please! What a nightmare. The two teams played in a snowstorm. Michigan won 9–3. There were 45 punts, many on first down to keep from fumbling, and the Wolverines didn't even make a first down. They scored by recording a safety and getting a touchdown on a blocked punt.

Legendary Coaches

There have been a slew of outstanding college football coaches over the years. But with no disrespect toward Pop Warner, Amos Alonzo Stagg, Frank Leahy, Bud Wilkinson, Bo Schembechler, Woody Hayes, or Bobby Bowden, we'll focus on Knute Rockne, Paul "Bear" Bryant, and Joe Paterno.

The Rock

Knute Rockne might be the most famous coach in college football history. For one, he coached Notre Dame and is responsible for the Fighting Irish becoming one of the most popular programs in the country. For another, he was a terrific motivator. His "Win One for the Gipper" speech, delivered at halftime of a 1928 game against Army, remains part of football lore. Maybe you saw the movie *Knute Rockne, All-American,* starring Pat O'Brien and a handsome young actor named Ronald Reagan.

But the main reason for Rockne's fame was his ability to coach. In 13 years at Notre Dame (1918–30), his teams won 105 games, lost 12, and tied 5. His .881 winning percentage is No. 1 all-time.

Rockne used his fame to land speaking engagements and commercial endorsements. This guy was way ahead of his time. His name was on footballs and helmets produced by Wilson Sporting Goods, and he was under contract to give motivational speeches for Studebaker Motors, based in South Bend, Indiana, where Notre Dame was located. Rockne's gift of gab earned him a top salary of $75,000, which was more than the president of the company.

Sadly, Rockne died in a plane crash in 1931 at the age of 43, prematurely ending one of the greatest coaching careers of all time.

Rockne was gone, but he would never be forgotten. In 1969, when a poll was taken among writers, coaches, and players to determine the best coach in the first 100 years of college football, Rockne finished on top.

The Bear

Coach Paul "Bear" Bryant got his nickname as a teenager after wrestling a bear in a traveling show. He was never paid the dollar a minute he was supposed to receive, but the nickname stuck.

Bryant as a head coach had the same commanding presence as a bear. He was a strict disciplinarian who demanded the most from his players. What he got in return was consistently excellent teams.

Bryant, known for his trademark hound's-tooth hat, was a head coach at the University of Kentucky and Texas A&M before taking over in 1958 at Alabama, where he enjoyed the lion's share of his success. He spent 25 seasons as coach of the Crimson Tide and led them to 13 Southeastern Conference titles and six national championships.

Bryant retired in 1982 as major college football's all-time winningest coach. His record was 323–85–17.

As luck would have it, Bryant recorded his 314th career victory, to pass Amos Alonzo Stagg as No. 1 on the all-time victory list, in 1981. It didn't come against the Little Sisters of the Poor; it came against Alabama's archrival, the Auburn Tigers. For Tide fans, it couldn't have been scripted any better.

Two-Minute Warning

You might think that Bear Bryant was such a great coach because of his innovations or his technical expertise. Not true. Bryant won because he worked harder, recruited better, and motivated his players as well as anyone ever has. "No coach has ever won a game by what he knows," said Bryant. "It's what his players have learned."

JoePa

By the time you read this, it's almost a lead-pipe cinch that Penn State's Joe Paterno will have overtaken Paul "Bear" Bryant as the winningest coach in major college football history. Entering the 2001 season, Paterno needed one win to tie and two wins to surpass the Bear's mark of 323 career victories.

Penn State coach Joe Paterno has coached the Nittany Lions to two national championships.

Photo: Reading Eagle Co.

Paterno, affectionately called JoePa, has been at Penn State for what seems like forever. He spent 16 years as an assistant coach, starting in 1950, and he took over as head coach in 1966. The 2001 season will be his 36th as head coach.

To put Paterno's longevity in perspective, he has been at Penn State through 11 presidential administrations, starting with Truman and continuing through George W. Bush. His success has been astounding:

➤ All-time leader in bowl game appearances (30) and victories (20)

➤ Only coach to win all four major bowls—Cotton, Orange, Rose, and Sugar

➤ Coached two national championship teams (1982, '86) and four undefeated teams that didn't win national titles

➤ Named American Football Coaches Association Coach of the Year a record four times

➤ The first football coach named *Sports Illustrated*'s Sportsman of the Year, in 1986

Paterno's commitment to excellence goes beyond the football field. He insists that his players attend class and keep up with their studies. He also has donated millions—yes, millions—to the university to endow faculty positions and scholarships and to support two building projects. That's in addition to the $250,000 he and his wife, Sue, donated to a library-expansion campaign.

But Paterno's devotion to academics, especially literature, isn't all that surprising when you find out that he graduated from Brown, likes opera, and was inducted into the Penn State chapter of Eta Sigma Phi, the national classics society. Talk about being a unique football coach!

The Inside Skinny

Joe Paterno will become the winningest coach in *major* college history. But he'll never coach long enough to surpass the victory total of former Grambling State coach Eddie Robinson, who coached for 55 seasons and won 408 games. Grambling State is a Division I-AA school, which is one step below the major college level.

Welcome to the Club

Each year in early December, the Downtown Athletic Club in New York City awards the *Heisman Trophy* to the most outstanding college football player in the United States. There are a slew of awards in college football each season, but the Heisman is the one that gets all the attention, including a live broadcast of the ceremony.

Jay Berwanger, a halfback from the University of Chicago, won the first award in 1935. Chris Weinke, a quarterback from Florida State, won the Heisman in 2000. In between, only one player—Archie Griffin, a halfback from Ohio State in 1974 and '75—repeated, and only 13 winners were juniors.

If you're a running back, history shows you have a distinct advantage. Of the 66 winners, 40 carried the ball. If you're a defensive player, good luck, because a defensive player has never won the Heisman.

The Fundamentals

The **Heisman Trophy** is named for John Heisman, who spent 36 years as a college football coach (1892–1927) and who was also the president of the Downtown Athletic Club (DAC). The trophy was first presented as the DAC Trophy, but was renamed in 1936 as a tribute to Heisman, who died of bronchial pneumonia.

The Least You Need to Know

➤ The first college football game took place November 6, 1869, between Princeton and Rutgers.

➤ Walter Camp is known as the father of American football.

➤ The Army–Navy game is among the most storied of all college football rivalries.

➤ Knute Rockne, who coached Notre Dame, was one of the game's most effective motivators.

➤ Paul "Bear" Bryant was a hard-nosed taskmaster who demanded the ultimate effort from his players.

➤ Penn State's Joe Paterno is a renaissance man who also happens to be a football coach.

Playing for Pay

The first version of the National Football League (NFL) was created in 1902 and was out of business after only one season. It took nearly a half-century before the league established itself for the long haul and developed into the version we know today.

Despite the chaos of those early days, the game produced some legendary figures—Jim Thorpe, Red Grange, and Bronko Nagurski, to name a few. In this chapter, we'll examine the origins of pro football and how it eventually overtook baseball as our national pastime. Now, some folks may argue the point about football being our national pastime, but when you consider how it's become such a television staple, how most teams play in sold-out stadiums each week and how the Super Bowl has turned into a happening, pro football, for my money, is No. 1.

Pro Football's Humble Beginnings

The first incarnation of the NFL was created by two baseball clubs in 1902. The Philadelphia Athletics and the Philadelphia Phillies each backed a football team. Those teams, along with the Pittsburgh Stars, comprised the NFL.

The league had no bylaws, no office, and no power to make schedules. All it had were three teams that played each other two or three times a season. They also played several games against independent teams.

For some reason, all three teams claimed the league championship, but league president Dave Berry named the Stars the champions—probably because the Stars won the championship game, beating the Athletics.

The first version of the NFL disappeared after one season.

Sports Strategies

Even though the original NFL folded after one season, the league did manage a milestone: The Philadelphia Athletics played the Kanaweola Athletic Club team in the first professional night game on Nov. 21, 1902, in Elmira, New York. Legend has it that huge searchlights were placed at each end of the field. The Athletics won 39–0.

Over the next 20 years or so, the pro game was focused first in western Pennsylvania and then in Ohio, where teams such as the Massilon Tigers and the Canton Bulldogs dominated. But by 1920, the game was pretty much a mess because of rising salaries, players switching teams to get bigger paychecks, and the use of college players still enrolled in school.

The solution to the problems was to form a league in which all teams followed one set of rules. The American Professional Football Conference was born in August 1920. But before the first game was played, the name was changed to the American Professional Football Association, which doesn't exactly roll off the tongue. The APFA operated for two years, before changing its name to the National Football League, which has done pretty well for itself.

There's no way to know for sure, but I'm guessing that the game's founding fathers would be stunned to see how wildly popular their league has became.

Pro Football's First Icons

Every league needs stars, and the National Football League was blessed with three bright ones in its early days. Even though they played way back when, and even though the game was still in its infancy, Jim Thorpe, Red Grange, and Bronko Nagurski rank among the greatest players in the history of the NFL.

Bright Path

You probably wouldn't know him by his Indian name, Wa-Tho-Huk ("Bright Path"), but just about everyone knows Jim Thorpe, who was as versatile as he was accomplished. There was nothing this guy couldn't do well.

Thorpe was born in 1887 in a one-room cabin in Indian Territory, now known as Oklahoma. He and his father, Hiram, didn't see eye to eye on things, and Hiram eventually sent his son to the Carlisle Indian Industrial School in Pennsylvania to become a tailor.

Jim Thorpe was one of professional football's first and biggest stars.

Photo: Icon Sports Media

Jim Thorpe was on the track and football teams at Carlisle. After graduating in 1912, he traveled to Stockholm, Sweden, for the Summer Olympics. He won gold medals in the decathlon and pentathlon.

Thorpe played professional baseball from 1913 to 1919, and from 1915 through 1920 he played football for the Canton Bulldogs. He sure could draw a crowd. Canton drew between 8,000 and 10,000 fans for every game, mostly because of Thorpe. He led the Canton Bulldogs to unofficial championships in 1916, 1917, and 1919.

In 1920, Canton joined the American Professional Football Association (the forerunner of the NFL), and Thorpe's NFL career began. It continued with the Oorang Indians, an all-Indian team that was sponsored by a company that owned dog kennels.

The Inside Skinny

Jim Thorpe was stripped of his Olympic medals by the International Olympic Committee, which found out he earned $125 a month for two years while playing minor league baseball. The medals were restored in 1982.

After two seasons with Oorang, he spent one year each with Rock Island, the New York Giants, and the Chicago Cardinals.

At 6' 1", 200 pounds, Thorpe was a punishing runner and devastating tackler. Here's what Knute Rockne, the famed Notre Dame football coach who also played for the Massilon Tigers, had to say about his unsuccessful attempt to tackle Thorpe: "It was as if a locomotive had hit me, and then been followed by a 10-ton truck rambling over the remains." It hurts just thinking about it.

Even though Thorpe was past his prime by the time he entered the NFL at age 33, he still made a significant enough impact to be a charter member of the Pro Football Hall of Fame in 1963.

The Galloping Ghost

As nicknames go, being a running back who's called the Galloping Ghost is as good as it gets. And Harold "Red" Grange was that good. He was graceful, speedy, and elusive. Would-be tacklers didn't have a chance, and sports fans couldn't get enough of him. And to think he almost decided not to play football at the University of Illinois, opting for basketball and track instead. Fortunately, for Grange and for football, some of his fraternity brothers talked some sense into him.

In his three seasons at Illinois, Grange rushed for 2,071 yards, averaged 5.3 yards a carry, and completed 40 of 82 passes for 575 yards. He scored 31 touchdowns, 16 of which were 20 yards or longer and nine of which were 50 yards or longer.

The day after he graduated from college in 1925, Grange turned pro, signing with the Chicago Bears for $3,500 a game, plus a percentage of the gate receipts—a pretty sweet deal in those days. The investment paid off handsomely. The Bears scheduled a barnstorming tour that included regular season games and exhibitions. Over the next 67 days, Grange played 19 games. The first 10 games were played in 18 days. He brought fans—65,000 in New York, 75,000 in Los Angeles—and credibility to pro football.

Not surprisingly, all those games took their toll on Grange, and knee injuries in 1927 and 1928 turned him into what he called an "ordinary runner." So what did he do? He helped the Bears by becoming a defensive back, and in the 1933 NFL Championship game against the New York Giants, he tackled halfback Dale Burnett to save the game for the Bears.

Grange, a charter member of the Pro Football Hall of Fame in 1963, would've been a fixture on highlight shows, had there been such things in those days. But as much as he's renowned for his fancy footwork on the field, he'll be remembered as much for the boost he gave pro football.

Bronko

You have to figure that anyone with a rugged, tough-sounding name like Bronko Nagurski was born to be a football player. And what a football player he was! At 6' 2" and 225 pounds, Nagurski was unstoppable as a runner and punishing as a tackler.

Supposedly, he was discovered by Doc Spears, football coach of the University of Minnesota. As legend has it, and no doubt this story is apocryphal, Spears stopped to ask directions from "a big farm boy plowing a field, and the boy picked up the plow and pointed with it."

Nagurski went on to play at Minnesota and, in 1930, became the only player to be named an All-American at two positions—fullback and defensive tackle.

Nagurksi signed with the Chicago Bears in 1930 and became the key to the team's offense. He cleared paths for the Bears' other runners, and when the Bears got within a few yards of the goal line, he cleared a path for himself.

But there was more to Nagurski's talents than blocking and running. He was an adept short passer—his pass to Red Grange in the 1932 NFL Championship won the game—and he was a fine *linebacker*.

The Inside Skinny

Separating fact from fiction when it came to Bronko Nagurski was difficult. One story had him running out of bounds at full speed and knocking over a policeman's horse. Then there was the time he collided with a (stationary) Model T and tore off a fender. Believe it or not.

The Fundamentals

Linebackers are smaller and more mobile and agile than defensive linemen, because they often cover pass receivers. Unlike linemen, who begin each play in a three-point stance, linebackers stand up. Defenses usually employ three linebackers, although sometimes four are used.

63

In fact, Nagurski returned to the Bears in 1943 to play linebacker and fill in at fullback—after six years of retirement. He did just fine, thank you, scoring a touchdown in the Bears' victory over the Washington Redskins. Not bad for a 35-year-old. When Nagurski finally retired for good, Clarke Hinkle of the Green Bay Packers called it "my biggest thrill in football."

Sports Strategies

The first player ever to gain 1,000 yards in a season was Beattie Feathers of the Chicago Bears in 1934. Feathers was a talented running back, but it's highly unlikely he would've reached his milestone without his fullback, Bronko Nagurski, opening holes for him like a pile driver.

The Fundamentals

Before the **college player draft,** the best players went to the highest bidders, meaning the rich got richer. Once the draft was instituted, teams drafted the players in inverse order of finish the previous season—that is, the worst teams got the first chance to pick the best players.

There are few players who could dominate a game no matter where they lined up on the field. Bronko Nagurski, a charter member of the Pro Football Hall of Fame, was one of them.

The NFL Emerges

Not everything went smoothly in the NFL's development. There were challenges from upstart rival leagues, gambling issues to be handled, and television—some newfangled invention—to be dealt with. But, luckily, the league's powers-that-be had a knack for selecting the right person to guide them through the choppy waters.

Bert Bell was named commissioner of the NFL in January 1946, and he guided the league through some of its toughest times and set the stage for the explosion that would come down the road.

After Bell died of a heart attack in 1959, the owners had a devil of a time agreeing on a replacement. But they finally decided on Pete Rozelle, who merely turned out to be the best thing that could've happened to the NFL.

Bert Bell

Before he became commissioner of the NFL, Bert Bell owned the Philadelphia Eagles. Early on, he also was the coach, the general manager, the ticket manager, and the public relations man. Obviously, Bert didn't have a lot of spare time.

The Eagles weren't a very good team, but it was their futility that led to Bell's coming up with what turned out to be a darn good idea. He proposed drafting college players to ensure competitive balance throughout the league. The first *college player draft* was held in 1936, and today it is one of the most anticipated events of the year for football fans.

Bell's first chore as commissioner was confronting the All-America Football Conference (AAFC), which began play in 1946. Because each league was overpaying to attract the best players, both leagues were in financial trouble.

The AAFC requested that the NFL participate in a common draft and hold an annual World Series of football. But Bell would hear none of it. He didn't even mention the rival league by name. His firm stand paid dividends when the AAFC folded in 1949, except for the three teams—Baltimore, Cleveland, and San Francisco—that joined the NFL.

Bell was hailed a genius, just as he was when he suspended New York Giants halfback Merle Hapes and later quarterback Frank Filchock for the 1946 NFL title game—not for gambling, but for not reporting that they were approached by gamblers. The message was clear: Don't mess with Bell.

Bell's most far-reaching move was taking steps to keep television under control. Television wasn't a big deal to the NFL back then. It was a relatively new phenomenon, kind of like a DVD player today. But Bell realized that if fans could watch games on TV, they might not go to the stadium. So he came up with the idea of televising road games to home cities, and televising home games only if they were sold out.

The Inside Skinny

The first pro football game to be nationally televised was the 1951 NFL title game between the Los Angeles Rams and the Cleveland Browns at the Los Angeles Coliseum. The DuMont Network paid $75,000 for the rights. It turned out to be a good show. The Browns won 30–28 on a last-minute field goal.

Fortunate Compromise

To say Pete Rozelle wasn't the overwhelming choice to replace Bert Bell in January 1960 would be a rather large understatement. He wasn't even one of the top two choices. One faction of the owners wanted Austin Gunsel, the NFL treasurer; another wanted Marshall Leahy, attorney for the San Francisco 49ers.

Well, after seven days and 22 ballots, neither of those guys could earn the three-fourths majority needed. Do you suppose they counted all the hanging chads?

Finally, a compromise candidate was nominated and elected on the 23rd ballot. Alvin "Pete" Rozelle, the general manager of the Los Angeles Rams, was the new NFL commissioner. Rozelle was only 33 and he was openly concerned about his qualifications—or lack thereof.

He was reassured by the owners, who promised he would grow into the job. What an understatement! All Rozelle did was make the NFL the envy of every other professional sport. He was a visionary who made all the right moves.

Pete Rozelle was one of the most innovative and forward-thinking commissioners in sports history.

Photo: Icon Sports Media

It was Rozelle who came up with the revenue-sharing plan that enabled small-market teams like the Green Bay Packers to compete with large-market teams like those in New York or Chicago. The key to the plan was a network television deal in which all teams shared the proceeds equally.

Rozelle also moved the NFL headquarters to New York City, so the league could take advantage of being in the nation's biggest media center.

"The Foolish Club"

With a name like "The Foolish Club," the success of your business venture is hardly a sure thing. But that's what the eight owners of the teams in the American Football League (AFL) were called.

The AFL was the brainchild of Lamar Hunt, an oilman from Dallas. He wanted to bring a team to the NFL, but was turned down. So he took matters—and money—into his own hands and created a rival league, with teams from Dallas, Denver, Houston, Los Angeles, New York, Buffalo, Boston, and Oakland.

The Inside Skinny

How's this for irony? On the same day Pete Rozelle was finally elected NFL commissioner—January 26, 1960—Lamar Hunt, the owner of the Dallas Texans, was elected as the first president of the American Football League.

Not many people, other than The Foolish Club, thought the AFL could compete with the NFL, but with its wide-open style of play and the television contract it signed with NBC, the new league fared far better than anyone expected—especially the NFL, which was having to print its own money to try to sign the best players.

Finally in 1966, after two months of secret negotiations, a merger of the two leagues was announced, starting with the 1970 season. The NFL and AFL held a combined draft in 1967, the same year teams from the two leagues began playing each other in preseason games.

One other provision came out of those negotiations: The institution of a championship game, starting after the 1967 season. It was called the AFL-NFL World Championship Game.

As names go, that one wasn't so catchy. You probably know it as the Super Bowl. Now *that* has a ring to it!

Sports Strategies

When the new National Football League began play in 1970, there were 26 teams playing in two conferences. The Baltimore Colts, Cleveland Browns, and Pittsburgh Steelers of the old NFL agreed to join the AFL teams to form the American Football Conference.

The Game That Became an Event

The Super Bowl has become an undeclared national holiday. It's the perfect excuse to have a party.

Oh, it's not that we're all that concerned about the football game; it's the nachos and chicken wings and guacamole dip that we're crazy about. We love to watch the commercials, too. Sometimes they're better than the game.

So, for a variety of reasons, the Super Bowl has become a red-letter day on all our calendars. But when the game was first conceived, no one had a clue it would become so popular.

The first game, between the Kansas City Chiefs of the AFL and the Green Bay Packers of the NFL, was held on January 15, 1967, in the Los Angeles Coliseum—which wasn't even full. Only 61,946 folks bothered to show up at the 94,000-seat stadium.

The game was, however, televised by two networks—CBS, which aired NFL games, and NBC, which aired the AFL. The Packers beat the Chiefs 35–10, but nobody seemed to pay all that much attention.

It wouldn't be long before that changed. The Super Bowl grew in popularity, with the biggest boost coming in Super Bowl III, won by the New York Jets in a stunning upset over the Baltimore Colts. It was the AFL's first victory and it changed the game forever. (We'll take a closer look at that game in Chapter 8, "Gridiron Classics.")

Two-Minute Warning

The advertisers don't always profit from their investment in Super Bowl ads. Of the 17 dot-com companies that paid $2 million or more for a 30-second spot for Super Bowl XXXIV in 2000, only six retained the same ad agency six months later, and one company went belly-up completely.

Over the years, the Super Bowl developed into a real plum for whichever network televised it, with commercial time in 2000 selling for more than $2 million for a 30-second spot. And usually, the advertisers got plenty of bang for their buck. Of the 50 all-time highest-rated television programs, the Super Bowl appears on that list 22 times.

Four Super Bowls rank in the top 10 highest-rated television programs of all time:

➤ 4. Super Bowl XVI (1982): 49ers 26, Bengals 21

➤ 5. Super Bowl XVII (1983): Redskins 27, Dolphins 17

➤ 7. Super Bowl XX (1986): Bears 46, Patriots 10

➤ 10. Super Bowl XII (1978): Cowboys 27, Broncos 10

For what it's worth, the three programs ranked higher than Super Bowl XVI are: No. 3, *Roots,* part 8; No. 2, the "Who Shot JR?" episode of *Dallas;* and No. 1, the final episode of *M*A*S*H.*

The Least You Need to Know

➤ The first two National Football League teams were backed by baseball teams: the Philadelphia Athletics and Philadelphia Phillies.

➤ Jim Thorpe, Red Grange, and Bronko Nagurski were among the game's early icons.

➤ As NFL commissioner, Bert Bell led the league through some of its most trying times.

➤ Pete Rozelle replaced Bell as commissioner and was a compromise candidate. He turned the league into the powerhouse it is today.

➤ The American Football League successfully challenged the National Football League. Eventually, the two leagues merged.

Chapter 7

Greats of the Game

In This Chapter

➤ Signal callers

➤ On the line

➤ Heavy hitters

➤ Catching on

➤ Run to daylight

➤ Coaching legends

We'll look at a few of the greatest players and coaches in the history of the game in this chapter. It is by no means the definitive list. You might even raise your eyebrows at some of my choices. What was I thinking to omit Brett Favre and include Dan Marino? How could I include Tom Landry and not Bill Parcells?

But that's part of the fun of sports: the discussion it creates. So let the debate begin!

The Field Generals

The quarterback position is the most glamorous on the field—by far. The quarterback gets the lion's share of the credit when things go well; when things go poorly he's the least popular guy in town. These four quarterbacks got way more praise than grief.

Sports Strategies

Among the many milestones and records set by Johnny Unitas, one stands above the rest because it's unlikely to be broken: Starting with the final game of the 1956 season, he threw touchdown passes in 47 straight regular season games. The streak ended in 1960.

The Inside Skinny

Joe Montana is the only player to be named Most Valuable Player in the Super Bowl three times. In his other appearance, Super Bowl XXIII, he didn't win the award, but he did win the game, driving the San Francisco 49ers 92 yards in the final three minutes. His touchdown pass to John Taylor beat the Cincinnati Bengals 20–16.

Johnny U

Johnny Unitas looked more like a 97-pound weakling than a Hall of Fame quarterback. He was skinny, stoop-shouldered, and wore high-top black shoes that made him look very uncool.

But in Unitas's case, looks were deceiving. Once he joined the Baltimore Colts in the 1956 season after being cut by the Pittsburgh Steelers, it wasn't long before he staked his claim to being the best quarterback of all time. Who knows? Maybe it was those shoes.

Unitas was at his best when the game was on the line. He always seemed to anticipate the defense, make the right call, and then deliver the ball precisely where it needed to be. It was as if he were born with a sixth sense.

Unitas won the NFL's Most Valuable Player Award three times, led the league in passing four times, and is a member of the Pro Football Hall of Fame.

If you're wondering how Unitas could be mentioned without reference to the 1958 NFL Championship Game, don't worry. We'll get to it in Chapter 8, "Gridiron Classics."

Magic Man

Joe Montana was a combination of Harry Houdini and David Copperfield in shoulder pads and a football helmet. No matter how dire or hopeless the situation appeared, Montana had enough up his sleeve to create something amazing. Time after time, he found a way to lead his teams to victory. He was cool, he was unflappable, and he thrived on pressure situations. The more pressure, the better.

Montana played his college ball at Notre Dame, where he started as the seventh-string quarterback. He was the starter by his senior year, and in his final game, he demonstrated his penchant for miracles. Against Houston in the Cotton Bowl game, Montana rallied the Fighting Irish from a 34–12 third-quarter deficit to a 35–34 victory and the 1976 national championship. Magic man, indeed!

But perhaps his most miraculous play came in the 1981 NFL Championship Game against the Dallas Cowboys. With 51 seconds left, Montana hit Dwight Clark with a pass in the back of the end zone to lift the 49ers to their first Super Bowl. Known as The Catch, it was the throw, which came after Montana was forced to scramble, that led to the drama.

And the magic.

Dan's the Man

Dan Marino never won a Super Bowl. Now, you're probably thinking that Marino's career is somehow tainted. Or that he doesn't deserve to be ranked among the best quarterbacks of all time.

Well, you could think that, but you'd be dead wrong.

Marino, who spent his entire career with the Miami Dolphins, had the misfortune of playing on teams plagued by ineffective running games, shoddy defenses, or both.

Dan Marino of the Miami Dolphins holds virtually every significant record for quarterbacks.

Photo: Diane Staskowski

But even though defenses knew the Dolphins couldn't run and that Marino was going to throw, it didn't keep him from rewriting the record book. He was that good.

Name a significant quarterback record and Marino owns it:

➤ Pass attempts: 8,358

➤ Completions: 4,967

➤ Passing yardage: 61,361 (the equivalent of 34.9 miles)

➤ Touchdown passes: 420

➤ Career 400-yard games: 13

➤ Career 300-yard games: 63

➤ Career 3,000-yard seasons: 13

You know the saying, records are made to be broken? Chances are pretty darn good that Marino's are safe.

The Comeback Kid

Think about John Elway and you think about comebacks. He was a master at bringing his team, the Denver Broncos, to victory with a fourth-quarter drive.

Forty-seven times Elway rallied the Broncos from a fourth-quarter deficit to either win or tie. And no wonder. He had it all: intelligence, leadership, toughness, agility, arm strength, and a warrior-like mentality.

The most famous of those comebacks—and the one that Cleveland Browns fans probably can't bear to recall—took place on January 11, 1986, in the AFC Championship Game. It's become known as The Drive.

Trailing the Browns 20–13 with 5:32 to play, Elway moved the Broncos 98 yards in 15 plays and threw the tying touchdown pass to Mark Jackson with less than 40 seconds to play. The Broncos went on to win the game in overtime and reach the Super Bowl.

Elway made it to five Super Bowls, but it wasn't until the last two in 1998 and 1999 that he came away a winner. He retired in April 1999. What a way to go out.

Sports Strategies

In 1984, Dan Marino had the most prolific season of any quarterback in NFL history. He completed 64.2 percent of his passes for single-season records of 5,084 yards and 48 touchdowns. He averaged 318 yards and three TDs a game. Unbelievable.

The Inside Skinny

John Elway spent his entire career with the Denver Broncos, but he was drafted by the Baltimore Colts. Elway, who went to Stanford, wanted to play for a team in the West. In effect, he forced the Colts to trade him by threatening to play baseball. Rather than lose him and get nothing in return, the Colts traded him to the Broncos.

Trench Warfare

The defensive linemen are usually the guys with the dirtiest uniforms and the most fearsome reputations.

They can hit and run, and they make a habit out of making life miserable for opposing quarterbacks and running backs, whom they pursue as if they had targets on their backs.

We'll look at two of the best defensive linemen of all time—a Minister, and a Mean Joe.

The Minister of Defense

Reggie White is an ordained Baptist pastor; hence his nickname, the Minister of Defense. But at 6' 5", 291 pounds, and blessed with strength, quickness, agility, and a nose for quarterbacks, he is probably unlike any pastor you're familiar with. In his NFL career, White has turned the *sack* into an art form.

After a standout career at the University of Tennessee and two seasons with the Memphis Showboats of the defunct United States Football League, White came to the NFL with the Philadelphia Eagles.

In 1992, White signed with the Green Bay Packers, where he was regarded as a savior. The year before White arrived, the Packers' defense ranked 23rd in the league. In his first season, the defense improved to second. How's that for making an impact?

White is the NFL's all-time leader in sacks with 198. He also holds the record for sacks in a Super Bowl (three) and sacks in one season (21). That season, by the way, was 1987, which was strike-shortened to just 12 games.

The Fundamentals

A **quarterback sack,** one of the most prized defensive statistics, is registered when a player tackles the quarterback behind the line of scrimmage while he's attempting to complete a pass.

Mean Joe

Mean Joe Greene, a defensive tackle, was renowned for his incredible quickness, his brute strength, and his starring role on the Pittsburgh Steelers' Steel Curtain defenses of the 1970s.

Yes, Greene helped the Steelers win four Super Bowls in the mid-'70s. And yes, he was named Defensive Player of the Year twice and an All-Pro eight times. But in spite of all those accolades, it's a TV commercial that made Greene famous to people who didn't know the first thing about football.

Remember? Greene trudging up the tunnel after a game and being offered a Coca-Cola by a little tyke, who walked away disappointed because Greene drank the Coke, but didn't acknowledge him. And then Greene yells, "Hey, kid," and tosses him his jersey.

It was a classic. Mean Joe was, too.

The Good-Hands People

Outstanding wide receivers have several things in common—good hands (duh), the ability to run precise pass routes, and the courage to catch the ball over the middle of the field with some hulking linebacker or head-hunting defender bearing down on them.

Don Hutson and Jerry Rice were from different eras, but they possessed all the talents to be considered at the top of a very short list of terrific receivers.

The Alabama Antelope

Don Hutson could stop on a dime, change directions, and drive defensive backs crazy with his perfect pass routes.

The Inside Skinny

There was no player draft in Don Hutson's day, the mid-1930s through the mid-1940s, and he signed a contract with each of the teams that showed interest—the Green Bay Packers and Brooklyn Dodgers. Joe Carr, president of the NFL, decided the contract that made it to the league office first would be in force. Green Bay's arrived 17 minutes before Brooklyn's.

He was tall and skinny and not much of a physical presence, but it didn't matter. Hutson, who played 11 years, led the league in catches eight times, touchdowns nine times, receiving yardage seven times, and scoring five times. Twice, he was named the NFL's Most Valuable Player. And he put up these numbers despite usually being double- and triple-teamed.

And as if his receiving ability wasn't enough, Hutson made 30 interceptions as a defensive back and was also a fine placekicker.

You probably won't be the least bit surprised to find out he was a charter member of the Pro Football Hall of Fame.

Simply the Best

It's almost impossible to believe, knowing what we know now, but in the 1985 NFL draft, there were two wide receivers taken before Jerry Rice.

Which is like choosing a Ford or a Chevy over a Rolls Royce. Rice is considered the best receiver in NFL history.

Rice, who played for the San Francisco 49ers from 1985 through 2000, before signing with the Oakland Raiders as free agent, owns just about every receiving record worth having. He was the NFL's Most Valuable Player in 1987, when he caught 23 touchdown passes for 138 points and led the league in scoring, which hadn't been done by a wide receiver since Elmer "Crazy Legs" Hirsch in 1951.

Rice holds records for career receptions (1,206), yardage (18,442), touchdown passes (169) and touchdowns (180).

Rice was also the Most Valuable Player in Super Bowl XXIII, when he caught 11 passes for 215 yards and one TD.

Make no mistake, Jerry Rice was blessed with a lot of God-given talent. But what made Rice into arguably the greatest receiver in NFL history was his tireless work ethic. As good as he was, Rice never stopped working to get even better.

Defensive backs who spent much of their careers chasing him can attest to that.

Sports Strategies

Jerry Rice didn't play his college football at one of the big football factories. He played at Mississippi Valley State, a small Division I-AA school. He was a consensus All-American as a junior and senior, and set 18 NCAA Division I-AA records.

The Hit Men

It is part of what makes the game so exciting: the bone-rattling, teeth-jarring tackles that sometimes are so powerful, you can feel them in your living room.

No two players are more renowned for punishing opposing ball carriers than Dick Butkus of the Chicago Bears and Lawrence Taylor of the New York Giants.

Butkus

The name sounds as if it were created for a football player, and Dick Butkus was a football player—as tough and ferocious as they came.

Butkus wasn't the biggest guy in the world at 6' 3", 245 pounds, but he was probably the most determined. Nothing kept him from the poor guy with the ball.

The Inside Skinny

To say Dick Butkus made an impact on the NFL would be a bit of an understatement. For instance, a poll of NFL quarterbacks paid him the ultimate respect by naming him the second-most feared player in the league. The poll was taken in 1985—21 years after Butkus retired.

Said MacArthur Lane, formerly a running back for the Green Bay Packers: "If I had a choice, I'd sooner go one-on-one with a grizzly bear."

It was an opinion shared by everyone who had the misfortune of being tackled by Butkus.

Sports Strategies

Lawrence Taylor was always conscious of his image, always concerned with seeming as tough as he really was. In high school, to cultivate that image, he insisted on being called Lawrence. The reason? He didn't think Larry sounded tough enough.

L.T.

Lawrence Taylor was a quarterback's nightmare. The sight of L.T., bearing down at full speed from his outside linebacker position, was enough to make a quarterback wish he had chosen a safer line of work—like alligator wrestling.

Taylor revolutionized the way the position was played, because he was such an effective pass rusher. Teams structured their entire game plans just to stop—or try to stop—Taylor.

Taylor led the Giants to seven appearances in the playoffs and two Super Bowl championships (1986, '90), and he is the only defense player ever to be named Player of the Year (1986).

When he retired after the 1993 season, besides making quarterbacks rejoice, he also ranked second all-time in sacks with 132.5.

Lawrence Taylor of the New York Giants redefined the linebacker position in the NFL.

Photo: Diane Staskowski

Ground Assault

Whenever a quarterback handed the ball off to Jim Brown or Walter Payton, it was practically a mortal lock that something wonderful was about to happen.

Brown and Payton were very much the same type runners: They relished contact, they ran hard, they were incredibly durable, and they were warriors.

The Standard

Jim Brown's NFL career was relatively short—only nine years. But what he accomplished during that time explains why he has become the measuring stick for running backs.

Think I'm exaggerating? See for yourself:

➤ He rushed for 1,000 yards in seven of nine seasons.

➤ In 1963, he rushed for 1,863 yards (an average of 6.4 yards per carry) and 12 touchdowns.

➤ His 5.2-yards-per-carry average is the all-time high.

➤ He rushed for 100 or more yards 58 times, nearly half of his total starts.

➤ His career rushing total was 12,312 yards. His 126 touchdowns was an NFL record that stood for more than two decades.

Two-Minute Warning

In case you thought that Jim Brown was only a football player, well, think again. At Syracuse University, Brown lettered in football, basketball, lacrosse, and track. In fact, he was an All-American lacrosse player.

And as if that wasn't enough, Brown punished tacklers, instead of the other way around. Defenders trying to bring down Brown were on the business end of a violent collision. More often than not, they hung on for dear life until help arrived. You bet he was the best ever.

Sweetness

Walter Payton's nickname, Sweetness, might give you the impression he was a finesse running back—someone who relied on moves, not toughness. Well, nothing could be further from the truth. Payton had all moves, but he also never shied away from contact.

If presented with the choice of going out of bounds to avoid a hit, or taking the hit and maybe getting an extra yard, Payton opted for the contact every time.

He was as complete a football player as ever played the game, and he always was ready to play. Payton missed only one game in his entire pro career with the Chicago Bears, and that was a coach's decision. Payton maintained all along that he was good to go.

Payton led the league in carries four straight seasons (1976–79), and through the 2000 season he was the NFL's all-time leading rusher with 16,726 yards.

Sadly, Walter Payton died on November 1, 1999, the result of a rare liver disease. His achievements—and the class and dignity with which he accomplished them—live on.

View from the Sidelines

One is recognized as the greatest motivator and disciplinarian in the history of the NFL; the other is the all-time winningest coach in the history of the NFL. Between them, they've won seven NFL championships and set the bar pretty darn high.

Vince Lombardi led the Green Bay Packers to glory, and Don Shula demonstrated consistent excellence with the Baltimore Colts and Miami Dolphins for more than three decades.

Lombardi

That Vince Lombardi was responsible for one of the most famous quotes ever— "Winning isn't everything, it's the only thing"—tells you all you need to know about him.

Sports Strategies

Vince Lombardi's career record was 98–30–4. The Packers' streak of three straight NFL titles hasn't been equaled since. His magic wasn't limited to Green Bay, either. After retiring from the Packers, he led the Washington Redskins to their first winning season in years.

He was demanding and intense, and ruled with an iron fist.

Of course, not all of his players were crazy about his attitude. When asked about how Lombardi treated the team, one player said everyone was treated the same: "like dogs."

But Lombardi got results. Oh, did he get results! He took over as the Packers' coach in 1959 and inherited a team that had just completed its ninth losing season in 11 years. But Lombardi led the Pack to a 7–5 record in 1959 and to the NFL title game in 1960, when they lost to the Philadelphia Eagles.

After that game, Lombardi promised his team would never again lose a title game. And it didn't. The Packers reached the championship game in five of the next seven seasons and won each one, including the first two Super Bowls in 1966 and '67.

Lombardi's teams didn't prosper because of some fancy offensive philosophy—you know, throwing the ball 30 or 40 times a game. The Packers won with a fundamentally solid running game, featuring their signature power sweep, and a punishing defense. They executed to near perfection on both sides of the ball. Their coach would have it no other way.

Top of the List

Don Shula wasn't just a great coach; he was a great coach over a long period of time. Players changed, the game changed, the times changed, everything changed. But all the while, Don Shula's teams won.

Shula, who spent seven seasons with the Baltimore Colts (1963–69), was the youngest head coach in NFL history when he took over at age 33. His youth didn't prove to be too much of a problem. The Colts won 73 percent of their games.

Shula experienced the bulk of his success with the Miami Dolphins. They got to three straight Super Bowls (1971–73), and won the last two. And his 1972 team was the only team in NFL history to complete an undefeated season. Seventeen games, 17 wins. Almost as impressive was the Dolphins' record over the 1972 and '73 seasons—32–2.

You want some evidence of how good a coach Don Shula was?

➤ More Super Bowl appearances than any other coach: 6

➤ One of only two coaches to reach three straight Super Bowls

➤ Playoff appearances in 20 of 33 seasons

➤ Ten-win seasons in 21 of 33 seasons

➤ All-time winningest coach in the NFL with a 347–173–6 record

Any wonder why Don Shula was a unanimous selection to the Pro Football Hall of Fame? I didn't think so.

The Inside Skinny

Don Shula eclipsed the Chicago Bears' George Halas as the winningest coach in NFL history on November 14, 1993, with his 325th victory, a 19–14 win over the Philadelphia Eagles at Veterans Stadium. Shula and Halas are the only NFL coaches to win 300 or more games.

The Least You Need to Know

➤ Johnny Unitas, after being cut by the Pittsburgh Steelers, rose to prominence with the Baltimore Colts.

➤ Reggie White is the all-time sack leader in the NFL with 198.

➤ Lawrence Taylor of the New York Giants changed the way the outside linebacker position was played.

➤ Jim Brown rushed for 1,000 yards or more in seven of his nine seasons.

➤ Vince Lombardi turned around the Green Bay Packers franchise, leading it to five championships in seven years.

Chapter 8

Gridiron Classics

In This Chapter

➤ A mauling by the Bears

➤ Brrr!

➤ Oh, Heidi!

➤ A brash prediction comes true

➤ Working overtime

Some games are memorable because they feature an extraordinary performance; others because the outcome isn't decided until the very last second; still others because they defy any semblance of logic in trying to figure them out.

For instance, championship games are supposed to be close and hard-fought; so how, pray tell, do you make any sense out of the Chicago Bears beating the Washington Redskins 73–0 in 1940?

Well, you can't, but that game, along with the others we'll look at in this chapter, has stood the test of time.

Skinned by the Bears

You could sift through the record books of every sport imaginable and you'd be hard-pressed to find a championship game as thoroughly one-sided as the NFL title game on December 8, 1940, between the Washington Redskins and the Chicago Bears.

Just three weeks before the title game, Washington had beaten Chicago 7–3. So there was no way to figure that in the rematch for the championship, the Bears would beat the Redskins 73–0.

73–0!

The Fundamentals

The **T-formation** used by the Bears had the quarterback directly behind the center and a fullback four or five yards behind the quarterback, flanked by two halfbacks. The key to the formation was one of the halfbacks going in motion, laterally and behind the line of scrimmage, before the snap.

The Inside Skinny

The 1940 NFL title game was noteworthy for a reason other than the final score: It was the last game played in which a player—Chicago end Dick Plasman—did not wear a helmet. The NFL made helmets mandatory in 1943, even though by then they were worn by everyone.

There were two main reasons for the turnaround: some ill-advised comments by Redskins owner George Marshall and the Bears' use of the *T-formation*.

Marshall got his team into trouble by shooting off his mouth. When the Bears complained that a penalty should've been called on the Redskins on the final play of the 7–3 Redskins victory, Marshall responded by calling the Bears a "bunch of crybabies" and "quitters."

Bad move, George. Chicago coach George Halas reminded his team of Marshall's comments every chance he got. The Bears entered the game with a bit of an attitude.

Halas also refined his version of the T-formation, which was just coming into vogue as an NFL offensive strategy. In the T-formation used by Halas, the quarterback took the snap from directly behind the center. A fullback, stationed several yards behind the quarterback, was flanked by halfbacks. The key to this whole setup was putting one of the halfbacks in motion before the snap.

The Redskins were clueless about how to stop the Bears, and the Bears took full advantage. Chicago scored three touchdowns in the first 13 minutes, and led 28–0 at the half and 54–0 in the third quarter.

Things got so bad that the officials asked the Bears to stop kicking extra points, because footballs were in short supply. Fans had not returned any of the first nine extra-point kicks.

After the game, George Marshall couldn't have been more gracious, calling the Bears "tremendous" and not taking them to task for running up the score.

But what would you expect? Marshall knew full well he'd have to play the Bears in the future.

The Ice Bowl

It can get pretty chilly in Green Bay, Wisconsin, in the dead of winter. Actually, it can get bone-chilling cold. On December 31, 1967, it got so cold that the heating system installed beneath Lambeau Field, home of the Green Bay Packers, froze. You can probably imagine what the playing surface was like. Concrete felt softer.

The high for the day was 13° below zero, and the wind chill factor was 48° below. A perfect day for football, and every seat at Lambeau was filled for the NFL Championship game between the Packers and the Dallas Cowboys.

The Packers took a 14–0 lead, but the Cowboys rallied to within 14–10 at the half. Early in the fourth quarter, Dallas, on a razzle-dazzle 50-yard *halfback option pass* from Dan Reeves to Lance Rentzel, went ahead 17–14.

The Packers mounted their final drive at their own 32-yard line with 4:50 to play. With 16 seconds left in the game, they had moved the ball to the one-yard line. It was third down.

Conventional wisdom had the Packers attempting a pass, which, if incomplete, would've stopped the clock and at least allowed time for a game-tying field goal. If the Packers attempted a running play and didn't score, the clock would not have stopped and Green Bay wouldn't have had time to attempt the field goal.

But quarterback Bart Starr told his coach, Vince Lombardi, that a quarterback sneak would work. Sure, it would be an all-or-nothing proposition, but if it worked, it would get everyone out of the cold.

Starr took the snap, put his head down, and wedged through a crease created by the blocks of center Ken Bowman and guard Jerry Kramer. Green Bay won 21–17.

The play turned out to be one of the most famous in NFL history. It's been replayed so often over the years, you'd think it would've worn off the film. Luckily, it hasn't.

The Fundamentals

A **halfback option pass** is a play in which the halfback takes a handoff from the quarterback and has the option to throw a pass or, if no receivers are open, to run.

Sports Strategies

The Green Bay Packers' victory over the Dallas Cowboys in the Ice Bowl earned them a trip to their second straight Super Bowl, in which they beat the Oakland Raiders. It was also their fifth world championship in seven years. It wasn't long after Super Bowl II that coach Vince Lombardi retired from the Packers.

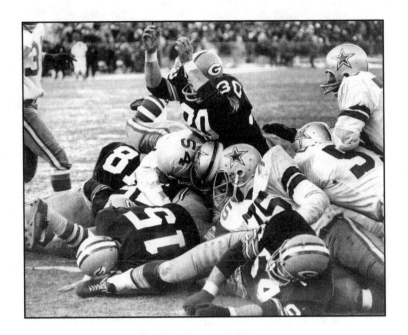

Bart Starr (15) of the Green Bay Packers scores the winning touchdown against the Dallas Cowboys in the "Ice Bowl."

Photo: Icon Sports Media

The Inside Skinny

The millions of viewers who were watching—then not watching— the conclusion of the New York-Oakland game were none too pleased with NBC's decision. The switchboards at the network were flooded, and when irate viewers couldn't get through to NBC in New York, they called the New York City police and the New York telephone company. NBC ended up issuing a public apology for its fumble.

The Heidi Game

This game was noteworthy not for what we saw, but what we *didn't* see. Imagine, you're sitting in your living room on November 17, 1968, enjoying a game between two of the American Football League's best teams and fiercest rivals—the New York Jets and the Oakland Raiders.

You've got your favorite snacks surrounding you, and perhaps a beverage in hand. The game goes back and forth until the Jets' Jim Turner kicks a 26-yard field goal with 1:05 to play, giving New York a 32–29 lead.

By this time, it's just about 7 p.m. on the East Coast, the start time for NBC's movie presentation of the evening, *Heidi*. So the network executives do some quick thinking—three-point lead, 65 seconds to play—and decide that the Raiders are finished, the Jets will win, and it's time to start showing *Heidi*. Which they did.

Well, as it turned out, the game wasn't quite as over as the NBC executives thought it was. The Raiders scored on a 43-yard pass with 42 seconds left to go ahead 36–32.

Then, on the ensuing kickoff, the Jets fumbled and the Raiders recovered for another touchdown, making it 43–32. Those two touchdowns were scored in a nine-second span.

The action was fast and furious. Unfortunately, what should've been Must See TV wasn't seen by anyone.

Brash Broadway Joe

Super Bowl III makes our list of great games not so much because of the action on the field, but because of what it meant to pro football's future.

This game marked the third time the American Football League champion would play the National Football League champion, and the first two games were blowouts won by the NFL champ. Green Bay won both, by an average of 22 points.

The third game looked for all the world to be another romp. Ho-hum. The Baltimore Colts of the NFL, who entered the game with a 15–1 record, faced the AFL's New York Jets and were favored by 18 to 21 points.

But in the week leading up to the game, Jets quarterback "Broadway" Joe Namath made a startling statement. He personally guaranteed a New York victory.

Well, obviously, everyone thought Namath had taken a few too many whacks to the noggin during the season, because there's no way he would say anything so outrageous if he were in his right mind. After all, the Colts were from the NFL, which everyone assumed was far superior, and it was for that reason alone that no one took the Jets seriously.

Guess what? Turns out Namath knew exactly what he was talking about. He played a nearly flawless game, picked apart the Colts' defense with the precision of a surgeon, and led the Jets to a 16–7 stunner of a victory. And as well as Namath played, the Jets defense was his equal.

The Jets win gave AFL instant credibility, and saved Joe Namath from eating a big, heaping plate of crow.

The Inside Skinny

When the NFL and AFL agreed to merge leagues in 1966, they also agreed to have their champions meet in what is now called the Super Bowl. But for the first two years of the game, it was called the AFL-NFL World Championship Game. It didn't become the Super Bowl, with Roman numerals, until the third game.

A Knock-Down, Drag-Out in Miami

By the time the first quarter of the American Football Conference divisional playoff game on January 2, 1982, between the San Diego Chargers and the Miami Dolphins was over, it was pretty obvious that it was going to be the Chargers' day.

85

When a team takes a 24–0 first-quarter lead like the Chargers did, you've got to like their chances.

Miami was forced to take its best-laid plans—geared toward running the football—and deep-six them, because the only way to climb out of a 24-point hole was to throw. A lot.

Which is what Dolphins quarterback Don Strock did—on almost every down. The Dolphins cut the lead to 24–10 and had the ball at the San Diego 40 with six seconds left in the first half. Instead of playing it safe, Miami got daring.

The Dolphins used the *"hook and ladder,"* which involves a receiver pitching the ball to a trailing teammate. It's something you'd expect to see on a playground, not in the NFL, but it resulted in a touchdown and made the score 24–17 at the half.

The Dolphins were pumped when they came out for the second half. Two more touchdowns, sandwiched around a San Diego score, made it 31–31—and it was only the third quarter.

The Fundamentals

To pull off a **hook-and-ladder play,** the quarterback has to complete the pass to one of his receivers. That receiver then laterals the ball to a teammate, who is running alongside or slightly behind. This is considered a gimmick play and is rarely used.

Both teams scored another touchdown. With the game tied at 38 and four seconds to play, the Dolphins reached the San Diego 25-yard line and set up for what would be the winning field goal. But San Diego tight end Kellen Winslow, all 6′ 5″ of him, deflected Uwe von Schamann's kick, and the game went into overtime.

The Chargers, who looked as if they had the game won in the first quarter, finally won it officially on Rolf Benirschke's 29-yard field goal with 13:52 gone in OT.

Both quarterbacks must've had sore arms. Strock threw for 403 yards and four scores; San Diego's Dan Fouts threw for 433 yards and three scores.

Winslow was so exhausted he needed to be helped from the field. He caught an NFL-playoff record 13 passes for 166 yards and a touchdown. But were it not for his blocked field goal, the Chargers might have let one get away.

The Immaculate Reception

Sometimes you just never know when the football gods might smile on you. Even though the situation looks hopeless, it's possible that, against all odds, the tide will turn in your favor.

Things couldn't have looked more dire for the Pittsburgh Steelers on December 23, 1972. They were making just their second postseason appearance—their first was way back in 1947—but it looked as if they had run out of time.

There were 22 seconds to play in an AFC divisional playoff game against Oakland. The score was 7–6 and the Steelers were down to their last play. On fourth-and-10 from the Pittsburgh 40, quarterback Terry Bradshaw was flushed out of the pocket while attempting one last desperation pass. As he scrambled around, searching for a receiver, he spied one of his running backs, John "Frenchy" Fuqua. Bradshaw threw. The ball got to Fuqua at precisely the same moment as Raiders safety Jack Tatum. The collision sent the ball flying into the air—and right into the hands of Fuqua's teammate, running back Franco Harris, who was several yards behind the play.

Harris chugged down the left sideline and scored one of the most improbable touchdowns in NFL playoff history.

At least the Steelers *thought* it was a touchdown. The Raiders were sure it wasn't, and the officials just weren't sure.

If the ball had touched Fuqua before Harris caught it, it would not have been a TD, because at that time, the rules prohibited two offensive players from touching the ball consecutively. But if the ball had ricocheted off Tatum, then the party could start in Pittsburgh.

After the referee, Fred Swearingen, talked it over with his supervisor, he returned to the field and signaled—drum roll, please—touchdown!

The Steelers kicked the extra point and won the game 13–7. Dubbed the "Immaculate Reception," the catch by Harris remains one of the great plays in NFL history.

Of course, only Fuqua knows who touched the ball immediately before Harris caught it. And he's not telling.

"I want to keep it 'Immaculate,'" said Fuqua in 1999.

Somehow, it's better that way.

The Inside Skinny

Unfortunately for Pittsburgh Steelers owner Art Rooney, he missed the fantastic finish that was the Immaculate Reception. Just before the play unfolded, he left the press box and was on the elevator to the locker room. Wasn't he pleasantly surprised when he got there?

Sports Strategies

From 1984 through 2001, 13 of the 18 Super Bowls played were decided by 13 or more points, and eight of those 13 were decided by 22 or more points. The average margin of victory in those 18 games was nearly 20 points.

The Longest Yard

For the most part, Super Bowls could be called Super Bores, because for all the hype and all the carrying on before the game, the game itself has more often than not been a letdown.

Some games have been so one-sided that the outcomes were determined by halftime. All that's left to do during the second half is to make sure there's no guacamole left over.

But on January 30, 2000, one of the greatest games in Super Bowl history took place, between two most unlikely participants—the St. Louis Rams and Tennessee Titans.

In the previous two seasons combined, the St. Louis Rams won a total of nine games, but in the 1999 season, thanks to a pass-happy offense engineered by quarterback Kurt Warner, they finished the regular season at 13–3.

Warner, who just five years earlier was working as a stock boy in a supermarket, was the ultimate rags-to-riches story. He became just the second quarterback in NFL history to throw 40 touchdown passes in one season and was named the league's Most Valuable Player.

Who knew stocking shelves could be such a good training ground for becoming an NFL quarterback?

As for the Titans, they had been 8–8 in each of the previous three seasons. In 1999, they finished 13–3, earned a wild card berth, and made it to the Super Bowl with victories over Buffalo, Indianapolis, and Jacksonville.

Sports Strategies

The NFL awards playoff spots to the six division winners (three each in the NFC and AFC). The three teams in each division with the next-best records receive wild card berths. In the first round of the playoffs, two of the wild card teams face each other; the third wild card team faces the division winner with the worst record. The other teams receive byes.

Super Bowl XXXIV was a battle between a high-powered offense and a stingy defense. And even though the Rams gained 294 yards of total offense in the first half, the Titans trailed only 9–0.

St. Louis went ahead 16–0 midway through the third quarter on a nine-yard TD pass from Warner to wide receiver Torry Holt.

But just when it looked as if another rout was brewing and attention would turn from the game to the snack table, the Titans rallied to tie the game at 16 with 2:12 to play. They got two short touchdown runs from Eddie George and a field goal from Al Del Greco.

The Rams, renowned as a team with quick-strike ability, struck quickly. It took them all of one play—a 73-yard touchdown pass from Warner to Isaac Bruce—to regain the lead at 23–16.

The Titans had 1:54 to score a touchdown. And they came oh-so close. They moved the ball from their own 12-yard line to the Rams' 10 with six seconds left. On the last play of the game, quarterback Steve McNair hit wide receiver Kevin Dyson with a pass.

Dyson made it to the one-yard line ... where he was tackled by linebacker Mike Jones. Dyson stretched the ball toward the goal line, but to no avail.

Final score: Rams 23, Titans 16. The game was one of the best ever. It was so good, the guacamole probably went untouched.

The Greatest Game Ever Played

Well, we've saved the game of all games for last. Besides being a riveting drama, the 1958 NFL Championship game between the New York Giants and the Baltimore Colts made an impact that changed the game forever.

Pro football was new to television in the 1950s, but on December 28, 1958, at Yankee Stadium, the suspense orchestrated by the Colts and the Giants, played out before a national TV audience, started something that continues to this day: Americans' love of football on the tube.

Part of the appeal of the game was the caliber of the participants: Twelve future Hall of Fame members were on the field that day. But mainly, the game resonated the way it did because it was the first championship game to be decided in *sudden death overtime.*

The Colts took a 14–3 halftime lead, only to see the Giants go ahead 17–14.

By the time the Colts took over for what would be their last chance, there was only 1:56 to play. Luckily, Baltimore's quarterback, Johnny Unitas, was a magician. The more tense the situation, the better. He was virtually unflappable. (See Chapter 7, "Greats of the Game," for more on Unitas.)

The Colts took over on their 14-yard line. Unitas completed three passes to wide receiver Raymond Berry, moving the ball into position for Steve Myrha's tying 20-yard field goal with six seconds left.

The Giants won the coin toss to start overtime, but were unable to advance the ball. The Colts took over on their 20, and once again it was Unitas who provided the magic.

In a career-defining performance, he moved the Colts 80 yards in 13 plays with a deft mixture of runs and passes. His clever play-calling confused the Giants; they never knew what was coming. The game ended with fullback Alan Ameche's one-yard touchdown plunge, the Colts winning 23–17.

The Fundamentals

When the 1958 NFL Championship went into **sudden death overtime,** it was the first time it ever happened. In **sudden death overtime,** the first team to score wins. Starting with the 1974 season, sudden death overtime play was added to regular season games. The overtime period lasts for 15 minutes, or the length of one quarter. If neither team scores within 15 minutes, the game is recorded as a tie.

How confident was Unitas about winning? At one point the Colts had the ball on the Giants' seven-yard line for what could've been an easy field goal—so easy that Myrha could've kept his eyes closed.

Instead, Unitas threw a pass to Jim Mutscheller that took the ball to the one, setting up Ameche's run.

Asked why he risked a pass when a field goal would've won, Unitas replied, "When you know what you're doing, you're not going to be intercepted."

And make no mistake, Johnny Unitas knew what he was doing.

The Least You Need to Know

➤ The Washington Redskins were on the receiving end of the most one-sided rout in NFL Championship history—73–0 by the Chicago Bears.

➤ In the Ice Bowl, with temperatures dipping to 13° below zero, the Green Bay Packers used a surprise quarterback sneak by Bart Starr to beat the Dallas Cowboys.

➤ The final frantic moments of a 1968 game between the New York Jets and Oakland Raiders went unseen by the viewing audience, because NBC cut away for the start of the movie *Heidi*.

➤ New York Jets quarterback Joe Namath shocked the world with his prediction that his team would beat the Baltimore Colts in Super Bowl III. Even more shocking was the outcome: Namath was right.

➤ The Immaculate Reception by Pittsburgh's Franco Harris lifted the Steelers to a most improbable 1972 playoff victory over the Oakland Raiders.

➤ Baltimore Colts quarterback Johnny Unitas defined his career with his clutch performance against the New York Giants in the 1958 NFL Championship game.

Game Time

In This Chapter

➤ Trivia quiz

➤ Making the grade

➤ Tidbits, facts, and figures

➤ Quotable quotes

➤ Super Bowl supermen

It's quiz time again. So put on your thinking caps and see how many answers you can come up with.

We'll also supply you with another collection of interesting tidbits of knowledge from college and pro football, some pithy quotes, and a look at some of the most impressive individual performances in the Super Bowl.

One of those performances was turned in by a most unlikely character. But you'll have to wait until the last section of this chapter to find out who it was.

First things first. Let's take the quiz.

Twenty Questions

It's time to kick off—get it?—our football quiz with some trivia about the college game and the NFL.

See how many questions you can answer—before peeking at the answers that follow in the next section.

Good luck!

1. Which teams played in the first college bowl matchup of unbeaten teams?

2. Which two NFL franchises are the only ones remaining from the *American Professional Football Association?*

3. Which two NFL franchises are the only ones remaining from the *All-America Football Conference?*

4. Which quarterback holds the record for most passing yards in a Super Bowl?

The Fundamentals

The **American Professional Football Association** was formed in 1920, but changed its name to the National Football League in 1922. The **All-America Football Conference** was a rival league with 14 teams that merged with the NFL following the 1949 season.

The Fundamentals

All-purpose yardage is the total of a player's rushing, receiving, and punt and/or kickoff return yardage.

5. Which city holds the record for playing host to the most Super Bowls?

6. Who is the oldest head coach to lead his team to a Super Bowl victory?

7. How many teams in the NFL have never played in a Super Bowl?

8. Who is the Super Bowl trophy named in honor of?

9. Which are the only two wild card teams to win a Super Bowl?

10. What was the longest NFL game ever played?

11. Which two coaches led teams to the Super Bowl and the Grey Cup, the Canadian Football League championship game?

12. What was the highest-scoring game in NFL history?

13. Who kicked the longest field goal in NFL history?

14. Who holds the single-game record for most yards rushing in a college game?

15. Which college team holds the record for most consecutive losses?

16. Who holds the record for most times leading the NFL in passing?

17. Who are the only running backs to rush for 2,000 or more yards in one season?

18. Who holds the record for most seasons played in the NFL?

19. Who leads the NFL in career *all-purpose yardage?*

20. Who holds the record for most consecutive NFL games played?

Twenty Answers

Well, there were some real brainteasers on that list. It's time to see how you did.

1. California beat Ohio State 28–0 in the 1921 Rose Bowl.

2. The Arizona Cardinals and the Chicago Bears. The Cardinals were the Chicago Cardinals in the American Professional Football Association. The Bears were the Decatur (Illinois) Staleys.

3. The San Francisco 49ers and the Cleveland Browns; both joined the NFL following the 1949 season.

4. Kurt Warner of the St. Louis Rams threw for 414 yards in a 23–16 victory over the Tennessee Titans in Super Bowl XXXIV, Jan. 30, 2000.

5. New Orleans has played host to eight Super Bowls (IV, VI, IX, XII, XV, XX, XXIV, and XXXI).

6. Dick Vermeil was 63 years old when he led the St. Louis Rams to the Super Bowl XXXIV title.

7. Through Super Bowl XXXV in January 2001, the Arizona Cardinals, Carolina Panthers, Cleveland Browns, Detroit Lions, Jacksonville Jaguars, New Orleans Saints, and Tampa Bay Buccaneers have never made it to the Super Bowl.

8. The trophy was named after Vince Lombardi, the legendary coach who led the Green Bay Packers to five NFL titles, including the first two Super Bowls.

9. The Oakland Raiders in 1981 and the Denver Broncos in 1998 are the only two Super Bowl winners who qualified for the playoffs as wild card teams. The Raiders beat the Philadelphia Eagles 27–10; the Broncos beat the Green Bay Packers 31–24.

10. On Christmas Day 1971, the Kansas City Chiefs and the Miami Dolphins met in a playoff game that lasted 82 minutes, 40 seconds. The Dolphins won 27–24 on a 37-yard field goal by Garo Yepremian at 7:40 of the second overtime period.

11. Bud Grant coached the Minnesota Vikings in four Super Bowls and the Winnipeg Blue Bombers in the Grey Cup. Marv Levy coached the Buffalo Bills in the Super Bowl and the Montreal Alouettes in the Grey Cup. Grant and Levy are each 0–4 in Super Bowls.

12. On November 27, 1966, the New York Giants routed the Washington Redskins 72–41. To save you the trouble of doing the math, that totals 113 points. Only

Sports Strategies

In case you're wondering, the college record for the longest field goal is 67 yards, held by three players: Steve Little, Arkansas, 1967; Russell Erxlaben, Texas, 1977; and Joe Williams, Wichita State, 1978. The reason the college record is longer than the pro record is because in college, kicking tees are used. Using a tee makes it easier for the holder to place the ball.

one other game has ever topped 100 points: The Oakland Raiders beat the Houston Oilers 52–49 in an AFL game on December 22, 1963.

13. Tom Dempsey of the New Orleans Saints kicked a 63-yard field goal on November 8, 1970, against the Detroit Lions. Jason Elam of the Denver Broncos equaled Dempsey's record boot on October 25, 1998, with a 63-yarder against the Jacksonville Jaguars.

14. LaDainian Tomlinson of Texas Christian University rushed for 406 yards against the University of Texas-El Paso in 1999.

15. Prairie View, a member of the Southwestern Athletic Conference, lost 80 straight games between 1989 and 1998. The slide finally ended with a 14–12 victory over Langston.

16. "Slinging" Sammy Baugh of the Washington Redskins and Steve Young of the San Francisco 49ers each led the league six times. Baugh did in 1937, '40, '43, '45, '47, and '49. Young did it in 1991–'94, and '96–'97.

17. O.J. Simpson of the Buffalo Bills was the first player to crack the 2,000-yard mark. He rushed for 2,003 yards in 1973. Barry Sanders of the Detroit Lions rushed for 2,053 yards in 1997. Terrell Davis of the Denver Broncos rushed for 2,008 yards in 1998. The single-season record-holder is Eric Dickerson, who rushed for 2,105 yards in 1984 with the Los Angeles Rams.

18. George Blanda, a quarterback and placekicker who spent most of his career with the Oakland Raiders, played for 26 seasons. So it figures that he also holds the record for most games played (340). Oh, one more thing—at 48, Blanda was the oldest player ever to play an NFL game.

19. The late Walter Payton, who played for the Chicago Bears, is the NFL's all-time leader in all-purpose yardage with 21,803 yards. The breakdown is 16,726 yards rushing, 4,538 yards receiving, and 539 yards in returns.

20. Jim Marshall, a defensive end for the Minnesota Vikings, played in 282 straight games. He is second in games played, also 282—which means he had perfect attendance.

Bet You Didn't Know ...

➤ The year 1996 was the first in which the four teams in the conference championship games were previous Super Bowl champs—Dallas and Green Bay in the NFC, and Pittsburgh and the Indianapolis Colts (formerly the Baltimore Colts) in the AFC.

➤ Michigan beat Stanford 49–0 in the first bowl game ever played—the 1902 Rose Bowl.

➤ The San Francisco 49ers have been Super Bowl champs five times. Believe it or not, 49ers quarterbacks—starters and reserves—have never thrown an interception in any of those five games.

➤ The first televised football game took place on October 22, 1939. The Philadelphia Eagles played the Brooklyn Dodgers at Ebbets Field. The telecast was primitive, to say the least. Every time a cloud passed over the field, the picture got darker.

➤ Byron "Whizzer" White, a running back for the University of Colorado, led the nation in rushing, all-purpose yardage, and total offense in 1937, when he also finished second in the voting for the Heisman Trophy. White went on to become a U.S. Supreme Court justice. He was appointed in 1962 by President John F. Kennedy.

➤ The University of Oklahoma owns the longest winning streak in the history of college football. The Sooners won 47 straight games between 1953 and 1957. The streak ended on November 16, 1957, in a 7–0 loss to Notre Dame.

➤ The longest unbeaten streak in college football was 63 games by the University of Washington, which won 59 games, lost none, and tied four between 1907 and 1917. The Huskies also saw their streak end with a shutout—27–0 against the University of California.

➤ The University of Michigan's stadium is officially known as Michigan Stadium. Its nickname is "The Big House," and for good reason. It seats 107,501, the largest capacity in the country.

Two-Minute Warning

If you're new to pro football or too young to remember anything before 1984, you might think the Indianapolis Colts have been around forever. But before moving to Indianapolis, the Colts were a fixture in Baltimore. Team owner Robert Irsay actually moved the team out of the city in the middle of the night in 1984, much to the disappointment of the loyal Baltimore fans.

➤ Cal Hubbard, a star tackle at Centenary College, is a member of the College Football Hall of Fame and the Pro Football Hall of Fame. In 1976, he was inducted into the Baseball Hall of Fame, not as a player, but as an umpire.

The Inside Skinny

Beginning with the 2001 college football season, there were four stadiums with seating capacity greater than 100,000. Michigan tops the list, followed by Neyland Stadium, University of Tennessee, 104,079; Ohio Stadium, Ohio State, 103,801; and Beaver Stadium, Penn State, 103,500.

Sports Strategies

While instant replay has become a staple for TV viewers, the NFL's use of the technology to help referees make the correct calls has been controversial. Instant replay was adopted in 1986, but voted out in 1992. In 1999, a "challenge" system of instant replay was instituted. A coach may challenge a referee's call, but if the call proves to be right, the challenging team loses a timeout.

➤ In a game between the Philadelphia Eagles and the Cleveland Browns on December 3, 1950, not a single pass was thrown. It goes without saying that that hasn't happened since.

➤ Instant replay, which we take for granted today, was used for the first time in 1963 by CBS during its telecast of the Army–Navy game.

➤ Tony Dorsett of the Dallas Cowboys holds the record for the longest run from scrimmage in NFL history—99 yards for a touchdown against the Minnesota Vikings on January 1, 1983.

➤ Florida State finished in the top four of the year-end Associated Press poll for 14 straight years, through the 2000 season.

Say What?

Unfortunately, football doesn't have any character as quotable or as funny as Yogi Berra of the New York Yankees.

But that doesn't mean memorable things haven't been said by football players and coaches about the game. Here are a few:

➤ John Heisman, former Georgia Tech coach and namesake of the Heisman Trophy: "What is it? A prolate spheroid, an elongated sphere, one in which the outer leather casing is drawn tightly over a somewhat smaller rubber tubing. Better to have died as a small boy than to fumble this football."

➤ Bob Zuppke, former Illinois coach: "Often an All-American is made by a long run, a weak defense, and a poet in the press box."

➤ Bill Parcells, former coach of the New York Giants, New England Patriots, and New York Jets: "This is private enterprise. The fans are entitled to the best product I can put on the field every Sunday, week in, week out, year in and year out if I'm lucky. How I put that product out there is my damn business."

➤ Dutch Moyer, former Texas Christian coach: "Fight them until hell freezes over, and then fight them some more."

➤ Eddie Erdelatz, former Navy coach: "I never thought the so-called skull sessions did much good. If you talk to the ends, the tackles doze off, and if you talk to the tackles, the ends lose interest."

➤ Roger Brown, former Detroit Lions defensive tackle, on Chicago Bears running back Gale Sayers: "Trying to bring Sayers down is like going rabbit hunting without a gun."

➤ Frank Gifford, former New York Giants half-back, then a sportscaster: "Pro football is like nuclear warfare. There are no winners, only survivors."

➤ Terry Bradshaw, former Pittsburgh Steelers quarterback, now a sportscaster: "This isn't nuclear physics, it's a game. How smart do you really have to be?"

➤ Norman Vincent Peale, on the impact of the Super Bowl: "If Jesus were alive today, He would be at the Super Bowl."

➤ Frank Leahy, former Notre Dame coach: "Egotism is the anesthetic that dulls the pain of stupidity."

➤ Duffy Daugherty, former Michigan State coach: "Football is not a contact sport. Football is a collision sport. Dancing is a contact sport."

➤ Vince Lombardi, former Green Bay Packers coach: "This is a game for madmen."

Sports Strategies

Bill Parcells was one of the NFL's most successful coaches. He is one of only two coaches to take two different teams to the Super Bowl. He won Super Bowl XXI and XXV with the New York Giants, and lost Super Bowl XXXI with the New England Patriots. The only other coach to manage such a double was Don Shula with the Baltimore Colts and Miami Dolphins.

Two-Minute Warning

When Terry Bradshaw joined the Pittsburgh Steelers in 1970 as the top pick in the NFL draft, he had the reputation of not being the brightest bulb on the tree, if you know what I mean. He was considered unintelligent and was the butt of many jokes. But he got the last laugh by being the only quarterback to lead his team to victories in four Super Bowls (IX, X, XIII, and XIV).

Supermen in the Super Bowl

Getting to the Super Bowl is the goal of every football player. Who wouldn't want to play a game on the biggest stage in all of sports? The Super Bowl is an event, a happening that the whole world watches.

And lucky for those players who not only get to the game, but also play the game of their lives. Here's a look at some of the great individual performances in Super Bowl history.

Mad Max

Max McGee's main claim to fame on the Green Bay Packers was his ability to get away with breaking curfew. After sneaking out—and sneaking back in—without being detected for 11 straight nights during training camp, McGee figured he held the NFL record.

Even on the night before the first Super Bowl game in 1967, McGee was out on the town, carousing, in spite of the $5,000 fine coach Vince Lombardi imposed.

Sports Strategies

To say that Max McGee was a small part of the Green Bay Packers offense would be a rather gross understatement. During the regular season, he caught only four passes for 91 yards. No wonder he was as surprised as anyone at his performance in the Super Bowl.

McGee, a wide receiver, returned to his room at about 7:30 the morning of the game. He was a bit worse for the wear, but he didn't think it mattered because he didn't figure he'd play. After all, he hadn't played in six weeks and wouldn't play unless Boyd Dowler, the starter, got hurt.

Guess what? Dowler got hurt on the second play of the game, and McGee, fuzzy head and all, was told he would play.

Guess what else? He played great. The 34-year-old McGee caught seven passes for 138 yards and two touchdowns in the Packers' 35–10 victory over the Kansas City Chiefs.

"The Chiefs are a good team, but we wore 'em down," said Lombardi. "We had a little more personnel. And what can you say about McGee. This was one of his finest games."

And he couldn't have picked a better time to have it.

Super 'Skins

The day before Washington Redskins quarterback Doug Williams was going to play in his first Super Bowl, he spent part of his time in the dentist's chair, undergoing an emergency root canal.

Talk about lousy timing—not that there's ever a good time for a root canal. But the day before Super Bowl XXII?

But Williams felt okay the day of the game, and it wasn't long before he proved it.

The Denver Broncos jumped out to a 10–0 lead, and then Williams took over. He led the Redskins to five second-quarter touchdowns—four of them TD passes—in five consecutive possessions. The 35 points is a Super Bowl record for points in a quarter.

Overall, Williams, named the game's Most Valuable Player, completed 18 of 29 passes for 340 yards and the four scores. His passing yardage total ranks third all-time, through the 2000 season. His four TD passes are tied for third all-time.

And Williams wasn't a one-man show for the Redskins. He got considerable help from a rookie running back named Timmy Smith, who has never been heard from since.

Smith, who rushed for 204 yards, a single-game Super Bowl record, and two touchdowns on 22 carries, might've been a flash in the pan. Actually, he was less than a flash, more like a little spark. His career lasted just two more seasons, in which he gained a grand total of 612 yards. Still, that doesn't detract from his record performance in Super Bowl XXII.

Joe Who?

Steve Young had the unenviable chore of following the legendary Joe Montana as the San Francisco 49ers quarterback.

In San Francisco, Montana was king, and for good reason. He led the franchise to four Super Bowl championships and did it with a flair and a style that set him apart.

Young was a terrific quarterback, who led the NFL in passing from 1991 to '94, but it still wasn't enough to make the 49ers faithful stop the comparisons to Montana.

Then came Super Bowl XXIX against the San Diego Chargers, following the 1994 season. Young had the kind of game a quarterback dreams about. He completed 24 of 36 passes for 325 yards and six touchdowns. And as if that wasn't enough, he also scrambled five times for 49 yards, making him the game's leading rusher.

Young's six TD passes broke Montana's record of five, and his passing yardage still stands as the sixth-highest total of all time. It goes without saying that Young was named the game's Most Valuable Player.

And while we're talking about great performances in Super Bowl XXIX, let's not overlook San Francisco wide receiver Jerry Rice. All Rice did was catch 10 passes for 149 yards and three touchdowns.

Young said Jerry Rice with one arm was better than any receiver in the league with two arms.

Young's arm was pretty good, too. It was strong enough to lift the monkey off his back.

San
ped

ut-
ce in

Photo: Diane Staskowski

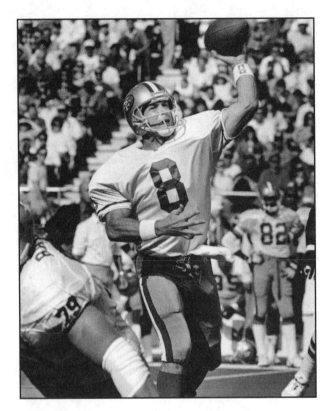

The Least You Need to Know

➤ St. Louis Rams quarterback Kurt Warner holds the record for most yards passing in a Super Bowl, with 414.

➤ New Orleans has played host to the most Super Bowls, eight.

➤ The Super Bowl trophy is named in honor of former Green Bay Packers coach Vince Lombardi.

➤ Tom Dempsey of the New Orleans Saints and Jason Elam of the Denver Broncos share the record for the longest field goal in NFL history: 63 yards.

➤ O.J. Simpson, Eric Dickerson, Barry Sanders, and Terrell Davis are the only players to rush for 2,000 or more yards in one season.

Part 3
Hoop Dreams

Over a hundred years ago, Dr. James Naismith was charged by his boss with coming up with a new activity to keep his students occupied during inclement weather. So he nailed a peach basket to a wall and—voilà—basketball was born.

Okay, it wasn't quite that simple, but you can read Chapter 10, "It Started with a Peach Basket," for the details. Since those early days, the rules have changed and the players run faster and jump higher. The peach basket has been replaced, too—good thing, because it wouldn't have stood a chance against a Wilt Chamberlain dunk.

Another thing that happened to change the game was the emergence of some guy named Jordan. You've probably heard of him.

It Started with a Peach Basket

For as American a game as basketball is (seeing how it was invented in Springfield, Massachusetts), you might be surprised to find out that the man considered the "Father of Basketball" was a native Canadian.

Dr. James Naismith, born November 6, 1861, in Almonte, Ontario, Canada, came up with the basics and the rules of the game he called "basket-ball" as a way to keep his YMCA students occupied during bad weather.

Based on how his experiment turned out, at the college and pro level, I'd say he did pretty darn good.

Introducing Dr. Naismith

So you're wondering how a guy who grew up in Canada and graduated from McGill University in Montreal came to invent basketball.

Well, his degree from McGill was in physical education and his first job out of college was as a physical education instructor at the School for Christian Workers in Massachusetts, now known as Springfield College.

It was there, in 1891, that he was challenged by his boss, Dr. Luther Gulick, to come up with a game that would keep students from being bored once the weather turned wintry, as it tends to do in New England.

The clock was ticking: Gulick gave Naismith 14 days.

At first, Naismith tried to bring outdoor activities indoors. But playing soccer and lacrosse within four walls and under a roof didn't work out, because the games were too physical and the space was too limited.

Then he remembered a childhood game called "Duck on the Rock" that required finesse and accuracy to become successful. The object was to throw balls into boxes.

Naismith took that idea and brainstormed. He got a soccer ball, two peach baskets, some nails, and a ladder. He nailed a basket to the lower rail of the balcony at each end of the gym, about 10 feet above the floor.

He then developed a set of 13 rules, and voilà—"basket-ball."

Rules of the Game

James Naismith's original rules of basketball follow. They were written in December 1891 and published in *The Triangle,* the Springfield College newspaper, a month later.

As you'll see, a whole lot has changed.

1. The ball may be thrown in any direction with one or both hands.

2. The ball may be batted in any direction with one or both hands.

3. A player cannot run with the ball. The player must throw it from the spot on which he catches it, with allowance to be made for a man who catches the ball when running at a good speed if he tries to stop.

Sports Strategies

Once James Naismith's rules of basketball were published in the Springfield College newspaper in January 1892, the game began to catch on quickly as copies of the rules were sent to YMCAs all over the United States.

4. The ball must be held in or between the hands; the arms or body must not be used for holding it.

5. No shouldering, holding, pushing, tripping, or striking in any way the person of an opponent shall be allowed. The first infringement of this rule by any player shall count as a foul, the second shall disqualify him until the next goal is made, or, if there was evident intent to injure the person, for the whole of the game, no substitute allowed.

6. A foul is striking at the ball with the fist, violation of Rules 3, 4, and such as described in Rule 5.

7. If either side makes three consecutive fouls, it shall count a goal for the opponents (consecutive means without the opponents in the meantime making a foul).

8. A goal shall be made when the ball is thrown or batted from the grounds into the basket and stays there, providing those defending the goal do not touch or disturb the goal. If the ball rests on the edges, and the opponent moves the basket, it shall count as a goal.

9. When the ball goes out of bounds, it shall be thrown into the field of play by the person first touching it. In case of a dispute, the umpire shall throw it straight into the field. The thrower-in is allowed five seconds; if he holds it longer, it shall go to the opponent. If any side persists in delaying the game, the umpire shall call a foul on that side.

10. The umpire shall be judge of the men and shall note the fouls and notify the referee when three consecutive fouls have been made. He shall have power to disqualify men according to Rule 5.

11. The referee shall be judge of the ball and shall decide when the ball is in play, inbounds, to which side it belongs, and shall keep the time. He shall decide when a goal has been made, and keep account of the goals with any other duties that are usually performed by a referee.

12. The time shall be two 15-minute halves, with five minutes' rest in between.

13. The side making the most goals in that time shall be declared the winner. In case of a draw, the game may, by agreement of the captains, be continued until another goal is made.

The Inside Skinny

As charming as they were, the peach baskets didn't last long. In 1892, Lew Allen of Hartford, Connecticut, began making cylindrical baskets out of heavy woven wire. It wasn't until several years later the baskets were made without bottoms.

It's Show Time

The day was December 21, 1891. The place was the YMCA in Springfield. The occasion was the first basketball game ever played.

It goes without saying that the original version looked as much like today's game as an eight-track tape (Remember them?) looks like a CD.

The uniforms, for one thing, hardly made a fashion statement. The boys wore long, gray pants, short-sleeved jerseys and gym shoes. And there was not a swoosh to be found on any of them.

Each team consisted of nine players, stationed in the following order from the basket—a goalkeeper, two guards (right and left), three centers (right, center, and left), two wings (right and left), and a home man.

And as if the court wasn't crowded enough, there was also a referee, an umpire, and a stepladder next to each basket for ball retrieval.

The Inside Skinny

Despite inventing the game, Dr. James Naismith only played it twice—in 1892 at the YMCA Training School Gym and in 1898, after he became an associate professor and chapel director at the University of Kansas. Asked why he didn't play more, Naismith said he just didn't get around to it.

Eventually, as the game became more popular, Naismith took a team of nine players and traveled throughout the East. It wasn't long before "basketball" went to college.

Hoops on Campus

The first official college basketball game took place February 9, 1895, between two "powerhouse" teams—Hamline College of St. Paul, Minnesota, and the Minnesota State School of Agriculture.

In case you're interested, Minnesota State School of Agriculture prevailed 9–3, using nine players a side.

In April 1895, women got into the act with their first college game. California faced Stanford, but unfortunately, no score was reported.

By 1905, basketball was a big game on campus with more than 80 schools having organized teams.

From there, the developments in the game took place rapidly. Here's a rundown of the events and decisions that helped shape college basketball:

➤ Yale defeated Pennsylvania 32–10 in the first official conference game between Ivy League schools in 1897. It was also the first official five-on-five college game on record.

➤ In 1900, the first college basketball conference was formed with Yale, Trinity College, and Wesleyan College. It was cleverly called the Triangle Conference.

➤ The Western Conference, which would later be known as the Big Ten, conducted its first formal league season in 1905. That same year, the rules of the college game were formalized by a governing body that would eventually become the NCAA.

➤ To cut down on rough play, a rule was adopted in 1908 to disqualify players after committing five personal fouls. Two years later, a second referee was added to further police the action.

➤ Naismith's game of "basket-ball" became "basketball" in 1918, as newspaper reports of games dropped the hyphen.

➤ In 1924, a rule was adopted to require that the player fouled take the free throw. Prior to 1924, designated free-throwers were used.

➤ Big news in 1928: A sporting goods company developed a basketball with the seams recessed. Players could now dribble without erratic bounces caused by the seams.

➤ Madison Square Garden in New York City launched its reputation as a basketball mecca by playing host to the first collegiate tripleheader. More than 16,000 people showed up January 19, 1931 to watch games involving Columbia, Fordham, Manhattan, New York University, St. John's, and Community College of New York.

➤ Up until the mid-1930s, most teams competed close to home, rarely leaving their geographic region. But in 1934, the first intersectional doubleheader was staged at Madison Square Garden, with New York University beating Notre Dame of South Bend, Indiana, in the opener.

➤ The first team from the West Coast to come east was Stanford in 1936. The Cardinal beat Long Island University at Madison Square Garden, ending LIU's 45-game winning streak.

➤ The first National Invitation Tournament (NIT) was held in 1938, with Temple beating Colorado at Madison Square Garden. The NIT was the first postseason tournament and for years was more prestigious than the NCAA Tournament, which began in 1939.

Sports Strategies

Hank Luisetti of Stanford was quite the attraction when Stanford came to Madison Square Garden. The forward is credited with developing the one-hand shot. Everybody shot the ball with two hands in those days. But he averaged 20 points a game in the 1935–36 season— quite a good scoring average back then—so it didn't take long for Luisetti's shot to be copied.

Now, let's check out the development of professional basketball.

Pro Leagues Come and Go

Today, the National Basketball Association (NBA) reigns as the ultimate in professional basketball worldwide. But it took a while before the NBA became the NBA.

The pro game often took one step forward and two steps back in its development. As quickly as some leagues started, they disappeared, only to have others take their place and succumb to the same fate.

The first pro league was formed way back in 1897. The National Basketball League debuted with six teams from the Philadelphia area, which wasn't very "national" at

The Inside Skinny

The first president of the Basketball Association of America was Maurice Podoloff, who also was the head of the American Hockey League. When he took over as BAA president, Podoloff had never even seen a basketball game. It didn't matter. He was put in place because of his business and marketing expertise.

all, when you think about it. A team from Trenton, New Jersey, won the first championship.

Four years after its start, the National Basketball League folded. Over the next several years the Eastern League, the Central League, the Hudson River League, and the New York State League would come and go. It wasn't until 1925, when the American Basketball League (ABL) was formed, that another serious attempt at basketball on the pro level was attempted.

Five years seemed to be the maximum any of these leagues lasted. The ABL was gone after five years, replaced by a second version of the National Basketball League (NBL) in 1937.

NBL II operated mainly in the Midwest. It had fine players—such as George Mikan, who would become the game's first great "big man"—but no place to showcase them. NBL games were played mostly in dumpy high school gyms in small, out-of-the-way towns.

That wasn't the case with the Basketball Association of America, which formed in 1946. The BAA was primarily an East Coast operation that was the idea of hockey-team owners, believe it or not.

It wasn't that these hockey-team owners were such huge basketball fans. It was that they were good businessmen. They saw that pro basketball was a burgeoning game. They also saw that it could fill their arenas when hockey games weren't scheduled.

The BAA got its biggest boost in 1948, when the Minneapolis Lakers switched leagues, forsaking the NBL for the BAA. That brought Mikan to the BAA and put the struggling NBL in a heap of trouble.

A year later, in 1949, the BAA and the NBL merged to form a 17-team league that was renamed the National Basketball Association. That would be the same NBA that exists today. Finally, a league that stood the test of time.

The NBA Takes Shape

The early days of the NBA were nothing to get excited about—literally. The games often dragged on … and on … because there were no rules in place to speed up play. Once a team got a lead, it wasn't unusual for it to hold the ball and slow down play in order to milk the clock.

Well, that got old after a few seasons. Thankfully, a guy named Danny Biasone came up with an idea that just might've saved the pro game.

Biasone, the owner of the Syracuse Nationals, did the math and suggested that teams be forced to shoot within 24 seconds of taking possession.

The 24-second clock debuted at the start of the 1954–55 season, and it made all the difference. The game was much more fast-paced and much more entertaining. The quicker tempo also helped distinguish it from the college game, which was played at the slower pace.

The other major improvement in the game was the result of a rule limiting the number of fouls a team could commit each quarter. After a team's fifth personal foul, a bonus foul shot was awarded. That put an end to all that intentional fouling.

Two-Minute Warning

Slow play wasn't the only problem that beset the NBA. No sirree. Rough-house tactics also made the game boring. Only one foul shot was awarded for a nonshooting foul, regardless of how many fouls had been committed. So teams would gladly put an opponent on the line to make one point instead of giving him the chance to make a field goal, which is worth two.

The Celtics Rule

The Boston Celtics were the greatest dynasty in the history of pro sports. You can debate that, if you like, but you'd be wasting your breath.

From 1957 through 1969, the Celtics won 11 NBA championships in 13 seasons. And in one of the years they didn't win, they made it to the finals and lost to the St. Louis Hawks (1958).

Now that I've piqued your interest, you're probably wondering about the other year they didn't win. Well, that was 1967, when the Celtics' archrivals, the Philadelphia 76ers, beat the San Francisco Warriors for the title.

The common denominator for those championship Celtics teams was a 6' 11" center named Bill Russell, who valued winning over individual statistics. He provided a defensive presence that, to this day, has never been surpassed.

We'll take a closer look at Russell's career in Chapter 12, "Basketball's Best," but he was, as they say in that Coors commercial, "an original."

The Celtics were far from a one-man team. They had great players such as Bob Cousy, John Havlicek, Sam Jones, and Bill Sharman, each of whom was voted one of the 50 greatest players in NBA history.

Their coach for nine of those championships, Arnold "Red" Auerbach, was an all-timer, too. Through the 2001 season, he ranked third all-time with 1,037 victories for a winning percentage of better than 65 percent—and a whole lot of his trademark victory cigars.

Sports Strategies

Bill Russell became the first African-American head coach in any major sport in 1966. As player-coach of the Celtics, he took over for the legendary Red Auerbach. Russell coached for three seasons and led the Celtics to the 1968 and 1969 NBA titles, before retiring as a player and coach in 1969.

The Inside Skinny

It was one of the most inspiring moments ever. Willis Reed, the Knicks center and one of the best players of all time, was injured and not expected to play in Game 7 against the Lakers in the 1970 NBA championship. He didn't participate in warm-ups, but just before the tip-off, Reed hobbled onto the court to a deafening ovation. He scored the first two baskets, and played sporadically thereafter, but his presence helped win the title.

Crucial Rebound

In the early '70s, the New York Knicks and the Los Angeles Lakers had some memorable battles for the championship. The Knicks beat the Lakers in 1970 and 1973; the Lakers beat the Knicks in 1972.

But in the mid- to late '70s, the league fell on hard times. Attendance was down and television ratings plummeted. It got so bad that the NBA championship series, usually a staple of prime time, was shown on tape delay, starting at 11:30 in the East.

Then, something "Magic"-al happened, and the league's popularity took off and soared like a "Bird."

Okay, sorry for the bad puns, but the arrival of Earvin "Magic" Johnson and Larry Bird in 1979 was an example of the right players arriving at precisely the right time.

In the spring of 1979, Johnson (Michigan State) and Bird (Indiana State) led their college teams to the national championship game, with Michigan State winning 75–64. By the way, that game is still the highest-rated college basketball game of all time.

Both players entered the NBA draft that June. Johnson was chosen first overall by the Lakers. Bird had been drafted sixth by the Celtics a year earlier, because there was a chance Bird would turn pro. He didn't, but they retained his rights for the 1979 draft. The rivalry they began in college continued in the NBA. And not only that, the way they played the game had fans taking notice.

Johnson, 6' 9" tall, was a *point guard*. Point guards usually stand from 6' 0" to 6' 3", so it goes without saying that he was the tallest point guard in NBA history. He was famous for his end-to-end rushes, his no-look passes, and his midair spins. He was razzle-dazzle, all right, but his showmanship was within the team concept. He made everybody better.

Bird was a throwback. He wasn't particularly athletic or quick. In fact, when he came into the league, there was even some question whether he'd be able to cut it in the NBA, which turned out to be a laughable notion.

Magic Johnson was the main reason his Los Angeles Lakers teams were referred to as "Showtime."

Photo: Icon Sports Media

Through a tireless work ethic, unending hustle, and fundamentals that were as solid as granite, Bird became one of the greatest players ever. And like all great players, he was at his best in the clutch.He led the Celtics to NBA titles in 1981, '84, and '86, and to the finals in 1985 and 1987.

Johnson didn't do too bad when it came to winning championships, either. The Lakers won titles in 1980, '82, '85, '87, and '88. They also made it to the finals in 1983, '84, '89, and '91.

Bird and Johnson did okay when it came to individual awards, too—each player was named Most Valuable Player three times.

The impact that Johnson and Bird had on the NBA transformed the league. It also set the stage for a guy named Jordan. We'll get to him in Chapter 12.

The Fundamentals

The **point guard** on a basketball team is the quarterback, the player who makes things go, a coach on the floor. His job is to call plays and make sure the ball gets to the right players. Scoring is not his main responsibility; playmaking is.

Larry Bird of the Boston Celtics relied on work ethic, hustle, and fundamentals to become one of the NBA's all-time greats.

Photo: Icon Sports Media

The Least You Need to Know

➤ Dr. James Naismith invented basketball in 1891 in Springfield, Massachusetts.

➤ The first official college basketball game took place Feb. 9, 1895, between Hamline College and the Minnesota State School of Agriculture.

➤ The first team from the West Coast to come east for a game was Stanford in 1936.

➤ After a number of pro leagues came and went, the NBA was formed in 1949.

➤ The Boston Celtics won 11 NBA championships in 13 years, from 1957 through 1969.

➤ Magic Johnson and Larry Bird injected new life and interest into the NBA.

School Days

As far as I'm concerned, college basketball is as good as it gets. The tradition, the rivalries, the emotion … it all adds up to a terrific sport.

In addition to checking out some of the best coaches and players in college basketball history, we'll also look at two of the sport's most stunning upsets, one of which was accomplished by a team that is said to have played not just a great game, but a perfect game.

Masters of the Game

Because the team rosters are constantly changing, college basketball is very much a coaches' game. It's the coaches who recruit the players, communicate their philosophies, and develop the programs.

There have been a lot of outstanding coaches over the years, but Dean Smith, Adolph Rupp, John Wooden, and Mike Krzyzewski stand out, for obvious reasons.

The Dean

Dean Smith's career was brilliant, remarkable, splendid, unsurpassed, distinguished, and any other superlative Roget bothered to put in his thesaurus.

In 36 years as the head coach at the University of North Carolina, Smith, who retired after the 1997 season, achieved a level of consistent excellence that is unparalleled.

Dean Smith, who coached the University of North Carolina for 36 seasons, is college basketball's all-time winningest coach.

Photo: Icon Sports Media

And to think, after his first season, when the Tar Heels finished 8–9, a group of dissatisfied students hung Smith in effigy, hoping to get him fired.

Thankfully, Smith stayed around and North Carolina basketball flourished. Check out this list of accomplishments:

➤ Winningest coach in college basketball history with 879 victories (879–254, a .776 winning percentage)

➤ Thirteen *Atlantic Coast Conference* Tournament titles, 11 Final Four appearances, two national championships (1982, '93)

➤ Twenty-seven consecutive seasons with at least 20 wins and 22 seasons with at least 25 wins

➤ The Tar Heels finished third or better in the always-competitive ACC for 33 straight seasons, including 17 firsts and 11 seconds

➤ The Tar Heels made 23 consecutive NCAA Tournament appearances

➤ From 1981 through 1993, the Tar Heels made the final 16 of the NCAA Tournament every year

➤ Named "Sportsman of the Year" by *Sports Illustrated* in 1997; winner of the Arthur Ashe Award for Courage in 1997

➤ Ninety-seven percent of his players have graduated from college

But more than just being a great coach, Smith was a teacher of the game. His teams were always well-schooled and fundamentally sound. More than 50 of his players went on to play pro basketball and 10 of his former assistants became head coaches.

Michael Jordan, who played at North Carolina from 1982 to '84 and experienced a fair amount of success in the NBA, gives Smith a lion's share of the credit for his brilliant career.

"Seriously, I would never have been able to be the scorer, passer, rebounder, defender, or team player that I (was) without Coach Smith," wrote Jordan in the foreword of *The Dean's List: A Celebration of Tar Heel Basketball and Dean Smith.*

Pretty high praise, wouldn't you say?

The Baron

For Dean Smith to become the all-time winningest coach, he had to pass the University of Kentucky's Adolph Rupp, who held that distinction for 30 years.

Rupp learned the game from legendary Kansas coach Phog Allen, who learned it from the guy who invented it, for goodness sakes—Dr. James Naismith. You can't get a better pedigree than that!

Rupp, known as the Baron, took over as Kentucky coach in 1931 and reigned for 41 years. His overall record of 876–190 computes to an 82.2 winning percentage.

The Fundamentals

The **Atlantic Coast Conference,** also known as the ACC, is one of the nation's foremost basketball leagues. Formed in 1954, it is made up of Clemson, Duke, Florida State, Georgia Tech, Maryland, North Carolina, North Carolina State, Virginia, and Wake Forest.

The Inside Skinny

Dean Smith made his mark on more than just the basketball court. He is credited with helping integrate Chapel Hill, North Carolina, site of the university, in 1965. Smith not only recruited Charlie Scott, the first African American ever to play for the Tar Heels, he took him to his church and insisted Scott be allowed to eat in a "whites only" restaurant. Guess what? Scott was served.

The Wildcats won four NCAA Tournament championships (1948–49, '51, '58), one National Invitation Tournament championship (1946), and 27 *Southeastern Conference* Tournament titles.

Rupp's career was not without its problems. There was a betting and point-shaving scandal in 1951 in which Rupp was never officially involved, although many questioned how it was possible that he had no knowledge of the gambling types his players were cavorting with.

The other knock against Rupp was the suspicion that he had racist tendencies, because during his tenure, the program recruited no African-American players.

Still, there is no denying his impact—on the Kentucky program and on college basketball as a whole.

As a Kentucky media guide put it, Rupp was "a man of consummate pride and a molder of powerful teams which for more than four decades made the name University of Kentucky synonymous with the game of basketball."

And it doesn't get much better than that.

The Fundamentals

The **Southeastern Conference,** formed in 1932, is made up of 12 teams split into two divisions. Florida, Georgia, Kentucky, South Carolina, Tennessee, and Vanderbilt are in the East. Alabama, Arkansas, Auburn, Louisiana State, Mississippi, and Mississippi State are in the West.

The Wizard of Westwood

John Wooden, coach of the UCLA Bruins, was known as the Wizard of Westwood. Never has a nickname fit so perfectly.

Think I'm kidding? Wooden led the Bruins to 10 NCAA Tournament championships between 1964 and 1975, including a run of seven straight.

During that storied run, UCLA was unbeaten four times and once-beaten three times. From 1967 through 1973, in addition to winning seven straight titles, the team's combined record was 205–5.

In 27 seasons at UCLA, Wooden, who retired after winning his 10th NCAA title in 1975, had a record of 316–68 and a winning percentage of .823.

Guaranteed, no college basketball team will ever come close—remotely close—to equaling the accomplishments of Wooden's teams. Yes, he was blessed with great players, most notably Lew Alcindor (now known as Kareem Abdul-Jabbar) and Bill Walton.

Sports Strategies

John Wooden was quite the player for Purdue University (1929–32). He led the Boilermakers to the 1932 national championship and was a three-time All-American. He was known as the Indiana Rubber Man, because of the way he bounced up off the floor after diving for a loose ball.

But it was Wooden's ability to teach the fundamentals and his insistence on selfless team play that were the main reasons for UCLA's sustained excellence. His teams weren't flashy or dominated by individuals interested in padding their scoring averages; they were five playing as one. And one, as in No. 1, is where Wooden's Bruins usually finished.

Coach K

When it comes to Wooden-like consistency and excellence, Duke coach Mike Krzyzewski is often compared to the Wizard of Westwood.

Known as Coach K because his name is a one-word spelling bee, Krzyzewski (pronounced *sha-shef-ski*) has made a habit of taking his Blue Devils to the Final Four. Nine times since 1986 Duke has been to the Final Four under Coach K. Only Dean Smith (12) and John Wooden (11) have more trips.

The Blue Devils won the national championship in 1991, 1992, and 2001, and Coach K's NCAA Tournament winning percentage of .800 is the highest of all time.

Coach K went to the U.S. Military Academy and coached at Army from 1975 to '80, before taking over at Duke.

Like all great teachers of the game, Coach K's teams are fundamentally sound and mentally disciplined. The Blue Devils play great defense, which means they're never out of a game—regardless of what the scoreboard says.

Duke coach Mike Krzyzewski has led the Blue Devils to three national championships.

Photo: Icon Sports Media

For instance, during the 2001 season, Duke trailed Maryland by 10 points with 54 seconds to play. The Maryland fans who headed to the parking lot to celebrate missed the Blue Devils tying the game in regulation and winning it in overtime.

Later in the same season, Maryland led Duke by 22 points in the second half. Guess what? Duke won that one, too.

The Inside Skinny

While at Army, Coach K played for Bob Knight, who went on to coach at Indiana and became the Texas A&M coach in 2001. Knight then offered Coach K a graduate assistant position at Indiana in 1974. A year later, Coach K took over as head coach at his alma mater, where he remained until 1980, when he moved to Duke.

That never-say-die attitude is a trademark of Coach K's teams. Given the Blue Devils' success, maybe he should be called Special K.

Give These Players an A+

Pete Maravich, Bill Bradley, and Bill Walton became fine pro basketball players, but college was where they made their names and their marks.

Maravich was a scorer and a consummate showman; Bradley almost single-handedly led Princeton to greatness; and Walton was a centerpiece of the UCLA dynasty. It didn't matter how tall they were—or weren't—all three were big men on their campuses.

Pistol Pete

Pete Maravich put up monster numbers for Louisiana State University, and he also put on the best show in college basketball.

What Pistol Pete did with a basketball qualified as magic. He dribbled behind his back and between his legs; he threw up crazy shots; he attempted passes that other players wouldn't think about; and he made moves that you weren't likely to see even on a playground.

But mostly, he put the ball in the basket and his name in the NCAA record books:

➤ Most points: 3,667

➤ Highest career scoring average: 44.2 points a game

➤ Most games scoring at least 50 points: 28

➤ Most points, single season: 1,381; highest scoring average, single season: 44.5 in 1970

Two-Minute Warning

Now, you might think 3,667 points would've translated into a championship, either in college or the NBA. But Pete Maravich, despite his prolific scoring ability, never won a championship. LSU's record during his career was only 49–35.

➤ Most field goals made: 1,387; most field goals attempted: 3,166

➤ Most free throws made, single game: 30, 1969

Maravich, with trademark floppy socks and hair that looked like it had been cut by one of the Beatles' barbers, was a three-time All-American (1968–70) and the college player of the year in 1970.

He spent his NBA career with four different teams. He was a five-time All-Star, averaged 24.2 points a game during his 10-year career, and was named one of the NBA's 50 greatest players in 1996 in a vote of a league-approved panel that included media, players, coaches, and team executives.

But as good as he was in the NBA, he was never as great as he was in college.

Dollar Bill

If you're on the short side of 30, the name Bill Bradley probably makes you think of the senator from New Jersey or the candidate for the 2000 Democratic presidential nomination.

If you're a little older, then you also remember Bill Bradley the basketball player, first at Princeton University and then for the New York Knicks.

Talk about the total package.

Through hard work and dedication, Bradley turned himself into a terrific basketball player. He wasn't a particularly gifted athlete, but he put lead in his sneakers to strengthen his legs and he practiced dribbling with blinders attached to a pair of glasses so that his lower vision was blocked.

Well, the practice paid off, and Bradley had one of the most outstanding college careers of all time.

At Princeton, Bradley was a two-time first-team All-American (1964–65). He averaged 30.2 points a game over his three years and led the Tigers to the 1965 Final Four. Even though Princeton lost in the semifinals, Bradley was named the tournament's Most Outstanding Player.

But that wasn't all. In 1964, he was a member of the USA's gold medal-winning Olympic team, and in 1965 he became the first college basketball player to win the Sullivan Award, given to the nation's outstanding amateur athlete.

Bradley's pro career was delayed for two years, because he was offered a Rhodes scholarship. But he

Sports Strategies

Because he was a straight–A student and averaged 27.4 points a game in high school, Bill Bradley was one of the most heavily recruited players. All the major schools offered scholarships, but Bradley turned down those offers and chose to pay his own way to go to Princeton, an Ivy League school that didn't offer scholarships.

joined the New York Knicks in 1967 and helped them win two world championships before retiring in 1977 and moving into politics.

The Maverick

As a collegian at UCLA in the early 1970s, Bill Walton was a bit of a rabble-rouser. He was anti-establishment, anti-Vietnam War, anti-Richard Nixon, and pro-Grateful Dead. He was also a vegetarian (not that there's anything wrong with that) and wore flannel shirts and multicolored headbands.

His coach, John Wooden, admitted to worrying about him off the floor. But on the floor, Walton was no problem at all. Unless you consider being one of the most dominant big men in college basketball history a problem. (I didn't think so.)

Walton led the Bruins to two national championships (1972–73), three Final Fours, and a record of 86–4 during his career. He was a three-time Player of the Year who also has the distinction of delivering arguably the best performance in NCAA championship history.

In the 1973 NCAA final against Memphis State, Walton was as close to perfect as possible. He made 21 of his 22 field goal attempts and both free throw attempts for 44 points, the most points ever scored in a final game.

Unfortunately, Walton's pro career was tainted by a variety of injuries. Still, he led the Portland Trail Blazers to the NBA championship in 1977 and was an important role player on the Boston Celtics' 1986 title team.

And when it came time for the NBA to choose its 50 greatest players, Bill Walton made the cut.

The Inside Skinny

Even if you've never seen Bill Walton play, if you're a basketball fan, you've surely heard his voice. Walton not only does commentary on NBA games for NBC Sports, he also worked for CBS Sports as an analyst for the 2001 NCAA Tournament. Regardless of which network he works for, he is never at a loss for words.

Monumental Upsets

On paper, the following games shouldn't have been close, because the favored teams were clearly superior to the underdogs.

But, thank goodness, games aren't played on paper. Otherwise, we would've been deprived of two stunning upsets.

Houston, You Have a Problem

The North Carolina State Wolfpack barely qualified for the 1983 NCAA Tournament with a mediocre 20-10 regular season record, and as a result, no one expected them to stay around for too long. In fact, they almost lost in the first round. The Wolfpack trailed Pepperdine by six with 1:10 to play, but rallied to win the game in overtime. It was a portent of things to come.

N.C. State went on to beat University of Nevada-Las Vegas, Utah, and Virginia to advance to the Final Four, then defeated Georgia in the semifinals to earn a matchup against the University of Houston. The Cougars were led by Akeem (now Hakeem) Olajuwon and Clyde Drexler, each of whom were named one of the NBA's 50 greatest players. This game figured to be no contest, which was confirmed early on when the Cougars went on a 17–2 run. With 10 minutes left to play in the game, they still led 42–35.

But then a not-so-funny thing happened to the Cougars. In trying to be careful with the ball and milk the clock, they stopped trying to win and started playing not to lose. Bad move. The Wolfpack slowly chipped away at the lead and with just over two minutes to play, Derek Whittenburg's jumper tied it 52–52.

N.C. State got the ball back and with 44 seconds left called a timeout to diagram a play that was never used. You know what they say about best-laid plans, right?

With the clock down to five seconds, Whittenburg had the ball. That was the good news. The bad news was that he was 35 feet from the basket. In desperation, he let it fly. The ball didn't come close to touching the rim, but it did fall right into the hands of Lorenzo Charles, who dunked it as the buzzer sounded. Final score: N.C. State 54, Houston 52.

Unbelievable.

Sports Strategies

The rules of the game, at the time, gave Villanova a big advantage against Georgetown. In 1985, the shot clock was used during the regular season, but not during the NCAA Tournament. Because Villanova could take as long as it wanted on each possession, thereby keeping the ball away from Georgetown, it was able to manage a miracle.

The Perfect Game

Rollie Massimino, the Villanova coach, admitted it the day before the 1985 NCAA championship game against Georgetown: It would take a perfect game for the Wildcats to beat the Hoyas.

Well, darned if Villanova didn't play the perfect game. Even though Georgetown was led by 7' 0" All-American Patrick Ewing, the Wildcats managed to win by shooting an unheard-of 78.6 percent from the field. Villanova took 28 shots from the field during the game and made—Are you ready for this?—22.

And the Wildcats' shooting performance didn't come against just any team. The Hoyas had the No. 1 defense in the country that year, limiting opponents to 39 percent shooting from the floor.

But Villanova doubled that—and had a national championship to show for it.

The Greatest of All Time?

Two heavyweight programs—Duke and Kentucky—played at the Spectrum in Philadelphia in the 1992 NCAA East Regional final. The winner would earn a trip to the Final Four.

Sports Strategies

Duke's Christian Laettner enjoyed more than a perfect ending to the NCAA East Regional final against Kentucky. He enjoyed a perfect night. Laettner scored 31 points without missing a shot. He was 10-for-10 from the floor and 10-for-10 from the foul line.

And for most of the game, it looked like the winner would be Duke. But Kentucky fought back from a 12-point deficit midway through the second half to send the game into overtime.

The last 32 seconds of overtime were classic. There were five lead changes, with Kentucky taking a 103–102 lead with 2.1 seconds to play.

Duke would inbound the ball under its basket, 94 feet from its goal. What happened next was not to be believed. Grant Hill threw a strike of a baseball pass to Christian Laettner, who caught the ball, dribbled, turned, and fired from just beyond the foul line. The ball was perfect from the moment it left his hands, and the Blue Devils managed a most improbable, thrilling 104–103 victory.

Said Duke Coach Mike Krzyzewski, "You hope someday you're a part of something like this, and I was."

If you missed it, you missed perhaps the most exciting college basketball game ever. But if you saw it, consider yourself lucky, because you'll never, ever forget it.

The Least You Need to Know

➤ Dean Smith is the all-time winningest coach in college basketball history.

➤ John Wooden led UCLA to 10 national championships in 12 years.

➤ Pete Maravich is the all-time scoring leader in NCAA history.

➤ North Carolina State and Villanova registered two of the biggest upsets in NCAA Tournament history.

➤ Duke's overtime victory over Kentucky in the 1992 NCAA East Regional final is regarded as one of the most exciting games of all time.

Basketball's Best

The best players in the NBA have become legends, not just in their sport, but in many cases, in all of sport.

From the epic battles between Wilt Chamberlain and Bill Russell to the singular dominance of Michael Jordan, the NBA has produced some of the greatest athletes of all time. We've already talked about Magic Johnson and Larry Bird in Chapter 10, "It Started with a Peach Basket." Here are some more of basketball's best.

Men in the Middle

There is an old adage in basketball: You can't teach height. That's why the center is one of the most important ingredients of any basketball team.

Whether it is making baskets or blocking shots, grabbing rebounds or providing a defensive presence, having a 7-footer at your disposal can mean a distinct advantage.

The Big Dipper

Wilt Chamberlain was the size of a small building. At a shade over 7 feet tall and weighing 275 pounds, he was virtually unstoppable on offense and impenetrable on defense.

How would you like to figure out a way to get a ball over or around him?

Chamberlain was able to score and rebound at will, and it didn't matter that defenses put two and three men around him. He was famous for his rim-rattling dunks and his feather-soft "finger roll," where the ball gently rolled off his fingers and into the basket.

After a stellar career at Overbrook High School in Philadelphia, where he averaged 44.5 points a game during his senior year, Chamberlain played two years of college ball at the University of Kansas. He averaged 29.9 points and 18.3 rebounds as a collegian and was a first-team All-American in 1957 and 1958.

He left KU after two seasons, because he was tired of the dirty tactics employed by opposing teams, and he wanted to hone his skills for the NBA. But the rules in those days kept him from playing in the NBA until his class graduated. So during the year he had to wait, he played for the Harlem Globetrotters and earned $50,000, which was better than bagging groceries or parking cars.

Chamberlain joined the Philadelphia Warriors in 1959, and the game was never the same. As a rookie, he averaged a league-leading 37.6 points and 27 rebounds. No, those numbers are not misprints.

For the next six seasons, Chamberlain led the NBA in scoring, averaging 38.4, 50.4, 44.8, 36.9, 34.7, and 33.5 points a game. He also led the league in rebounding 10 times.

The Inside Skinny

Wilt Chamberlain was known as Wilt the Stilt, which he hated, and the Big Dipper, which he liked. He got the nickname when he was a kid, playing basketball with some buddies in the basement of a vacant house. He injured his eye on a low-hanging pipe and his buddies kidded him about having to dip under it. The name stuck.

In 1962, Chamberlain did the unthinkable. He scored 100 points in a game against the New York Knicks, played in Hershey, Pennsylvania. He made 36 of 63 shots from the field and 28 of 32 from the foul line, which was particularly impressive considering he was a lousy foul shooter throughout his career.

Other than the foul shooting, the other knock on Chamberlain was not playing on more championship teams. He played on two—Philadelphia (1967) and Los Angeles (1972). His main rival, Boston's Bill Russell, played on 13.

But championships or not, there is no doubt about Chamberlain's statistical dominance:

➤ Second all-time in career scoring: 31,419

➤ Second all-time in scoring average: 30.1

➤ First all-time in rebounds: 23,924 (22.9 average)

➤ First in single-season scoring average: 50.4, 1962

➤ First in single-season field goal percentage: .727, 1973

➤ First in single-season rebounding average: 27.2, 1961

➤ Most rebounds, single game: 55, 1960

➤ Most career games with 50 or more points: 118

➤ Most games in one season with 50 or more points: 45, 1962

Wilt Chamberlain was inducted into the Naismith Memorial Basketball Hall of Fame in 1978. Given his impact on the game, he should've gotten his own wing.

The Winner

Bill Russell was synonymous with winning championships. No matter what level he played, he led his team to a title.

In college, at the University of San Francisco, Russell led the Dons to 55 straight wins and two NCAA championships (1955–56). At the 1956 Olympic Games, he led the United States to the gold medal. And with the Boston Celtics, he set a championship standard that will never be eclipsed.

Russell was the force behind the Celtics dynasty that won 11 NBA championships in 13 years, including a run of eight straight from 1959 through 1966. The last two titles, in 1968 and 1969, were won with Russell serving as player-coach. The guy did it all.

Russell, unlike his chief rival, Wilt Chamberlain, who was known for his scoring, was famous for his defense and rebounding. He epitomized the team concept. Individual statistics meant nothing to him. All that mattered was winning.

He averaged 15 points a game—solid, but not spectacular for someone 6' 9" tall and weighing 230 pounds. But Russell, a five-time NBA Most Valuable Player, excelled on the boards, averaging 22.5 rebounds a game throughout his 13-year career and ranking second all-time, to Chamberlain.

If you're wondering how many shots Russell blocked, it's anybody's guess, because the NBA didn't count blocks as an official statistic until 1973.

Sports Strategies

Of all the records and distinctions that Wilt Chamberlain has, one stands out, because it's so unexpected. He played in 1,205 games, regular season and play-offs, and never fouled out—unbelievable given what a physical presence he was.

Two-Minute Warning

Despite the greatness he achieved in college and in the NBA, Bill Russell didn't start out as a can't-miss basketball prospect. He was the third-string center on his junior varsity team in high school. Actually, he was worse than third string. The team had 15 uniforms and 16 players. Russell alternated wearing the 15th uniform.

But suffice it to say, his defensive presence and his shot-blocking ability changed the way the game was played.

"No one had ever played basketball the way I played it," said Russell. "They had never seen anyone block shots before. I like to think I originated a whole new style of play."

One that resulted in winning—like no one before or since.

The Inside Skinny

Lew Alcindor had been a Muslim since college. In 1971, his second year in the NBA, he changed his name to Kareem Abdul-Jabbar, which means "noble, powerful servant." Many fans were unhappy with his decision, but the controversy didn't affect his play in the least.

Sports Strategies

Even though he stood more than 7 feet tall, Kareem Abdul-Jabbar didn't dominate because of sheer physical strength. Unlike most centers, Abdul-Jabbar relied on his grace and versatility. He had a soft shooting touch and was an excellent passer, defender, and shot blocker.

The Skyhook Reigns

He came to prominence as Lew Alcindor; early in his pro career, he changed his name to Kareem Abdul-Jabbar. But no matter what he was called, he dominated the game at every level with one of the great weapons in all of sport—the skyhook.

The skyhook was virtually unstoppable. Jabbar, who stood 7' 2" tall, would take a little jump and shoot a hook shot *down* and into the basket. Goodness knows, that shot served him well, and for a long time.

Jabbar (then Alcindor) played his college ball at UCLA. He led the Bruins to three straight national titles (1967–69) and an overall record of 88–2.

It figured that he would win some individual hardware for his efforts, and he won enough to fill a small outbuilding—three-time first-team All-American, two-time National Player of the Year, and three-time Most Outstanding Player in the NCAA Tournament.

Jabbar began his NBA career in 1970 with the Milwaukee Bucks, and in just his second season, he did what came naturally: He led them to a championship, what else?

And there would be more titles to come, only not for the Bucks. Jabbar was traded to the Los Angeles Lakers in 1975 and led them on an incredible run of successes—five NBA titles and seven NBA Finals appearances in an eight-year stretch, beginning in 1980.

Jabbar, who retired in 1989 after 20 seasons, scored a few points along the way, too—more than anybody else in the history of the game. His 38,387 points are No. 1 all-time. He also tops the charts in most seasons of 1,000 or more points (19), minutes played (57,446), and most field goals (15,387).

John Wooden, Jabbar's coach at UCLA, summed up his greatness by saying, "Kareem was the finest truly big man ever to play basketball. He could do anything you asked of him, and do it almost to perfection."

Which pretty much says it all.

Up, Up, and Away

They soared through the air with the greatest of ease—and there wasn't a trapeze in sight. Elgin Baylor and Julius Erving seemed to live in midair. They combined grace, agility, explosiveness, athleticism, and gravity-defying creativity. You'd swear they could hang in midair forever.

And the moves they used to shed their opponents and get the ball in the basket had to be seen to be believed.

Baylor, at 6′ 5″, 225 pounds, was the first acrobat the game had ever seen, a show unto himself. A forward, he began his NBA career in 1959 with the Minneapolis Lakers, who moved to Los Angeles one year later. In his 14-year career, he averaged 27.4 points a game, fourth-highest all-time, and in 1960, he scored 71 points in a game against the New York Knicks.

Unfortunately, Baylor's career was plagued by injuries. You name it, he hurt it—both knees, kneecap, finger on his shooting hand, torn Achilles tendon. He also had the misfortune to play in the NBA during the Boston Celtics dynasty. The Lakers made it to the NBA Finals eight times during Baylor's career and lost all eight, including the first seven to the Celts.

But championship or not, there is no denying his greatness or the way he changed the game.

Baylor retired early in the 1972 season, and as he left, Julius Erving was just getting started. Erving, a.k.a. Doctor J or the Doctor, began his pro career in 1971 in the *American Basketball Association,* which was a short-lived rival to the NBA.

Erving, a forward, spent five seasons in the ABA, then joined the Philadelphia 76ers of the NBA. Like Baylor, he was a highlight film, with moves that were indescribable. He was the guy who invented hang time. He could spin and scoop and slam and do things that you'd swear required superhuman talents. And there were those who would make the case that the Doctor was superhuman.

Erving, the NBA's Most Valuable Player in 1981, led the Sixers to the NBA Finals three times, finally

Sports Strategies

Elgin Baylor's 71-point effort against the New York Knicks in 1960 makes him one of only four players to score at least 70 in one game. Wilt Chamberlain did it six times (100, 78, 73, 73, 72, 70); David Thompson (73) of the Denver Nuggets and David Robinson (71) of the San Antonio Spurs did it once each.

The Fundamentals

The **American Basketball Association** began play in 1967 with 10 teams. The league used a red, white, and blue ball and the three-point basket. The ABA lasted nine seasons before going under. Four ABA teams—Denver Nuggets, Indiana Pacers, New York Nets, and San Antonio Spurs—were absorbed into the NBA in 1976. The NBA also adopted the 3-point shot, used by the ABA, in 1979.

winning a championship in 1983. He was the first non-center to score 30,000 points in the pros—11,662 ABA, 18,364 NBA—and he averaged 24.2 points a game during his 16-year career.

The other thing about Erving, besides his uncanny ability to draw oohs and ahhs, was the class and dignity with which he carried himself. Said Dominique Wilkins, an All-Pro himself: "I never heard anybody knock him or express jealousy. Never one negative word. I can't name you one other player who has that status."

Julius Erving was the total package—on and off the court.

On Guard

There have been a slew of great guards in the NBA over the years. Bob Cousy, the first great playmaker; Magic Johnson, who redefined the point guard position; John Stockton, the all-time assist leader.

The list is lengthy, and the players on it are terrific talents. But all pale in comparison to Michael Jordan.

His Airness

What Michael Jordan accomplished during his college and NBA careers is enough to fill a book all by itself. How does this sound? *The Complete Idiot's Guide to Michael Jordan*. It might have to be a two-volume set.

What Michael Jordan meant to the NBA can't be overstated. He set a slew of individual records, but he was the consummate team player as well. His teammates were better just because they were on the floor with him.

And while he's best known for his high-flying dunks, he was also a terrific defender and one of the best players of all time with the game on the line.

The only thing he was missing was an *S* on his chest.

All that fame on the basketball court translated into commercial endorsements and even a full-length feature film. He sold everything from Nike shoes to Ray-O-Vac batteries, from MCI long distance to Gatorade. And in the movie *Space Jam,* he starred with Bugs Bunny and the Looney Tunes gang.

Jordan became one of the best-known sports celebrities of his time. Strike that. Make it *the* best-known celebrity. Even if you didn't know a jump shot from a jump rope, you sure as heck knew who Michael Jordan was.

Michael Jordan led the Chicago Bulls to six NBA championships in eight years.

Photo: Diane Staskowski

Jordan played his college ball at the University of North Carolina, where he was one of the few freshmen ever to earn a spot in the starting lineup.

The Tar Heels reached the 1982 NCAA championship game in Jordan's freshman year, and he provided a hint of things to come when he sank the winning jump shot with 17 seconds to play to beat Georgetown.

Jordan left North Carolina after his junior season (but returned to get his degree in geography) and was the third pick in the 1984 NBA draft. Now, I know what you're thinking. *Third? You mean two players were picked before Michael Jordan?* Hard as it is to believe, the Houston Rockets picked Hakeem Olajuwon and the Portland Trail Blazers picked Sam Bowie. The Bulls grabbed Jordan next.

The first several years of Jordan's career resulted in lots of points and four straight NBA scoring titles (1987–90), but no championships. And people thought that maybe Jordan was just a showman and not a winner.

129

Two-Minute Warning

As difficult as it is to fathom, Michael Jordan wasn't a great player when he first began to play basketball. Believe it or not, he was cut from his Laney High School team in Wilmington, North Carolina, when he tried out as a sophomore. He was disappointed but not demoralized, and he used that disappointment to fuel his desire to improve.

Sports Strategies

After the Bulls' 1993 title and with nothing left to prove, Michael Jordan announced his retirement from the NBA. He also began a new pursuit: making the Chicago White Sox as an outfielder. Jordan spent a season in the minor leagues and 17 months away from basketball. He returned to the Bulls in March 1995.

Starting in 1991, he proved he was both. He won three more scoring titles, and he also led the Bulls to three straight NBA championships.

Jordan left the game for nearly two seasons to play professional baseball, but when he came back in March 1995, it didn't take him—and the Bulls—long to pick up where he left off.

Jordan won scoring titles and the Bulls won championships in 1996, '97, and '98. That makes six NBA titles in all, if you're keeping score at home.

And in what turned out to be Jordan's final game, Game 6 of the 1998 NBA Finals against the Utah Jazz, he hit the winning shot with 6.6 seconds left. What a perfect ending to a brilliant career.

Here's how brilliant:

➤ Fourth all-time in points: 29,277

➤ First all-time in scoring average: 31.5

➤ Most scoring titles: 10

➤ Third all-time in steals: 2,306

➤ Most playoff points: 5,987

➤ Highest playoff scoring average: 33.4

➤ Most points in one playoff game: 63

➤ All-NBA first team: 10 times

➤ All-Defensive first team: nine times

➤ Most Valuable Player: five times

And it's just possible that those totals could be added to. By the time you read this, Michael Jordan may have decided to make another comeback. Stay tuned.

The Big O

The term *triple-double* didn't become a part of basketball lingo until Magic Johnson came along. Because he was so proficient in so many areas of the game, and because he registered double figures in three different statistical categories, the triple-double was a stat that carried special significance.

During the 1961–62 season, Oscar Robertson of the Cincinnati Royals averaged a triple-double for the year, which has to rank as one of the greatest single-season performances ever. The 6' 5" guard averaged 30.8 points, 12.5 rebounds, and 11.4 assists a game that season.

Overall, Robertson, known as the Big O, scored 26,668 points (25.7 average), which ranks seventh all-time and more than any guard in NBA history except Michael Jordan. He also ranks third in assists (9,887, 9.5 average), behind John Stockton and Magic Johnson.

Robertson was traded to the Milwaukee Bucks in 1970. A year later, he teamed with Kareem Abdul-Jabbar to win his only NBA championship.

And let's not forget about Robertson's college career at the University of Cincinnati, where he was the first player ever to lead the nation in scoring three years in a row (1958–60). He averaged 35.1, 32.6, and 33.7 points a game, respectively.

After all these years, he still ranks seventh all-time among college players with 2,973 points.

Sports Strategies

Michael Jordan scored a single-game playoff record 63 points against the Boston Celtics in 1986. Of the nine highest single-game point totals in the history of the playoffs, Jordan has five of them. He scored 55 points three times and 56 points once.

Mr. Clutch

When the game was on the line and the clock was winding down, there was no question whom the Los Angeles Lakers wanted to take the crucial shot—Jerry West, the guy they called "Mr. Clutch."

The nickname fit like Spandex on a super model. Time and time again, Jerry West proved himself with his cool, calm, and collected demeanor, and that deadly accurate jump shot.

One of his most famous shots came in Game 3 of the 1970 NBA Finals against the New York Knicks. With the Lakers trailing by two, time about to expire and West 60 feet from the basket, he let fly with a prayer that was answered, sending the game into overtime.

The Fundamentals

The **triple-double** came into being as a result of Magic Johnson's all-round talent. To register a triple-double is to reach double figures in any three statistical categories. For instance, 35 points, 12 rebounds, and 10 assists would be a triple-double.

Jerry West became an NBA icon. In addition to his jump-shooting ability, he also was a fundamentally sound player whose intensity and toughness was widely respected, as was the class with which he played the game. So it figured when the NBA needed a silhouette for its logo, it used Jerry West as the model.

West became the third player in NBA history to surpass the 25,000-point mark. He finished with 25,192 points, an average of 27 points a game, which ranks fifth all-time.

Hard as it is to believe and as great a player as West was, he rarely was satisfied with his level of play. He took losses to heart and expected nothing less than perfection from himself.

It didn't help that the Lakers happened to have great teams at the same time the Boston Celtics dynasty ruled. From 1962 through 1970, the Lakers made it to the NBA Finals seven times, losing six times to the Celtics and once to the New York Knicks.

Finally, in 1972, everything came together for the Lakers. They won an NBA-record 33 straight games and compiled a 69–13 mark—at the time, the best single-season record ever.

In the NBA Finals against the Knicks, the Lakers won in five games, and Jerry West finally had his championship.

The Least You Need to Know

➤ Bill Russell led the Boston Celtics to 11 NBA titles in 13 seasons.

➤ Wilt Chamberlain was an unstoppable offensive force.

➤ Julius Erving and Elgin Baylor brought high-flying athleticism to the game.

➤ Kareem Abdul-Jabbar is the NBA's all-time leading scorer.

➤ Michael Jordan led the Chicago Bulls to six NBA titles and is widely regarded as the greatest player ever to play the game.

➤ Oscar Robertson averaged a triple-double during the 1961–62 season.

Game Time

We've reached that time again. So get your No. 2 pencil, keep your eyes on your own paper, and try to answer these trivia questions.

After the questions, we'll give you the answers, followed by some pithy quotes, some nuggets of information with which you can impress your friends, and a look at basketball, distaff style.

Twenty Questions

It's time for a quiz on college and pro basketball. Good luck.

1. Who holds the record for most times leading the NBA in free throw percentage?
2. Which of these players led the NBA in blocked shots at least once? a.) Patrick Ewing; b.) Shaquille O'Neal; c.) George Johnson; d.) Elvin Hayes.
3. Who is the NBA's all-time leader in games played?

4. Who is the only player to be named Most Valuable Player in the ABA and the NBA?

5. Who is the only coach to win championships in the American Basketball League (ABL), ABA, and NBA?

6. Which seven players have played on NCAA, Olympic, and NBA championship teams?

7. Which team won the first *National Invitation Tournament?*

8. Which 12 players from nonchampionship teams were named Most Outstanding Player in the NCAA Tournament?

9. Which team has the most NCAA Tournament appearances of all time?

10. What three teams were led to the NBA championship finals by player-coaches?

11. What year was the dunk declared illegal in college basketball?

12. Which team has the most appearances in the NBA Finals?

13. Which seven college teams have won the national championship and finished their season undefeated?

The Fundamentals

The **National Invitation Tournament** began in 1938 and was the first postseason basketball tournament. Until 1977, the 32-team tourney was played entirely in Madison Square Garden in New York. But in 1977, the games were moved to on-campus sites, with the semifinals and final being played in the Garden.

14. Which six players have been named Player of the Year in college basketball and Most Valuable Player in the NBA?

15. Which three players have led the NCAA in scoring and rebounding in the same season?

16. What is the all-time record for victories in one college basketball season?

17. Who holds the record for most times being named the Most Valuable Player in the All-Star Game?

18. Who was the first player to lead the NBA in steals?

19. What two players have been named the NBA's Rookie of the Year and Most Valuable Player in the same season?

20. Which team had the best regular season record in NBA history?

Twenty Answers

OK, let's see how you did and whether you were fooled by question No. 2.

1. Bill Sharman of the Boston Celtics led the NBA in free throw shooting seven times—1953–57, '59, and '61.

2. A bit of a trick question. George Johnson led the NBA in blocked shots three times—1978 (New Jersey), and 1981–82 (San Antonio).

3. Robert Parish, who spent the bulk of his career with the Boston Celtics, played 1,611 games over 21 seasons.

4. Julius Erving won three Most Valuable Player awards in the ABA (1974–76) with the New York Nets and one in the NBA (1981) with the Philadelphia 76ers.

Julius Erving led the Philadelphia 76ers to the 1983 NBA championship.

Photo: Icon Sports Media

5. It's the same person who was such a good foul shooter. Bill Sharman won the ABL title in 1962 with the Cleveland Pipers, the ABA title in 1971 with the Utah Stars, and the NBA title in 1972 with the Los Angeles Lakers.

Sports Strategies

Julius Erving first made his name in the American Basketball Association. He led the ABA in scoring three times and was its Most Valuable Player twice. His flamboyant style of play not only was credited with carrying the league, but it was a main reason the NBA decided to absorb four ABA teams when the league folded in 1976.

Two-Minute Warning

Even though Villanova's Howard Porter was the key to the Wildcats' march to the 1971 NCAA Tournament final, his participation that season was not without controversy. Because Porter signed with an agent before the end of the season, Villanova's runner-up finish to UCLA was forfeited.

6. The seven players who have managed the NCAA, Olympic, and NBA trifecta: Clyde Lovellette (Kansas 1952; Olympics 1956; Minneapolis 1953, Boston 1963–64), K.C. Jones (University of San Francisco 1955; Olympics 1956; Boston 1957, '59–66), Bill Russell (University of San Francisco 1955–56; Olympics 1956; Boston 1957, '59–66, '68–69), Jerry Lucas (Ohio State 1960; Olympics 1960; New York Knicks 1971), Quinn Buckner (Indiana 1976; Olympics 1976; Boston 1984), Magic Johnson (Michigan State 1979; Olympics 1992; Los Angeles 1980, '82, '85, '87–88), and Michael Jordan (North Carolina 1982; Olympics 1984, '92; Chicago 1991–93, '96–98).

7. Temple defeated Colorado 60–36 in 1938.

8. The 12 NCAA tournament players who were named Most Outstanding Player while playing for a nonchampionship team were Jimmy Hull, Ohio State, 1939; B.H. Born, Kansas, 1953; Hal Lear, Temple, 1956; Wilt Chamberlain, Kansas, 1957; Elgin Baylor, Seattle, 1958; Jerry West, West Virginia, 1959; Jerry Lucas, Ohio State, 1961; Art Heyman, Duke, 1963; Bill Bradley, Princeton, 1965; Jerry Chambers, Utah, 1966; Howard Porter, Villanova, 1971; and Akeem Olajuwon, Houston, 1983.

9. Kentucky leads the way with 43 appearances, through the 2001 tournament. UCLA is next with 37, followed by North Carolina with 35.

10. The three teams led to the NBA Finals by player-coaches: Baltimore Bullets, 1948, Buddy Jeannette, guard; Syracuse Nationals, 1950, Al Cervi, guard; and Boston Celtics, 1968–69, Bill Russell, center.

11. The dunk was outlawed in 1967. It returned, much to the fans' delight, in 1975.

12. Through the 2001 season, the Minneapolis-Los Angeles Lakers have appeared in the NBA Finals 26 times. (The team moved from Minneapolis to L.A. for the 1960–61 season.) The Lakers have won 13 championships.

13. The seven undefeated national champions: San Francisco, 29–0, 1956; North Carolina, 32–0, 1957; UCLA, 30–0, 1964, '67, '72–73; and Indiana, 32–0, 1976.

14. Six players have hit the daily double, winning Player of the Year in college and Most Valuable Player in the NBA: Bill Russell (San Francisco 1956; Boston Celtics 1958, '61–63, '65), Oscar Robertson (Cincinnati 1958–60; Cincinnati Royals 1964), Kareem Abdul-Jabbar (UCLA 1967, '69; Milwaukee Bucks 1971–72, '74; Los Angeles Lakers 1976–77, '80), Bill Walton (UCLA 1972–74; Portland Trail Blazers 1978), Michael Jordan (North Carolina 1984; Chicago Bulls 1988, '91–92, '96, '98), and Shaquille O'Neal (Louisiana State 1991; Los Angeles Lakers 2000).

Shaquille O'Neal was the most valuable player of the 2000 NBA regular season, playoffs, and All-Star Game.

Photo: Diane Staskowski

15. The three players to lead the NCAA in scoring and rebounding in the same season: Xavier McDaniel of Wichita State in 1985 (27.2 points, 14.8 rebounds), Hank Gathers of Loyola Marymount in 1989 (32.7, 13.7), and Kurt Thomas of Texas Christian in 1995 (28.9, 14.6).

Sports Strategies

The Loyola Marymount teams of the Hank Gathers era were point-producing machines. Four Loyola teams rank among the 10 highest-scoring teams of all time. The 1990 team led the way, averaging 122.4 points a game. That's nearly 10 points a game higher than the 1989 Loyola team that ranks second.

16. University of Nevada-Las Vegas in 1987, and Duke in 1999 and 1986 had 37 wins in their respective seasons. Ironically, none of those teams won a national championship.

17. Bob Pettit of the St. Louis Hawks was named Most Valuable Player in the All-Star Game four times—1956, '58–59, and '62.

18. The NBA first kept steals as an official statistic in 1974. The first player to lead the league, with an average of 2.68 steals per game, was—are you ready for this?—Larry Steele of the Portland Trail Blazers.

19. Wilt Chamberlain of the Philadelphia Warriors in 1960 and Wes Unseld of the Baltimore Bullets in 1969 are the only players to be named Rookie of the Year and Most Valuable Player in the same season.

20. The Chicago Bulls finished the 1995–96 regular season with a 72–10 record. They are the only team in NBA history to reach 70 wins in the regular season.

Sports Strategies

The all-time leader in blocked shots is Hakeem Olajuwon of the Houston Rockets with 3,740, through the 2001 season. Bill Russell and Wilt Chamberlain, arguably the two best shot-blockers of all time, are not on the list. But that's because the blocked shot didn't become an official NBA stat until 1973.

Bet You Didn't Know ...

➤ Elmore Smith of the Los Angeles Lakers holds the NBA single-game record for most blocked shots—17 against the Portland Trail Blazers in 1973.

➤ The dimensions of an NBA basketball court are 94 feet long by 50 feet wide. The NBA three-point line is 23 feet, 9 inches away; the college and high school line is 19 feet, 9 inches away.

➤ Wilt Chamberlain, Bob Pettit, and Jerry Lucas are the only three players to average 20 points and 20 rebounds a game for an entire season.

➤ Jerry West of the Los Angeles Lakers, named Most Valuable Player of the 1969 NBA Finals, is the only person so honored who did not play on the championship team.

➤ The Washington Wizards changed their nickname from the Washington Bullets in 1997, because team owner Abe Pollin didn't like the connotation of bullets as they related to crime in the Washington D.C. area.

➤ Nate Archibald is the only player to lead the NBA in scoring and assists in the same season. Playing for the Kansas City-Omaha Royals in 1975, he led the league with 34 points and 11.4 assists a game.

➤ George Mikan, a 6' 11" center, was the game's first dominant big man. He led the Minneapolis Lakers to four NBA championships and was voted the Greatest Basketball Player of the First Half Century by the Associated Press.

➤ In 1953, Clarence "Bevo" Francis scored 116 points for Rio Grande of Ohio against Ashland Junior College of Kentucky. The following year, he scored 113 points against Hillsdale College of Michigan.

➤ In 1966, Texas Western defeated Kentucky to win the NCAA Tournament title. The game was significant because it pitted an all-black Texas Western team against an all-white Kentucky team. As discussed in Chapter 11, "School Days," Kentucky was coached by Adolph Rupp, who never recruited black athletes.

➤ The Larry O'Brien Trophy is presented to the NBA champion. It is named in memory of the former NBA commissioner, who served from 1975 to '84.

➤ The Converse Rubber Co. developed the first "official" basketball shoe in 1917. It was named the All-Star.

➤ The first conference champion in college basketball history was Yale, which won the Ivy League title in 1902.

The Inside Skinny

The Kansas City-Omaha Royals were just one stop for a franchise that has been on the move. Beginning as the Rochester Royals in 1945, the team moved to Cincinnati from 1958 to '72, to KC-Omaha from 1972 to '75, to Kansas City from 1975 to '85, and to Sacramento from 1985 to the present. The team became the Kings in 1972.

The Inside Skinny

Larry O'Brien's successor as NBA commissioner, David Stern, took over in 1984 and is widely regarded as an innovator, a revolutionary thinker, and the most effective commissioner of the four major professional team sports.

➤ The oldest college arena in the country still in use is the Rose Hill Gym at Fordham University. It opened in 1925 and seats 3,470.

➤ John Wooden and Lenny Wilkens are the only two people inducted into the Naismith Memorial Basketball Hall of Fame both as a player and a coach.

➤ Just three players—Oscar Robertson, John Havlicek, and Clyde Drexler—have managed 20,000 points, 6,000 rebounds, and 6,000 assists in their careers.

Say What?

Legendary UCLA coach John Wooden was one of the game's great teachers and philosophers (see Chapter 11). Here are some samples of the gospel, according to Wooden:

➤ "I always tried to make clear that basketball is not the ultimate. It is of small importance in comparison to the total life we live. There is only one kind of life that truly wins, and this is the one that places faith in the hands of the Savior. Until that is done, we are on an aimless course that runs in circles and goes nowhere."

➤ "Sports do not build character, they reveal it."

➤ "Be more concerned with your character than with your reputation. Your character is what you really are, while your reputation is merely what others think you are."

Two-Minute Warning

John Wooden may have been quoted as saying, "I don't know whether always winning is good," but his UCLA teams seemed to win all the time. In fact, from 1971–74, the Bruins won 88 straight games. The streak was ended Jan. 19, 1974, by Notre Dame.

➤ "Don't mistake activity for achievement."

➤ "Ability may get you to the top, but it takes character to keep you there."

➤ "I don't know whether always winning is good. It breeds envy and distrust in others and overconfidence and a lack of appreciation very often in those who enjoy it."

➤ "For an athlete to function properly, he must be intent. There has to be a definite purpose and goal if you are to progress. If you are not intent about what you are doing, you aren't able to resist the temptation to do something else that might be more fun at the moment."

➤ "(Pro basketball) is great if you want to watch individual play, but I like team play. The lack of hustle and thinking bothers me on some pro teams. Heck, if I want to watch great individual play, I'll watch golf or track."

John Wooden wasn't the only quotable basketball person. Here is a sampling of other hoopsters with something to say:

➤ Red Auerbach, former Boston Celtics coach: "Basketball is like war in that offensive weapons are developed first, and it always takes a while for the defense to catch up."

➤ "Hot" Rod Hundley, former player-turned-broadcaster: "My biggest thrill came the night Elgin Baylor and I combined for 73 points in Madison Square Garden. Elgin had 71 of them."

➤ Bill Bradley, former New York Knicks forward: "The point of the game is not how well the individual does, but whether the team wins. That is the beautiful heart of the game, the blending of personalities, the mutual sacrifices for group success."

➤ Michael Jordan, Chicago Bulls guard: "Talent wins games, but teamwork and intelligence win championships."

➤ More Jordan: "I know that fear is an obstacle for some people, but it is an illusion to me. Failure always made me try harder next time."

Sports Strategies

In addition to being a terrific offensive player, Hot Rod Hundley also was known as a combination court jester and clown prince. Among his crowd-pleasing antics: dribbling with his knees and his elbows, punching layups into the basket with a clenched fist, and shooting free throws over his shoulder with his back to the basket. Hundley went on to a successful career as a broadcaster.

Belles of the Ball

It was a long time coming, especially if you ask the pioneers of the game, but in 1996, a professional women's basketball league finally debuted. The American Basketball League (ABL) began with eight teams and high hopes. But it lasted only two seasons before folding.

But in 1997, the Women's National Basketball Association (WNBA), owned and operated by the NBA, had its inaugural season. The good news is, the WNBA has not only lasted, it's prospered.

The WNBA started with eight teams, expanded to 10 teams in 1998, then 12 in 1999 and 16 in 2000. Each team is located in an NBA city. It shouldn't be too tough to remember the winners of the first four WNBA championships (1997–2000): The Houston Comets, led by Cynthia Cooper.

Unfortunately, the WNBA came too late for some of the giants of the women's game to take advantage. But whether they were able to play or not, their contributions made a significant impact.

Carol Blazejowski

Carol Blazejowski, known as Blaze, led the nation in scoring in 1977 and 1978 and was a three-time All-American at Montclair (New Jersey) State College. She went to work for the NBA in 1990 and helped develop the concept of the WNBA.

The Inside Skinny

Nancy Lieberman-Cline learned the game, growing up in Queens, by playing against boys and men. So it figured that if someone was going to make history by being the first female to play in a men's pro league it would be Lieberman-Cline. She played two seasons with the Springfield Fame of the United States Basketball League, a minor league.

The Inside Skinny

Ann Meyers and former Los Angeles Dodgers pitcher Don Drysdale got married in 1976. They formed the first husband-and-wife team in any Hall of Fame. Drysdale died on July 3, 1993.

Blazejowski was one of the all-time great shooters in the women's game. She averaged 31.7 points a game during her three years at Montclair State College, and in March 1977, she scored 52 points against Queens College, a Madison Square Garden record for either sex.

Nancy Lieberman-Cline

Nancy Lieberman-Cline probably had the biggest impact on women's basketball. She was tough and tenacious, and she played the game with considerable flair, as evidenced by her nickname, "Lady Magic."

Lieberman-Cline was a three-time All-American at Old Dominion University (1978–80), played for the Phoenix Mercury in the WNBA in 1997, then became the coach and general manager of the Detroit Shock.

Ann Meyers

Ann Meyers was the first woman ever to receive a full athletic scholarship to UCLA, where she was a four-time All-American.

Meyers led the Bruins in rebounding, assists, steals, and blocked shots in each of her four seasons. And she is the only player in school history, male or female, to record a quadruple-double—20 points, 14 rebounds, 10 assists, and 10 steals in 1978. Now that was a good night's work.

Meyers also recorded another first: She was the first woman to sign a contract with an NBA team. The Indiana Pacers gave her a three-day tryout in 1979.

Cheryl Miller

Cheryl Miller learned the game by playing against her brothers, one of whom is Reggie Miller, a future Hall of Famer who plays for the Indiana Pacers.

Miller averaged nearly 33 points a game through four years in high school at River-side Polytechnic in Riverside, California, once scored 105 points in one game, and led her team to a 132–4 record in four years. She played her college ball at the University of Southern California, where she continued to dominate.

Miller led the Trojans to national championships in 1983 and 1984, and to an overall record of 112–20 in four years. She was a four-time All-American, a three-time Player of the Year, and the first basketball player—male or female—at Southern Cal to have her number retired.

But we're not quite finished with her resumé, which is novel-length.

Miller led the U.S. Olympic team to a gold medal in 1984; she returned to her alma mater as head coach in 1993, compiling a 44–14 record in two seasons; and then she went on to a successful career in television, where she registered yet another first. In November 1996, she was the first female commentator ever to work on a nationally televised NBA game.

Oh, yeah, one more thing: In 1997, Miller was named head coach and general manager of the Phoenix Mercury of the WNBA.

So having paid tribute to the players who laid the groundwork for the WNBA, the players who are reaping the rewards shouldn't be overlooked.

The college players who now have a pro league in which to continue their careers have become more athletic and more skilled. The growth of the women's college game in the '90s has been remark-able.

Two programs have been dominant—Tennessee, coached by Pat Summitt, and Connecticut, coached by Geno Auriemma. Tennessee's Lady Volunteers won four national championships in the '90s, and Connecticut two, including an un-defeated team in 1995.

Sports Strategies

Cheryl Miller has a trophy case full of hardware, everything from two Broderick Cups, emblematic of the best women's college player in the nation, to gold medals from the Olympics, the Pan-Am Games, and the Goodwill Games. And even though she didn't win the Sullivan Award in 1986 as the best amateur athlete in the nation, she was the first women's basketball player to be nominated.

The Least You Need to Know

➤ Julius Erving is the only player to be named Most Valuable Player in the ABA and the NBA.

➤ Seven teams have finished the college basketball season as undefeated national champions.

➤ Wilt Chamberlain and Wes Unseld are the only players to be named Rookie of the Year and Most Valuable Player in the same season.

➤ College basketball outlawed the dunk in 1967 and returned it in 1975.

➤ John Wooden and Lenny Wilkens are the only two people inducted into the Naismith Memorial Basketball Hall of Fame as both a player and a coach.

➤ The WNBA, owned and operated by the NBA, began play in 1997.

Part 4

Going It Alone:
Golf, Tennis, and Boxing

Granted, golf and tennis don't have much in common with boxing. Golf and tennis are steeped in tradition; boxing isn't. Golf and tennis are played at country clubs; boxing probably isn't allowed on televisions at some country clubs.

But what they share is individualism. Jack Nicklaus standing over a crucial putt. Rod Laver needing to win a critical point. Muhammad Ali looking for that knockout punch. In this part, we'll find out about the athletes who excelled in these individual sports and what it took to help them reach the top.

Fore!

The game of golf is old, very old. We know it dates back to at least 1457, because James II of Scotland authorized an Act of Parliament to ban golf and football. Seems these sports were interfering with archery practice by those charged with defending the country. They were more interested in golf than archery.

Shame on them.

Today, a lot of nongolfing wives might like to ban the game, because of all the time their husbands spend on the links. But the game is here to stay.

Birthplace of the Game

It's generally accepted that golf was born in Scotland during the fourteenth or fifteenth century. And even though James II, king of Scotland, put the kibosh to the game in 1457, no one paid much attention.

Early in the sixteenth century, James IV took up the game, and then his granddaughter, Mary, who would become Mary Queen of Scots, began playing. Once royalty got involved, everyone followed. Well, not everyone; golf was played primarily by those of affluence.

In 1744, the first golf club was formed. The Honourable Company of Edinburgh Golfers put together the first rules of golf, among them:

➤ You are not to change the ball which you strike off the tee.

➤ You are not to remove stones, bones, or any break club for the sake of playing your ball, except on the fair green, and that only within a club's length of your ball.

➤ If you should lose your ball, by its being taken up, or any other way, you are to go back to the spot where you struck last and drop another ball and allow your adversary a stroke for the misfortune.

And my personal favorite:

➤ If a ball be stopp'd by any person, horse or dog, or anything else, the ball so stopp'd must be played where it lyes.

Soon other clubs popped up—the Society of St. Andrews Golfers in 1754 and the Royal Blackheath, near London, in 1766.

Golf balls way back when were hand-stitched leather and filled with boiled feathers. And in case you're wondering, they traveled farther than you might think. In dry weather, those feather balls flew about 180 yards.

The next major advance in golf balls came in the mid-1800s, when a substance called gutta-percha was used.

Gutta what? Gutta-percha was a milky liquid that came from trees in Malaysia. The substance was softened by boiling, and molded into a ball, after which it was allowed to harden.

The only problem was the ball tended to veer in flight. But it flew much straighter after it picked up some nicks and scratches. That's when the ball makers started putting dimples in the ball with a hammer.

The gutta-percha ball was used until 1901, when a rubber core was inserted, with the gutta-percha molded around it. While golf ball technology has advanced light years since that time, seemingly in the last few months, a core surrounded by a durable cover has remained the basic formula.

Sports Strategies

The Society of St. Andrews Golfers changed its name in 1834 to the Royal and Ancient Golf Club of St. Andrews, also known today as the R & A. The Royal and Ancient is the governing body of golf throughout the world, except for the United States and Mexico, which are governed by the United States Golf Association.

Sports Strategies

The size requirements for a golf ball? A ball must have a diameter of no less than 1.68 inches and weigh not more than 1.62 ounces. Aren't you glad you know?

As for golf clubs, the heads of the earliest clubs were made from beech, holly, dog-wood, pear, or apple trees. The shafts were ash or hazel, because those woods gave the clubs more whip. Eventually, iron clubs were forged to provide more loft.

The Father of American Golf

Golf wasn't such a big deal in this country in the early part of the twentieth century, because a.) most of the best players in the world were British, and b.) it was perceived to be a game only for the wealthy.

But then along came a 20-year-old amateur who shocked the world and changed the perception of the sport.

Francis Ouimet had already taken time off from his job at a sporting goods company to play in the 1913 U.S. Amateur, where he lost in the second round. He entered the U.S. Open, because Robert Watson, the president of the United States Golf Association, asked him to. What he didn't tell Watson was that he had no intention of taking more time off to play golf.

But when Ouimet's supervisor saw his employee's name on the entry list, Ouimet ended up playing. Good thing, as it turned out.

The tournament was held at the Country Club in Brookline, Massachusetts, which Ouimet knew quite well, having caddied there since he was 11. Unfortunately, as a youth he never got to play the entire course, because the greenskeeper would chase him off before he was finished.

But it didn't matter that he never played all the holes, because you couldn't tell by the way Ouimet played the course. After the regulation 72 holes, Ouimet, Ted Ray, and Harry Vardon, the latter two Englishman, were tied, forcing an 18-hole playoff. With two holes to play, Ouimet led Vardon by one and Ray by two. Ouimet *birdied* the 17th, whereas Vardon *bogeyed*, and Ouimet went on to become the first amateur to win the Open.

Ouimet was a hero, and golf earned a spot on the front pages of the newspaper. As Herbert Warren Wind, the legendary golf writer, noted: "Here was a person all of America, not just golfing America, could understand—the boy from the 'wrong side of the street,' the caddie, the kid who worked during his summer vacations from high school—America's idea of an American hero."

Ouimet's title of the Father of American Golf was well-deserved.

The Fundamentals

Each hole is assigned a par, based on distance, of three, four, or five, figuring an average of two shots to reach the green on par threes and par fours and three shots to reach the green on par fives, plus two putts. The pars for individual holes are added to get the course's par. A **birdie** is completing a hole in one stroke under par. A **bogey** is completing a hole in one stroke over par.

149

Greats of the Game

Pro golfers are defined by how they perform in the game's four major championships. The Masters, the U.S. Open, the British Open, and the PGA Championship make up golf's Grand Slam.

In this section, we'll take a look at six golfers who have distinguished themselves and defined their careers by their performances on golf's most significant stages.

Golf's All-Time Amateur

So, you think you need the most expensive equipment on the market to learn the game? Well, not necessarily. Bobby Jones learned to play golf with an old ball and a cut-down club, and he became the only player in the history of golf to win the Grand Slam.

In 1930, Jones won the four major championships, which at the time were the U.S. Open, British Open, U.S. Amateur, and British Amateur. He is still the only player to manage the feat.

Jones retired from competition following the 1930 season. He spent his retirement filming instructional movies—some of which can still be seen on the Golf Channel—and creating his most enduring legacy: He designed Augusta National Golf Club, site of the Masters, which began in 1934.

The Iceman

For a guy who grew up in Dublin, Texas, a small town of about 2,500 people and no golf courses, Ben Hogan fared pretty well. Thanks to his tireless work ethic and unwavering determination, Hogan became one of the all-time greats and maybe *the* greatest ball striker ever.

Hogan turned pro in 1931, at age 19, but didn't find his way to the winner's circle until 1940. But once he broke through with that first win, there was no stopping him. He won five times in 1941 and never finished lower than fifth in 26 events.

Hogan won the U.S. Open in 1948, and the PGA Championship in 1946 and 1948.

Then, tragedy struck. Hogan was involved in a serious head-on car crash with a Greyhound bus in 1949. He suffered a double fracture of the pelvis, a broken collarbone, and a broken left ankle. Forget about playing golf again; most people assumed Hogan would never walk again.

But in 1950, Hogan, having relearned how to walk and swing a golf club, returned to competition. And in 1950, he won the U.S Open. He went on to win five more major championships, for a total of nine. He is one of only five players to win each of the four Grand Slam tournaments.

The Streak

Byron Nelson is responsible for one of the most remarkable streaks in sports history. In 1945, he won 11 PGA Tour events in a row. That's so unbelievable it's probably even beyond Tiger Woods's abilities.

Starting with the Miami Four-Ball tournament March 11 and continuing through the Canadian Open August 4, Nelson didn't lose.

Just to show how radically things have changed on the PGA Tour, Nelson's earnings for those 11 victories totaled $63,335—in war bonds. These days, the first prize for winning one tournament is usually in the neighborhood of $800,000, which would be considered the high-rent district.

The Inside Skinny

Byron Nelson's winning streak actually reached 12 tournaments in a row. So why is he not given credit for 12? An event in Spring Lake, New Jersey, won by Nelson, wasn't counted as part of the streak because the purse was below the PGA Tour minimum.

Nelson entered 30 events in 1945. He won 18 tournaments in all, including the PGA Championship; finished second in seven others; and never finished out of the top 10.

There are also four other major championships on Nelson's resumé: the 1937 and '42 Masters, the 1940 PGA Championship, and the 1939 U.S. Open. His 52 PGA Tour victories rank him fifth all-time.

The King

Arnold Palmer isn't the greatest golfer in the history of the game, but he has made the most impact.

Palmer, nicknamed the King, entered his prime in the late '50s and early '60s, just as the game was becoming a staple on television. His charisma and go-for-broke style was a real hit with viewers and allowed the game to get a foothold with the masses.

But what the fans really liked were Palmer's charges—his ability to come from behind to win tournaments.

One of the most famous came at the 1960 U.S. Open at Cherry Hills Country Club in Denver. He entered the final round in 15th place, seven shots behind the leader, Mike Souchak.

The talk in the clubhouse was that Palmer was too far back, even for one of his patented charges. But he proved the doubters wrong by shooting a six-under 65 and winning by two strokes.

Palmer, who won four Masters, one U.S. Open, and two British Opens, remains one of the most revered and adored athletes. He's also one of the most recognizable and highly paid through commercial endorsements. No athlete—yes, golfers are athletes—has been more marketed, licensed, promoted, or loved.

Sports Strategies

It's one thing to win major championships, which Jack Nicklaus did with regularity throughout his career. But when he didn't win, he usually contended. In addition to his 18 wins, Nicklaus also has 19 seconds, 48 top-three finishes and 56 top-five finishes.

The Golden Bear

Jack Nicklaus is the greatest golfer of all time. Now you're probably thinking: "Geez, isn't that a pretty bold statement? Could it possibly be that cut-and-dried? Isn't there anyone else in the running for that distinction?"

To answer those questions in order: No, yes, no.

Nicklaus, nicknamed the Golden Bear, has won 18 professional major championships—four U.S. Opens, three British Opens, five PGA Championships, and six Masters.

Jack Nicklaus, winner of 18 professional major championships, is widely regarded as the greatest player of all time.

Photo: Diane Staskowski

To put Nicklaus's greatness into perspective, his 18 majors are seven more than Walter Hagen, 11 more than Ben Hogan and Gary Player, 12 more than Tom Watson, and 13 more than Arnold Palmer.

Of all Nicklaus's major championship victories, one stands out because it was the least expected. In 1986, at age 46, Nicklaus became the oldest ever to win the Masters, and he did it in spectacular style. Trailing by six shots with eight holes to play, he shot a six-under 30 on the back nine to win his sixth Masters championship.

The reaction from the gallery at Augusta National was deafening. But there's much more to Nicklaus's career about which to cheer:

➤ Two-time winner of the U.S. Amateur

➤ Appeared in 44 straight U.S. Opens (1957–2000)

➤ Appeared in 154 consecutive major championships

➤ Won 71 PGA Tour events, including at least one a year for 17 straight seasons

➤ Five-time PGA Tour Player of the Year

➤ Eight-time PGA Tour leading money winner

➤ Named Golfer of the Century by *Golf* magazine

After many golfers tried and failed to be the "next Nicklaus," Tiger Woods looks to be the guy who will mount a serious challenge to the Golden Bear's remarkable record. By any standard, Tiger's got a tough act to follow.

The Heir Apparent

At the ripe old age of 24, Tiger Woods became the youngest player to complete the career Grand Slam. Entering 2000, he already had won the Masters (1997) and the PGA Championship (1999). He added the two missing trophies by winning the U.S. Open by an unheard of 15 shots, and the British Open by eight.

The Inside Skinny

In addition to being the best golfer of all time, Jack Nicklaus is also an accomplished designer of golf courses. More than 150 courses throughout the world have been designed, codesigned, or redesigned by Nicklaus. More than 20 of his courses have regularly appeared on the top-100 lists of various publications.

Sports Strategies

When Tiger Woods won his first Masters in 1997, he did so in record-breaking fashion. He shot rounds of 70, 66, 65, and 69 for an 18-under 270 total, one better than the previous mark held by Jack Nicklaus and Raymond Floyd. Also, at 21 years, 3 months, and 14 days, Woods was the youngest Masters champion ever and the first major championship winner of African or Asian heritage.

In the year's final major, the PGA Championship, Woods successfully defended his title, defeating journeyman Bob May in a stirring three-hole playoff.

Now, winning three majors in one year—the first player since Ben Hogan in 1953 to do so—would be enough for most players, but Woods isn't most players. He was virtually invincible during 2000. He won a total of 10 tournaments—eight on the PGA Tour and two internationally—and earned nearly $10 million worldwide.

When the 2001 season started, Woods didn't win right away, and all people could talk about was his "slump." Well, he ended that "slump" by winning three tournaments in the spring, including his second Masters.

That victory in the Masters meant Woods held the titles in each of the four major championships simultaneously (2000 U.S. Open, British Open, and PGA Championship, and the 2001 Masters). Technically, it wasn't a Grand Slam, because the wins didn't occur within the same calendar year. But it was an incredible achievement, just the same.

Ever since Michael Jordan retired, people wondered who would be the next Jordan. Little did anyone know it would be a golfer.

Like Jordan, Tiger Woods is the best player of his time; he's blessed with style and charisma that make him unbelievably popular; and he picks up all kinds of extra loot for his many commercial endorsements, the most memorable of which was the Nike commercial where he bounced the golf ball off the face of a wedge.

Tiger Woods transcends his sport. Not bad for a guy in his mid-20s.

Sports Strategies

In 1950, the first year of the LPGA Tour's existence, there were 14 tournaments on the schedule, with the total prize money—total—being $50,000. By the end of the decade, there were 26 tournaments worth $200,000. In 2001, the schedule included 40 events worth more than $42 million.

Ladies Day

The first attempt at organizing a women's professional golf tour was the Women's Professional Golf Association (WPGA) in 1944. The U.S. Women's Open was first played two years later.

In 1950, the WPGA became the Ladies Professional Golf Association (LPGA) and was chartered in 1950 by a group of brave, trail-blazing women to whom today's players owe a large debt.

They were brave, because in those days, golf was very much a man's world. (Some would argue that hasn't changed all that much, but that's another story.) The founders of the LPGA persevered, bound and determined to make their tour a success.

Players such as Peggy Kirk, Patty Berg, Louise Suggs, Marilynn Smith, and Betsy Rawls were instrumental in helping the tour establish roots. And they did much more than play. They planned and organized the events, helped prepare the golf courses, drafted the bylaws, and supervised the membership—in other words, just about everything except selling hot dogs at the concession stands.

But their efforts paid off. Today, the LPGA Tour is the world's longest-running women's professional sports organization.

Here's a look at some of the players who are responsible for making the LPGA Tour what it is today.

The Babe

Babe Didriksen Zaharias was a real character and a terrific player. Bold and brash, the Babe talked a good game and backed it up on the golf course. As an amateur, she won 17 tournaments in a row in 1946–47.

As a pro, she won 31 of the 128 events she entered, including 10 *major championships*. A former Olympic champion—she competed in the javelin, 80-meter hurdles, and high jump—her presence on the tour gave it credibility. She died in 1956 at age 43 from cancer.

The Fundamentals

The **major championships** on the LPGA Tour have changed over the years. During Babe Zaharias's day, the majors were the U.S. Women's Open, still played today, and the Titleholders and the Western Open, which disappeared. The LPGA Championship was inaugurated in 1955 and remains today, along with the Nabisco Championship, the U.S. Women's Open, and the Women's British Open.

What a Swing!

Mickey Wright had a swing that was smooth, efficient, rhythmic, and powerful; in short, she had a swing that was flawless. Her record wasn't too shabby, either.

Wright won 82 LPGA Tour events, 71 of them within a 10-year span (1959–68). In 1963, she won 40 percent of LPGA Tour events—13 of 32 tournaments. Now there's a feat that will never be duplicated.

Among those 82 victories were four U.S. Women's Opens, four LPGA Championships, three Western Opens, and two Titleholders.

All-Time Win Leader

Kathy Whitworth is the all-time leader in career victories with 88. Her first win came in 1962, her last in 1985. No one, man or woman, has ever won more. She also won six major championships—a Titleholders, three LPGA Championships, and a Western Open—and was the first LPGA player to surpass $1 million in career earnings.

About the only thing she failed to win was the U.S. Women's Open, the only hole in an otherwise exemplary resumé.

Personality Plus

To say Nancy Lopez made a big splash during her rookie season on the LPGA Tour would be a bit of an understatement, sort of like saying the Grand Canyon is a big hole.

Nancy Lopez, winner of 48 LPGA Tour events, is a member of the LPGA Hall of Fame.

Photo: Diane Staskowski

Lopez won nine tournaments in 1978, including a record five in a row. In addition to fattening her bank account, she also brought unprecedented attention to the LPGA Tour with her engaging personality and bright smile.

Today's Best

Annika Sorenstam and Karrie Webb have taken turns dominating the LPGA Tour since 1995.

Sorenstam won back-to-back U.S. Women's Opens in 1995 and 1996, was the leading money winner in 1995, '97, and '98, and won more tournaments than any other LPGA Tour player in the '90s.

Webb won 13 events in 1999 and 2000, including three major championships—the 1999 du Maurier Classic (no longer a major), the 2000 Nabisco Championship, and the U.S. Women's Open. She also set a single-season earnings record in 2000 with $1,876,853 and was the tour's leading money winner in 1996, '99, and 2000.

After two years of watching Webb lead the way, Sorenstam took over once again in 2001. She opened the season with five wins (including four straight), two second-place finishes, and one third-place finish in 10 events. She also became the first woman ever to shoot a 59, which is golf's magic number.

Two-Minute Warning

To many people, Nancy Lopez *is* women's golf. You might think she's won everything, but she hasn't. Lopez has won only one of the four major championships—the LPGA Championship, three times. Her near-miss in the U.S. Women's Open in 1997, when she finished second, was ironic in that she became the only player in Women's Open history to shoot four rounds in the 60s (69-68-69-69). But she fell one stroke short.

The Least You Need to Know

➤ The birthplace of golf was in Scotland in the fourteenth or fifteenth century.

➤ Francis Ouimet, who won the U.S. Open in 1913, is known as the Father of American Golf.

➤ Bobby Jones won the Grand Slam in 1930, the only time it's ever been accomplished.

➤ Byron Nelson won 11 consecutive tournaments in 1945.

➤ Arnold Palmer is largely responsible for golf's initial—and enduring—popularity.

➤ Jack Nicklaus has won 18 professional major championships.

➤ Nancy Lopez was to women's golf what Arnold Palmer was to men's.

Love of the Game

Major Walter C. Wingfield is credited with creating the game of tennis that we know in 1874. But the game, in one form or another, has been around since the Middle Ages in France.

Back then, tennis was called *jeu de paume* (game of the palm), because the ball was hit with the hand. And for good reason—rackets hadn't been invented yet.

Much about the origin of the game remains a mystery, for reasons which are a mystery. Apparently someone forgot to take notes. But in this chapter, we'll look at what we know about how the game began, as well as some of the sport's best players.

Introducing Major Wingfield

The game began in France in the twelfth century. Because players hit the ball with their hand, they wore gloves. Eventually, they used rackets of varying sizes and shapes. It wasn't until the mid-1700s that rackets began to look like they do today.

That version of the game, known today as real tennis, was played in Great Britain in the sixteenth and seventeenth centuries. The version of the game that we're most familiar with—the Brits called it lawn tennis—was invented in 1874 by Major Walter Clopton Wingfield, who devised the rules, applied for a patent, and sold the equipment necessary to play.

Sports Strategies

The U.S. National Lawn Tennis Association (USNLTA) was formed in 1881. It became the sport's governing body and was the first sports organization of its kind. Eventually, the name was changed to the U.S. Lawn Tennis Association and then to the U.S. Tennis Association, which is how it remains today. Dr. James Dwight was the organization's president for 21 of its first 31 years.

The Fundamentals

The **open era** in tennis began in 1968, when professionals and amateurs were allowed to compete in the same tournaments. Prior to the open era, professionals were prohibited from entering any of the four Grand Slam events.

After Wingfield's patent expired in 1877, many of his original rules were modified and the court was reconfigured to today's dimensions of 78 feet long and 27 feet wide for singles play and 36 feet wide for doubles play. The net is three feet high at the center and 3$\frac{1}{2}$ feet wide at either end.

The game made it to the United States within months after Wingfield's "invention." Either Mary Outerbridge of Staten Island or Dr. James Dwight of Boston introduced the game in the U.S. of A. No one's quite sure, which isn't all that surprising given the uncertainty about any of the game's history.

But regardless of who was first—and neither claimed credit—Dwight is known as the Father of American Lawn Tennis because of the leadership he demonstrated and his involvement in organizing tournaments.

In the late 1920s, the pro game became profitable, with players touring the country in groups and playing for pay. The Grand Slam tournaments were open to amateurs only, a situation that existed until 1968, the start of the *open era,* when pros and amateurs were allowed to play for the game's most prestigious titles.

The Grand Slammers

Just like in golf, a player's place in tennis history is measured by his or her performance in the *Grand Slam* events. Those four tournaments mean more than the entire rest of the year's tournaments combined.

Unlike golf, tennis has more than one winner of the Grand Slam. Don Budge, Rod Laver, Maureen Connolly Brinker, Margaret Court, and Steffi Graf have each won all four major championships in the same calendar year. Laver managed it twice—once as an amateur and once as a pro.

Don Budge

Don Budge came to prominence in 1937, when he won Wimbledon and the U.S. Nationals, and led the U.S. to its first *Davis Cup* title in 11 years.

Because Budge was the No. 1 player in the world in 1938, he was under quite a bit of pressure to turn pro. But he remained an amateur, a decision that earned him a place in tennis history.

Budge became the first player to win the Grand Slam. He beat John Bromwich to win the Australian Open, Roderich Menzel to win the French Open, Bunny Austin to win Wimbledon, and Gene Mako to win the U.S. Nationals.

The term Grand Slam was not part of the tennis vocabulary at the time, but Alison Danzig, the legendary tennis writer for *The New York Times,* coined the phrase to describe Budge's feat.

The Fundamentals

The **Grand Slam** of tennis is made up of the Australian Open, played in January on hard courts; the French Open, played in June on clay courts; Wimbledon, played in late June and early July in England on grass; and the U.S. Open, played in late August/early September, now on hard courts. Each tournament lasts two weeks, with men and women competing simultaneously.

Rod Laver

Rod Laver did the unthinkable, winning the Grand Slam twice, seven years apart, as an amateur in 1962 and as a pro in 1969.

Nicknamed the Rocket, Laver, a left-hander, was a tireless worker and a complete player who tried to get to the net at every chance.

While winning the Grand Slam in 1962 was a remarkable achievement, he was playing only against amateurs. The best players in the world had turned pro. But in 1969, he was playing against the best in the world.

Laver beat Andres Gimeno in the Australian Open, Ken Rosewall in the French Open, John Newcombe at Wimbledon, and Tony Roche in the U.S. Open.

For the record, Laver won 17 tournament titles in 1969 and had a match record of 106–6. His 11 career Grand Slam singles titles ties him for third behind Pete Sampras (13) and Roy Emerson (12).

The Fundamentals

The **Davis Cup** is a team competition for men that began in 1900 and is still played today. Four-man teams represent their countries, playing two singles the first day, a doubles match the second, and two singles the third day, with the opponents reversed. All matches are best-of-five sets. The U.S. is the all-time leader in Davis Cup championships with 31.

Maureen Connolly Brinker

Maureen Connolly Brinker, known as Little Mo, was the first woman to win the Grand Slam. In 1953, she beat Julie Sampson to win the Australian Open and Doris Hart to win the French Open, Wimbledon, and the U.S. Nationals.

Brinker won 10 of 12 tournaments in 1953 and had a record of 61–2. Overall, she won nine major championships.

Margaret Court

Margaret Court was at her best in major championships. Her total of 62 Grand Slam titles, in singles, doubles, and mixed doubles, is by far the best of all time for men and women.

Her Grand Slam season came in 1970, when she beat Kerry Melville to win the Australian Open, Helga Niessen to win the French Open, Billie Jean King to win Wimbledon, and Rosie Casals to win the U.S. Open. Only Casals was able to win a set during Court's run.

Steffi Graf

Steffi Graf not only won the Grand Slam in 1988, she went one better and made it a Golden Slam. She won the four major championships, plus an Olympic gold medal at the 1988 Games in Seoul, South Korea.

Graf, one of the most athletic and accomplished players in women's tennis history, won 11 of 14 tournaments in 1988 and had a match record of 73–3. She was nearly as good in 1989, when she won Wimbledon and the U.S. Open, 14 of 16 tournaments, and 86 of 88 matches.

In all, Graf won 22 Grand Slam singles titles, second all-time to Margaret Court. And between 1987 and 1990, she reached the final of all 12 Grand Slams, winning 10.

Under the Big Top

Every now and then, a sporting event takes place with ramifications that go way beyond the boundaries of sport—Jackie Robinson breaking the color barrier in Major League Baseball, for instance.

When Billie Jean King met 55-year-old Bobby Riggs in a much-ballyhooed battle of the sexes in September 1973, a sea of change was effected. The match gave tennis a tremendous boost that would last for more than a decade, and women's sports also benefited, because King, a longtime crusader for women's rights and equality, helped make the point that women could play.

Riggs, the 1939 Wimbledon champ, was a hustler, a showman, a self-proclaimed "king of male chauvinist pigs" who wanted to prove that a 55-year-old man could beat a top women's player. The 29-year-old King refused to take the bait, but after he beat Margaret Court handily on Mother's Day in 1973, she felt she had no choice but to accept his challenge.

The Battle of the Sexes was held in the Houston Astrodome before a record tennis crowd of 30,472 and televised nationally in prime time. King, two months shy of her 30th birthday, won 6–4, 6–3, and 6–3 in thoroughly dominant fashion and struck a blow for women and for her sport.

"She changed the nature of sport in America," said Richard Lapchick, founder and director of the Study of Sport and Society in Boston. "There were a lot of women desiring to participate in sports, a lot of men resisting them, and very few men embracing them. She stood in the face of those men and wiped away the stereotypes and cobwebs."

Not a bad night's work.

Sports Strategies

Besides being a crusader, Billie Jean King was also a terrific tennis player. But you probably already knew that. She won 12 Grand Slam singles titles, including six at Wimbledon. Her 20 titles at Wimbledon (six singles, ten doubles, four mixed doubles) is a record for men and women. King was the No. 1–ranked player in the world six times.

Fire and Ice

Rivalries are the lifeblood of any sport, and tennis has been lucky enough to have some of the best ever.

Chris vs. Martina

Chris Evert rarely ventured from the baseline. She could hang back there all day and return shot after shot as if she were a backboard. Martina Navratilova had a big serve, played an attacking game, and couldn't wait to get to the net.

Chris Evert won 154 tournaments in her career, which ranks second all-time.

Photo: Icon Sports Media

Their rivalry was as good as it got. Starting in 1973 and ending in 1988, Evert and Navratilova played 90 times with Navratilova holding a 47–43 edge. They met 10 times in Grand Slam finals, with Navratilova winning six.

They also rank 1-2 in tournaments won—Navratilova 167, Evert 154. And speaking of 1-2, from 1975 through 1986, one of them was ranked No. 1 in the world, and seven times the other was ranked No. 2.

They brought out the best in each other and gave their best to us.

Sports Strategies

The 1980 Wimbledon final between Bjorn Borg and John McEnroe was one of the most compelling matches in Wimbledon history. The match went five sets, but it was the fourth-set tiebreaker, won 18–16 by McEnroe, that everyone remembers. Borg, by the way, won the match for his fifth straight Wimbledon title.

The Calm vs. the Storms

Bjorn Borg was the epitome of serenity. No matter how tense the situation or how tight the match, his demeanor never changed. He was unflappable.

Jimmy Connors and John McEnroe were as volatile as powder kegs. The least little thing could set them off. They could be brash, boorish, and vulgar; they could also play brilliantly.

When Connors or McEnroe matched up against Borg—they were the preeminent players of their time—you knew you were in for something special. From the mid-'70s through the early '80s, the trio dominated the game.

Borg won a record five straight Wimbledons and six French singles titles. McEnroe won three Wimbledons and four U.S. Opens. Connors won an Australian Open, two Wimbledons, and five U.S. Opens.

Borg led his rivalry with Connors 10–7; he and McEnroe split their 14 matches.

But McEnroe and Connors scored wins over Borg in the tournament he wanted to win the most: the U.S. Open. Borg failed in 10 attempts to win the Open. He reached the final four times, losing twice to Connors and twice to McEnroe.

Fab Five

So far, we've checked out the Grand Slam winners, the time the circus came to tennis, and some of the best rivalries in the sport.

Let's learn about five more players who would be included on any list of tennis's greatest players: Andre Agassi, Arthur Ashe, Ken Rosewall, Bill Tilden, and Pete Sampras.

Andre the Giant

It seems as if Andre Agassi has had several different careers, the way he's been up and down and up again. But since 1997, when he plummeted to the lowest ranking of his career—141st in the world—Agassi has been up.

He rededicated himself to the game, got in better shape, and made history. With his victory in the 1999 French Open, Agassi became only the fifth player—Rod Laver, Don Budge, Roy Emerson, and Fred Perry are the others—to win each of the four Grand Slam singles titles. He previously had won Wimbledon in 1992, the U.S. Open in 1994, and the Australian in 1995.

Overall, Agassi has won seven Grand Slam singles through May 2001. His groundstrokes and especially his return of serve rank right up there with the best of all time.

Two-Minute Warning

Although these days Andre Agassi wears more conventional tennis attire, he wasn't always so conforming. When he first joined the tour, he wore wildly colored shirts and shorts and black shoes. You can imagine how that went over with the tennis purists. But his sense of style, while controversial with some purist fans, was a huge hit with others.

Sports Strategies

Arthur Ashe was about much more than tennis. He was an outspoken advocate of racial equality and a vigorous protester of apartheid in South Africa. Ashe was granted a visa to South Africa in 1973 and became the first African American to win a title there.

A Gentleman and a Champion

Arthur Ashe was one of the game's great players and goodwill ambassadors. As an African American, he overcame racial prejudice and segregation to rise to the top of his sport and become one of the most popular players in the world.

And speaking of popular, his victory in the 1975 Wimbledon final over Jimmy Connors might be the most popular win in tennis history. Ashe entered the final against Connors, the defending champion and top seed, as a heavy underdog. But he played an intelligent match—not hitting his shots as hard and mixing spins and pace—to stun Connors in four sets.

Ashe, the only African-American male to win three Grand Slam singles titles (1968 U.S. Open, 1970 Australian, and 1975 Wimbledon), had his best season in 1975. He won nine tournaments and was ranked fourth in the world.

Sadly, Ashe contracted AIDS through a 1988 blood transfusion. He kept his condition a secret until 1992, when he announced it at a press conference. He died on February 6, 1993.

Muscles

Ken Rosewall was nicknamed Muscles, which, considering he stood just 5' 7" and weighed 135 pounds, was a bit of misnomer. But in spite of his lack of size, Rosewall became one of the game's most successful and enduring stars.

Ken Rosewall, one of the most consistent players ever, won every major title except Wimbledon.

Photo: Diane Staskowski

He was ranked in the top 10 in the world in three different decades, beginning in 1952 and running through 1975. Two of the major reasons for his success were his fitness and his backhand, which was as reliable and lethal a stroke as ever existed in tennis.

Rosewall won eight Grand Slam singles titles and 18 Grand Slam titles in all, including doubles and mixed doubles. About the only thing he didn't win was a Wimbledon title, although he reached the final four times. He is probably the best player never to have won at Wimbledon.

"Big Bill" Tilden

Bill Tilden was the dominant player of his time and certainly one of the greatest players of all time—and no wonder. He had a powerful serve, a powerful forehand, and a powerful backhand. How's that for a deadly combination?

But Tilden didn't just overpower opponents. He also had finesse in his arsenal.

Wrote Will Grimsley of the Associated Press: "He was more than a mere striker of the ball. He was a tactician, an artist. The racket was like a violin in his hands."

Tilden was pretty much unbeatable between 1920 and 1926. He won Wimbledon the only two times he entered it (1920–21); he won the U.S. Nationals six straight times, beginning in 1920; and he led the U.S. to seven straight Davis Cup titles.

And as if that wasn't enough, he also wrote a book, *Match Play and the Spin of the Ball,* which is considered a tennis classic.

Tilden was ranked in the top 10 in the world from 1919 through 1930, including six years at No. 1. He was the No. 1 player in the United States a record 10 times (1920–29). He turned pro in 1931, revived the pro tour, and was such a big name that he played professionally until he was nearly 50.

The Inside Skinny

Ken Rosewall won the last professional title of his career in November 1977 at a tournament in Hong Kong, where he defeated Tom Gorman. The victory, which occurred two weeks after his 43rd birthday, made Rosewall the second-oldest player to win a title in the open era (since 1968). The oldest was Pancho Gonzalez at 43 years, 9 months.

The Inside Skinny

Bill Tilden's life contained some hardship, too. In 1947, he was sent to jail on a morals charge, and in 1949, he was back in jail for a parole violation. Each term lasted less than a year. Tilden died of a heart attack at age 60 on June 5, 1953, his bags packed and ready to go to Cleveland to compete in the U.S. Pro Championships.

The Best Ever?

Pete Sampras is in the process of staking his claim as the best player of all time. That's a mouthful, I know, but a pretty strong case can be made for Sampras, starting with Wimbledon.

Two-Minute Warning

Winning the Wimbledon singles title wasn't nearly as physically grueling way back when. From 1878 through 1921, the tournament operated under the challenge-round system, meaning the defending champion played only one match, the final. The opponent was the challenger who won what was called an all-comers tournament.

He's owned the place, winning seven titles in eight years, through 2000. The only year he failed to win was in 1996, when he was eliminated in the quarterfinals by Richard Krajicek, the eventual champion. Those seven titles, by the way, are a modern record.

Sampras, who relies mainly on a powerful serve, has done pretty well at other Grand Slam tournaments, too.

He's won two Australian Opens and four U.S. Opens, the first of which was won in 1990 at age 19, making him the youngest U.S. Open champ ever.

The 13 Grand Slam singles titles make him the all-time leader in that category. He has one more than Roy Emerson.

Like Ken Rosewall, who never won Wimbledon, and Bjorn Borg, who never won the U.S. Open, Sampras also has an event that has eluded him—the French Open. The slow, red clay on which it's played isn't suited to his powerful style. But even if he never wins it, Sampras's Grand Slam total makes a pretty strong case for his place in history.

The Least You Need to Know

➤ Don Budge, Rod Laver (twice), Maureen Connolly Brinker, Margaret Court, and Steffi Graf won the Grand Slam.

➤ Bjorn Borg won five straight Wimbledon titles, a modern record.

➤ Billie Jean King defeated Bobby Riggs in the Battle of the Sexes on September 20, 1973.

➤ Pete Sampras is the all-time leader in Grand Slam singles titles with 13.

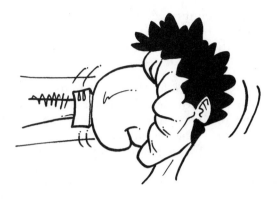

Chapter 16

Put Up Your Dukes

In This Chapter

➤ The first punches

➤ Boxing primer

➤ The heavyweight of all heavyweights

➤ Champions for the ages

It's not a sport known for the purity of its characters. Truth be told, the fight game has a pretty awful reputation. But, that said, boxing's been around in one form or another forever, going all the way back to the ancient civilizations of Egypt, Greece, and Rome.

Boxing as we know it today dates back to the eighteenth century in England, where fighters went at it without gloves. These days, gloves are standard issue. But that still doesn't keep bouts from deteriorating into street fights—or worse. After all, would a guy bite off a piece of an opponent's ear in a street fight, as Mike Tyson did to Evander Holyfield? Probably not.

Still, there is nothing more exciting or compelling than the atmosphere that surrounds a championship fight. It's electric.

The Opening Bell

The first boxing champions were recognized in England during the eighteenth century in what was called the bare-knuckle era. These matches were not for the faint of heart. Besides fighting without gloves, the boxers also fought without referees, time limits, or rules. Doesn't that sound like a blast?

The fights, which lasted for hours, didn't end until one of the participants was down for good. In addition to using fists, fighters also strangled each other, gouged eyes, kicked, and used foreign objects. Apparently, these fights were also the forerunner to professional wrestling.

Sports Strategies

James Figg is known as the Father of Boxing because he was the first recognized champion, played a major role in popularizing the sport, and helped teach boxing. He established Figg's Amphitheatre, which was one of the most popular venues in London to watch fights. He claimed the bare-knuckle championship in 1719 and held it until his retirement in 1734.

The boxing that we know today began to take shape in 1867, when John Graham Chambers, an Englishman, came up with a set of rules that removed some of the chaos. Known as the Queensberry Rules because they were sponsored by the Marquess of Queensberry, they set a time limit on each round—three minutes with one minute's rest in between—and mandated that gloves be worn.

John L. Sullivan, born in Boston and the first great American boxer, was the last to hold the bare-knuckle heavyweight title (1882–89) and the first to be crowned champion under the Queensberry Rules (1885–92).

By the time the twentieth century rolled around, boxing had become a popular sport in America. There were problems with fights being fixed, but the institution of an athletic commission to oversee fights in New York State was copied by other states and the sport continued to prosper.

Fights became a staple on radio, as did fight coverage in newspapers. But with the increased exposure came a confusing number of weight classes and a proliferation of boxing organizations.

Boxing Alphabet and Weighty Subjects

If it seems like every time you peruse the newspaper or tune into *SportsCenter* that a whole bunch of world boxing titles are being won and lost, join the club.

With all the different weight classes and the alphabet soup of boxing organizations, it's almost impossible to keep things straight.

But I'll do my best to try and bring some semblance of order to all the numbers and letters.

Getting on the Scales

Back in England, when fighters first began trying to knock each other silly, there were no restrictions on weight. It wasn't until the early part of the twentieth century that weight classes were established. At first there were eight—heavyweight (over 190 pounds), light heavyweight (169–175), middleweight (155–160), welterweight (141–147), lightweight (131–135), featherweight (123–126), bantamweight (116–118), and flyweight (109–112).

Today, there are 17 weight classes. No wonder it's tough to keep them all straight. Okay, let's find out what class you'd be fighting in:

➤ Heavyweight—over 190 pounds

➤ Cruiserweight—176–190

➤ Light heavyweight—169–175

➤ Super middleweight—161–168

➤ Middleweight—155–160

➤ Junior middleweight—148–154

➤ Welterweight—141–147

➤ Junior welterweight—136–140

➤ Lightweight—131–135

➤ Junior lightweight—127–130

➤ Featherweight—123–126

➤ Junior featherweight—119–122

➤ Bantamweight—116–118

➤ Junior bantamweight—113–115

➤ Flyweight—109–112

➤ Junior flyweight—106–108

➤ Strawweight—Under 105

Two-Minute Warning

Before flyweights debuted in England, paperweights, a 105-pound division, was used in the United States. Paperweights eventually became known as flyweights in the U.S., but not until 1920.

What Do All Those Letters Mean?

These days, there are four major boxing organizations, each of which crowns champions in all 17 weight classes. To save you the trouble of doing the math, that computes to 68 champions. However, that doesn't necessarily mean there would be 68 different champions, because champions could hold titles for more than one organization.

The four biggies are the World Boxing Association (WBA), the World Boxing Council (WBC), the International Boxing Federation (IBF), and the World Boxing Organization (WBO).

But within the last several years, a few others have popped up—the World Boxing Union (WBU), the International Boxing Organization (IBO), and the Intercontinental Boxing Council (IBC).

Is it any wonder there's so much confusion?

The Greatest

You might not know the first thing about boxing. You might not know that the ring is really a square or that it takes 10 to be counted out. But regardless of what you don't know about boxing, you more than likely do know that Muhammad Ali was "the Greatest."

Muhammad Ali relied on speed and quickness, not brute strength, to become one of the greatest heavyweight champs of all time.

Photo: Icon Sports Media

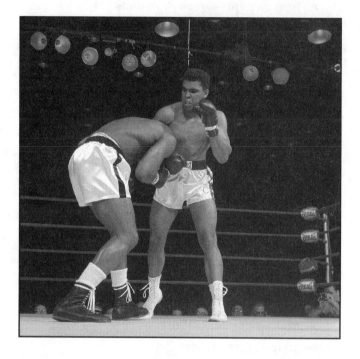

The Fundamentals

In boxing, a **jab** is a short, quick punch thrown into an opponent's body or face. The other major weapon is an **uppercut,** which is thrown from the waist or below the waist.

Ali used his birth name, Cassius Clay, until 1964. That's when he joined the Nation of Islam and was given the name Muhammad Ali. Just to keep things simple, he'll be referred to Ali throughout this book.

Ali was arguably the greatest heavyweight of all time, and he was also as colorful and controversial a character as the sports world has ever seen. He was brash, outspoken, and very much at home in the limelight.

What he wasn't was the typical heavyweight. Instead of relying on brute force and punching power, Ali used quickness and agility to run circles around his opponents. He could flick his *jab* as he danced around the ring on his toes, and he had the uncanny ability to avoid an opponent's punch by leaning just beyond its reach.

Ali rose through the ranks, winning Golden Gloves titles, a national amateur tournament, in 1959 and 1960, and the gold medal in the light heavyweight division at the 1960, Olympics in Rome. By 1964, he was a top contender in the heavyweight division and on February 25, 1964, had earned a shot at the world championship. What a night that turned out to be.

Ali Shocks the World

No one gave Muhammad Ali much of a shot against Sonny Liston, the heavyweight champion of the world. Liston was a big, burly, sullen guy, who also was an ex-con. He figured to overpower Ali. But to overpower him, Liston had to catch him, and that proved to be a bit of a problem.

Ali danced all around the ring, forcing Liston to chase him, but by the time the third round was over, Liston was one tired fellow. He was exhausted.

But after the fourth round, Ali had a problem: pain in both eyes. It seemed someone doctored Liston's gloves with something that caused Ali's pain. Despite wanting to pack it in, Ali answered the bell for Round 5, which he survived. In Round 6, his eyes clear, Ali began to hit Liston. Eight straight times he pounded him at one point. Liston returned to his corner after the round—and stayed there.

Ali was the new heavyweight champion of the world, having beaten Liston by a *technical knockout* in the seventh round.

Ali and Liston fought a rematch in May 1965 in Lewiston, Maine. For those folks who got delayed waiting in line for a hot dog, they might've missed the fight, which lasted all of one round. Ali knocked out Liston with a so-called "phantom punch." Liston didn't see it, and neither did anyone else. But wherever it came from, it did the trick.

Over the next two years, Ali successfully defended his title eight times, but he lost it in 1967—not to another fighter, but because he was stripped of it. Ali refused to be inducted into the Army on religious grounds. He was inactive while the case was being litigated, meaning he lost nearly four years in the prime of his career. Finally, in 1971, the U.S. Supreme Court ruled in his favor.

The Inside Skinny

Muhammad Ali's boxing career got its start thanks to a thief. That's right, when he was 12 years old, someone stole his brand new Schwinn bicycle. Joe Martin, the policeman that Ali talked to about his bike, also ran a gym. When Martin heard Ali talking about getting revenge, he suggested coming to the gym for boxing lessons. The rest, as they say, is history.

The Trilogy

Muhammad Ali and Joe Frazier fought three of the most famous, most compelling fights ever. They were opposites in style: Ali was the dancer, Frazier the relentless attacker. The contrast produced three classic bouts.

The first came on March 8, 1971, in Madison Square Garden in New York City. In a brutal battle, Frazier won a 15-round decision and handed Ali his first loss.

The second, also in Madison Square Garden, took place on January 28, 1974. This time, Ali evened the score, winning a 12-round decision.

The final meeting, dubbed the Thrilla in Manila and considered by many to be the greatest fight of all time, took place on October 1, 1975, in the Philippines. Ali led early, and Frazier caught up during the middle rounds.

In the 12th round, Ali battered Frazier, cutting his mouth and swelling his eye shut. Ever the warrior, Frazier battled for two more rounds, before his trainer stopped the fight after the 14th.

The Fundamentals

A **technical knockout,** also known as a TKO, occurs when a fight is stopped by the referee because one fighter is injured, unwilling to continue, or unable to continue in the referee's judgment.

Sports Strategies

The first fight between Muhammad Ali and Joe Frazier at Madison Square Garden did huge business. More than 300 million people watched on closed circuit television or satellite, and the promoters grossed approximately $23 million. The 1974 fight, also at the Garden, set a nontitle indoor gate record of more than $1 million.

Rope-a-Dope

Prior to the final fight with Joe Frazier, Muhammad Ali regained the title by defeating George Foreman. Yes, the same George Foreman who advertises mufflers and sells the Lean, Mean, Fat-Reducing Grilling Machine.

The fight, held in October 1974 and dubbed the Rumble in the Jungle, was held in Kinshasa, Zaire. Foreman was a much more powerful puncher than Ali, but Ali was craftier. He employed the so-called "Rope-a-Dope" strategy, and it made all the difference.

Ali leaned on the ropes, covered up, and allowed Foreman to wail away—to no avail. Foreman eventually tired and Ali won by an eighth-round knockout.

Ali held on to the title until February 1978, when he lost a 15-round decision to Leon Spinks. In September 1978, Ali regained the title by beating Spinks in a rematch.

Ali announced his retirement, but then fought twice more, losing both bouts, before packing it in for good. His record was 56–5–0, with 37 knock-outs. Today, Ali suffers from Parkinson's disease, but continues to be one of the most accomplished and admired athletes of all time.

Powerful Figures

Although Muhammad Ali was the Greatest, he had plenty of company in the "great" category.

Jack Dempsey, Joe Louis, Rocky Marciano, and Sugar Ray Leonard rank right up there among the very best of all time, regardless of weight class. Pound for pound, they were terrific fighters.

The Manassa Mauler

As legend has it, Jack Dempsey quit school after the eighth grade, went from town to town looking for work, and added to his income by challenging customers in saloons to fights. Legend also has it that he was undefeated.

Whether he was undefeated or not, he did well enough to turn pro in 1914. By July 1919, he was the heavyweight champion of the world. He took the title from Jess Willard, who outweighed him by 58 pounds. No matter: The Manassa Mauler knocked him down seven times in the first round.

Dempsey held the title until September 1926, when he lost a 10-round decision to Gene Tunney. The rematch, held a year later, remains one of the most famous fights ever.

The fight took place at Soldier Field in Chicago before 102,000 fans. Dempsey knocked Tunney down in the seventh, but was slow in moving to a neutral corner, as mandated by Illinois boxing rules. Tunney got to his feet by the count of nine, but he was actually down for about 14 seconds. The extra time allowed him to recover and win a decision. A few months later, Dempsey called it quits.

The Inside Skinny

Even though in 1996, he was some 20 years past his prime, Muhammad Ali proved he could still get people's attention. Ali provided the highlight of the opening ceremonies of the '96 Summer Olympics in Atlanta, when he lit the Olympic torch; his role had been kept secret. It was a moment that will be remembered forever.

Two-Minute Warning

He was known as Jack, but he was born William Harrison Dempsey in Manassa, Colorado. He and his two older brothers, also fighters, called themselves Jack Dempsey, as a tribute to a fighter actually named Jack Dempsey, who fought from 1883 to 1895 and was nicknamed the Nonpareil. When his brothers retired, he kept the name.

The Inside Skinny

Joe Louis was the first African-American heavyweight champ since Jack Johnson in the early 1900s. But he was much more accepted than Johnson, because his managers instructed him to behave respectfully and modestly so that he would appeal to white America. He was so popular that Jimmy Cannon, a newspaper columnist, wrote that Louis was "a credit to his race—the human race."

Sports Strategies

Rocky Marciano's childhood dream was to become, not a boxer, but a baseball player. Marciano was a catcher and was good enough to get a tryout with a minor league team after World War II. But a sore arm ended his career and he turned to boxing, where he made other people sore.

The Brown Bomber

Joe Louis's mother had wanted him to play the violin. Joe Louis had other ideas. He used the 50 cents his mother gave him for violin lessons and rented a locker at Brewster's Gym in Detroit instead. That was in 1934, when Louis was 17.

Three years later, Louis turned pro, and a year after that, he was the No. 9 contender for the heavyweight title. So much for those violin lessons.

Louis's path to the championship was delayed slightly, when he suffered his first loss, to Max Schmeling, who knocked him out in the 12th round before 60,000 fans in Yankee Stadium on June 19, 1936.

It took six more victories before the Brown Bomber won the title, in June 1937, by knocking out James J. Braddock in the eighth round.

Louis got a chance for revenge against Schmeling in June 1938 in a fight that was much more than a fight. Schmeling was held up as a symbol of Aryan superiority by German leaders. Louis met with President Franklin D. Roosevelt the night before the fight, which let everyone know there was a lot riding on the outcome.

Some 75,000 fans packed Yankee Stadium, and they didn't have to wait long for the outcome. Louis won by knockout in the first round.

Louis retained his title until retiring in 1948. But like most fighters, Louis's retirement didn't last long. He fought Ezzard Charles for the title in September 1950, but lost a 15-round decision. After winning eight more fights, he was knocked out by Rocky Marciano in the eighth round. After that, he retired for good.

The Brockton Blockbuster

Rocky Marciano had 49 professional fights and 49 professional victories, 43 by knockout. Well, you can't do much better than that, can you?

Marciano started his boxing career in the Army and had a successful career as an amateur in New England. He turned pro in 1947, won his first 42 bouts and finally got a title shot in 1952.

Facing Jersey Joe Walcott for the heavyweight title, Marciano was knocked down in the first round, but rallied to score a 13th-round knockout. Marciano successfully defended his title six times, including a first-round knockout of Walcott in their rematch. He retired in September 1955.

Marciano was killed in a plane crash in 1969 in Des Moines, Iowa.

Sugar Ray

Sugar Ray Leonard first got our attention by winning the gold medal in the light welterweight division at the 1976 Summer Olympics in Montreal. Not only was he a terrific fighter, but he had style and charisma that made him exceedingly popular.

And had things gone according to plan, he would've landed some endorsement deals, helped his parents out financially, and then gone to college.

But when the endorsements didn't happen, Leonard decided to keep fighting to earn a living. He turned pro in February 1977 and had one of the best careers of the modern era.

Sugar Ray Leonard, an Olympic gold medalist, won world championships in five different weight classes.

Photo: Icon Sports Media

After winning his first 25 fights, Leonard beat Wilfred Benitez in November 1979 to win the WBC welterweight championship. He went on to win world titles in four more weight classes—WBA junior middleweight, 1981; WBC middleweight, 1987; WBC light heavyweight, 1988; and WBC super middleweight, 1988–90.

It had appeared Leonard's career was over in 1982, after he underwent surgery for a detached retina. He even went so far as announcing his retirement. But as it turned out, he was just getting started.

The Least You Need to Know

➤ Boxing as we know it got its start in England in the eighteenth century.

➤ There were originally only eight weight classes. Today there are 17.

➤ Muhammad Ali won the championship with a stunning upset of Sonny Liston in 1964.

➤ Jack Dempsey lost to Gene Tunney in the famous "long count" fight in 1926.

➤ Rocky Marciano, with a 49–0 record, is the only undefeated professional boxer.

Game Time

It's that time again—time to take another quiz. I'll test your knowledge about golf, tennis, and boxing. As always, try not to peek at the answers immediately.

After the quiz, I'll provide a grab bag of interesting facts, figures, and anecdotes. We'll finish up with a look back at Tiger Woods's incredible run of four consecutive major championships and the records he set along the way.

But right now, it's test time.

Twenty Questions

OK, folks, put on your thinking caps and see how much you know.

1. Who was the first male golfer to earn $1 million in one season?

2. Who was the first female golfer to earn $1 million in one season?

3. Which active female golfer has won the most major championships?

4. What golfer has won the most British Open championships?

5. What golfer was responsible for the "shot heard 'round the world?"

6. What is the regulation number of clubs a golfer can carry in his or her bag?

7. Which three golfers won the same event four consecutive years?

8. Who was the last amateur to win a PGA Tour event?

9. Who was the youngest golfer ever to compete in a U.S. Women's Open?

10. What was the longest sudden death playoff on the PGA Tour?

11. Who holds the women's record for most singles and doubles tournaments played in a career?

Sports Strategies

Tennis is played on four different surfaces—grass, clay, hard courts, and indoor synthetic surfaces, also called carpet. Grass, which used to be a much more predominant surface, is used primarily at Wimbledon and the tune-up events leading up to Wimbledon. Clay and hard courts are used almost exclusively outdoors.

12. In tennis, what's a bagel? (Hint: It has nothing to do with breakfast.)

13. Who was the only player to win the U.S. Open on three different surfaces?

14. Who is the youngest player to win the Wimbledon men's singles title?

15. Which five tennis players have won both the NCAA men's Division I singles championship and the Wimbledon singles title?

16. Who is the only boxer to hold titles in three weight classes simultaneously?

17. Who holds the record for being named Fighter of the Year the most times by *Ring* magazine?

18. Who is the all-time leader in career knockouts?

19. Who is the all-time leader in total bouts?

20. What match was the biggest upset in the history of heavyweight championship fights?

Twenty Answers

Did you think that quiz was tough? Let's see how you fared.

1. Curtis Strange who won $1,147,644 in 1988.

2. Karrie Webb earned $1,002,000 in 1996.

3. Juli Inkster has won nine major championships—one U.S. Women's Open, two LPGA Championships, one du Maurier Classic, two Nabisco Championships, and three U.S. Amateurs.

4. Harry Vardon has won the British Open six times—1896, '98–99, 1903, '11, and '14. Four players—James Braid, J.H. Taylor, Peter Thomson, and Tom Watson—have five British Opens.

5. Gene Sarazen, in the 1935 Masters, holed his second shot on the par-five 15th hole for a *double eagle*. The ball was 220 yards from the flagstick. Sarazen used a 4-wood and the ball never got more than 30 feet off the ground.

6. Fourteen is the number of clubs a golfer can carry, according to the *Rules of Golf*.

7. Laura Davies, Walter Hagen, and Gene Sarazen each won the same events four years in a row. Davies won the Standard Register Ping tournament from 1994 to '97; Hagen won the PGA Championship from 1924 to '27; and Sarazen won the Miami Open from 1926 to '30. (The event was not held in 1927.)

8. Phil Mickelson won the 1991 Northern Telecom Open as an amateur.

9. Beverly Klass was 10 years, 7 months, and 21 days old when she teed it up in the 1967 U.S. Women's Open held at Virginia Hot Springs Golf and Tennis Club in Hot Springs, Virginia.

10. At the 1949 Motor City Open, Cary Middlecoff and Lloyd Mangrum played 11 holes of sudden death and were declared co-winners by mutual agreement.

11. Rosemary Casals played in 685 singles and doubles tournaments in her career.

12. A bagel in tennis refers to a shutout set, 6–0, because the loser's score looks like a bagel.

13. Jimmy Connors won the 1974 Open on grass, the 1976 Open on clay, and the 1978, '82, and '83 Opens on hard courts.

14. In 1985, Boris Becker was 17 years, 7 months. The oldest, in case you're wondering, was Arthur Gore in 1909. He was 41 years, 6 months.

The Fundamentals

A **double eagle** is one of rarest accomplishments in golf. It means holing your second shot on a par five. An eagle, less rare, but still a feat, would be holing your third shot on a par five or your second shot on a par four. A double eagle is three under par for that hole; an eagle is two under par.

Sports Strategies

The U.S. Nationals, the precursor of the U.S. Open, was played at the West Side Tennis Club in Forest Hills, New York, from 1924 through 1977. The surface was grass until 1975. In 1978, the Open moved to the National Tennis Center. The National Tennis Center occupies the grounds used for the 1964 World's Fair and is next to Shea Stadium, home of the New York Mets.

15. Tony Trabert, Alex Olmedo, Arthur Ashe, Jimmy Connors, and John McEnroe have won both the NCAA men's singles title and a Wimbledon championship. For your information, since the NCAA began crowning a women's singles champ in 1982, no winner has gone on to win any of the four Grand Slam singles titles.

Two-Minute Warning

Unlike today, when most top-level fighters are in action maybe two or three times a year, there once was a time when fighters fought constantly. "Homicide Hank" Armstrong, for example, had 27 bouts in 1937. He won them all, by the way. In March, July, August, and September, he had three fights in each month.

16. "Homicide Hank" Armstrong was the featherweight, lightweight, and welterweight champion in 1938. The weight range of those three classes ranged from 126 to 147 pounds.

17. Muhammad Ali was named Fighter of the Year five times—1963, '72, '74, '75, and '78. Joe Louis was next with four.

18. Archie Moore, a light heavyweight, registered 130 knockouts between 1936 and 1963. The ever-popular Young Stribling, a heavyweight who fought in the 1920s and '30s, was next with 126.

19. Len Wickwar, a light heavyweight, fought 463 bouts between 1928 and 1947.

20. On Feb. 10, 1990, Buster Douglas, a 42-1 underdog, knocked out Mike Tyson in the 10th round. Tyson had been previously unbeaten.

Bet You Didn't Know ...

➤ The term caddie originated from Mary Queen of Scots, who is known as the first woman golfer. She was raised in France and returned to Scotland when she was 19. Her assistants, who retained their French titles, were called cadets (*ka-day* in French). They carried her clubs and handed them to her when she was ready to hit her shot.

➤ The term fore, used in golf to warn other golfers that a ball is headed in their direction, was first used by artillerymen in the British military. They would yell "Beware before" to warn of enemy cannonballs, which would do considerably more damage than an errant Titleist.

➤ The lowest 72-hole score in PGA Tour history was carded by Mike Souchak in the 1955 Texas Open. He shot a 27-under 257.

➤ The most strokes under par in a PGA Tour event was John Huston, who shot a 28-under 260 in winning the 1998 Hawaiian Open.

➤ Sam Snead's 81 PGA Tour victories is an all-time record. Kathy Whitworth holds the LPGA Tour record with 88 wins.

➤ The du Maurier Classic, a Grand Slam event on the LPGA Tour from 1973 through 2000, was discontinued because du Maurier, a tobacco company, was prohibited from sponsoring sporting events, according to Canadian law. It was replaced by the Women's British Open.

➤ Only three women—Babe Zaharias in 1950, Mickey Wright in 1961, and Pat Bradley in 1986—have won three Grand Slam events in the same year. No woman has ever won a Grand Slam.

➤ Harry Vardon not only holds the distinction of winning six British Opens, he's also the namesake of one of the most popular ways to grip a golf club. The Vardon grip requires the little finger of the right hand to overlap the space between the forefinger and middle finger on the left hand (for a right-handed golfer). He developed it near the end of the nineteenth century. What's more, the Vardon Trophy is also named after him. It's given annually to the PGA Tour player with the lowest stroke average.

➤ The Vare Trophy, which goes to the LPGA Tour player with the lowest stroke average, was named after Glenna Collett Vare, who won the U.S. Women's Amateur championship six times from 1922 to 1935.

➤ The *Ryder Cup,* a team competition, was originally for male professionals from the U.S. and England. In 1979, the competition was expanded to pit the U.S. against Europe.

➤ In 1974, Billie Jean King became the first woman to coach a professional team that included men. King was the player-coach of the Philadelphia Freedom of the World Team

The Inside Skinny

Sam Snead, nicknamed Slammin' Sammy, was renowned for having one of the most fluid swings ever. It was a swing that stood the test of time. He holds the record for the most wins after the age of 40 (17) and the most years between victories (27, 1938–65) and was the oldest to win a PGA Tour event (52 years, 10 months, 8 days).

The Fundamentals

The **Ryder Cup** began as an unofficial match between players from the United States and England. Samuel Ryder, who was a British seed merchant, enjoyed the competition so much, he donated the Ryder Cup to be given to the winning team. The first Ryder Cup was played in 1927. The U.S. holds a 24–7–2 lead in the series. The women's version of the Ryder Cup, known as the Solheim Cup, began in 1990. It was named after Karsten Solheim, the inventor of Ping golf clubs.

Tennis league, which she was instrumental in establishing and which continues today.

➤ Althea Gibson was the first African American to win a Grand Slam singles title. She won the 1956 French championship, and followed that with the Wimbledon and U.S. championships in 1957 and 1958.

➤ The longest match, time-wise, in tennis history came at the 1982 *Davis Cup*. John McEnroe defeated Mats Wilander 9–7, 6–2, 15–17, 3–6, 8–6 in a match taking 6 hours, 32 minutes. (Tiebreakers are not played in Davis Cup competition.)

➤ The longest women's match lasted 6 hours, 31 minutes between Jean Hepner and Vicki Nelson-Dunbar, who won 6–4, 7–6 in the first round of a tournament in Richmond, Virginia in 1984. The tiebreaker, the score of which was 13–11, lasted 1 hour, 47 minutes. One point of that tiebreaker lasted 29 minutes and 643 strokes.

➤ Suzanne Lenglen, who won six Wimbledon and six French singles championships, caused an uproar at Wimbledon in 1919, when she played in a dress cut just above the calf. Typically, women played in dresses that reached the shoe tops.

➤ Some of the biggest fashion news to be made at Wimbledon occurred in 1949, when Gussie Moran had the nerve to wear panties trimmed with lace under her tennis skirt.

The Fundamentals

Until 1920, if the fight ended with both fighters still standing, the result was a no decision. The reasoning behind the no-decision rule was to keep gamblers from trying to fix fights. But newspaper reporters would print who they thought won the fight. Those results were cleverly known as **newspaper decisions.**

➤ Joe Frazier and George Foreman are the only two fighters to win both an Olympic gold medal and a world championship in the heavyweight division.

➤ Boxing is responsible for some of the most colorful nicknames in all of sports. A sampling: Georges Carpentier, the Orchid Man; Kid Chocolate, the Cuban Bon Bon; James J. Jeffries, the Boilermaker; Ezzard Charles, the Cincinnati Cobra; Archie Moore, the Old Mongoose; and Fritzie Zivic, the Croat Comet.

➤ Harry Greb, known as the Pittsburgh Windmill, was one of the fiercest competitors and most frequent fighters in boxing history. He fought 299 times, winning 264, including *newspaper decisions*, which were rendered in the early twentieth century. He was knocked out only twice, once in his first year as a fighter and once when he broke his arm while throwing a punch.

➤ The fighter with the most career losses is Arnold "Kid" Sheppard, a welterweight, who lost 154 bouts between 1926 and 1939. He won 96 and had 36 draws. Of his 286 total bouts, 222 went the distance.

Say What?

There are probably more memorable quotations about golf than any other sport. Here are a few, along with some tennis and boxing quotes.

➤ Sam Snead, winner of seven major championships: "You know those two-foot downhill putts with a break? I'd rather see a rattlesnake."

➤ Bobby Jones, winner of the Grand Slam in 1930: "Golf is a game that is played on a five-inch course—the distance between your ears."

➤ Gary Player, winner of each of the four Grand Slam events: "Golf is a puzzle without an answer."

Gary Player is one of five players to have won each of the four Grand Slam tournaments.

Photo: Diane Staskowski

➤ Ben Hogan, four-time U.S. Open champion: "This is a game of misses. The guy who misses the best is going to win."

➤ Byron Nelson, winner of 11 consecutive tournaments in 1945: "This game is like a horse ... if you take your eye off it, it'll jump back and kick your shins for you."

➤ Sam Snead, on comparing golf with baseball: "In golf, when we hit a foul ball, we got to go out and play it."

➤ Miller Barber, the all-time leader in Senior PGA Tour appearances with more than 550: "I don't say my golf game is bad, but if I grew tomatoes, they'd come up *sliced.*"

The Fundamentals

In golf, when you **slice** the ball it has nothing to do with a knife. A slice, for a right-handed player, means the ball starts to fly straight, but then curves to the right. A **hook** does just the opposite: The ball starts off straight, but curves to the left.

The Inside Skinny

Billie Jean King, who had a career filled with milestones and records, was the first female athlete ever to earn more than $100,000 in a year ($117,000 in 1971) and the oldest ever to win a pro tournament (39$\frac{1}{2}$ in 1983).

➤ Craig Stadler, 1982 Masters champion: "The game just embarrasses you until you feel inadequate and pathetic. You want to cry like a child."

➤ Arnold Palmer, four-time Masters champ: "What other people may find in poetry or in art museums, I find in the flight of a good drive—the white ball sailing up and up into that blue sky, growing smaller and smaller, almost taking off in orbit, then suddenly reaching its apex, curving downward, falling ... and finally dropping to the turf to roll some more, just the way I planned it."

➤ Jack Nicklaus, winner of 20 major championships, on Tiger Woods: "I don't think we've had a whole lot happen in what, 10 years? I mean, some guys here have come on and won a few tournaments, but nobody has sustained and dominated. I think we might have somebody now."

➤ Billie Jean King, winner of a record 20 Wimbledon titles in singles, doubles, and mixed doubles: "It's really impossible for athletes to grow up. On the one hand, you're a child, still playing a game. But on the other hand, you're a superhuman hero that everyone dreams of being. No wonder we have such a hard time understanding who we are."

➤ Billie Jean King again: "Tennis is a perfect combination of violent action taking place in an atmosphere of total tranquility."

➤ Jimmy Connors, five-time U.S. Open tennis champion, on the competitiveness of a match: "People don't seem to understand it's a damn war out there."

➤ Chris Evert, three-time Wimbledon champ, on comparing winning to mother-hood: "The great high of winning Wimbledon lasts for about a week. You go down in the record book, but you don't have anything tangible to hold on to. But having a baby—there isn't any comparison."

➤ Althea Gibson, the first African American to win the U.S. and Wimbledon championships: "In sports, you simply aren't considered a real champion until you have defended your title successfully. Winning it once can be a fluke; winning it twice proves you are the best."

➤ Muhammad Ali, former heavyweight champion of the world: "I'm not the greatest; I'm the double greatest. Not only do I knock 'em out, I pick the round."

➤ George Foreman, former heavyweight champion of the world: "There ain't nothing like being in the corner, and the trainer is whispering in your ear and another guy is putting in your mouthpiece. Five seconds to go, then boom! The bell. It's more exciting than looking down a cliff."

➤ Joe Louis, former heavyweight champion of the world: "Once that bell rings, you're on your own. It's just you and the other guy."

Sports Strategies

Not only was Muhammad Ali a great champion, he was also quite the character. Ali would play to the cameras, tell everyone how "pretty" he was, talk in rhyme and predict, usually accurately, what round the fight would end. "They all fall in the round I call," he would say. When he first burst onto the scene, his act put off a lot of people, but over time, he became one of the most beloved athletes ever.

Tiger's Excellent Adventure

Jack Nicklaus called it the most remarkable achievement he's seen in golf, which is saying something because he's accomplished a slew of remarkable things.

But what Tiger Woods accomplished in 2000 might never be repeated—unless he does it himself.

Woods had one of the greatest single seasons in golf history, primarily because he won three of the four Grand Slam events. Not since Ben Hogan in 1953 has anyone managed that feat.

His major achievement is worth a recap.

Tiger Woods's three major championship victories in 2000 ranks as one of the greatest achievements in golf history.

Photo: Icon Sports Media

U.S. Open

The U.S. Open was played at historic Pebble Beach, California, a difficult venue—for everyone but Woods. He shot rounds of 65-69-71-67 for a 12-under 272 total and a 15-shot victory. If you're wondering, the old record margin of victory in a major championship was 13 shots, set by Tom Morris Sr. in 1864 at the British Open.

Woods's score tied the Open record, held by Jack Nicklaus and Lee Janzen, and it broke the Open record in relation to par (held by Nicklaus, Janzen, and Hogan) by four strokes. His opening-round 65 was the lowest round ever shot in an Open.

Turns out, Woods was just getting started.

The British Open

Different tournament, different continent, same result. Woods dominated—again. This time, he broke the British Open and the major championship record with a 19-under 269 total. He won by eight shots.

The British Open was played at the Old Course at St. Andrews, one of the most hallowed and demanding layouts in the game.

If you want a clue as to just how well Woods played, this should do the trick. The Old Course features 112 bunkers, which are areas filled with sand. Woods avoided every one of them on all four days of the tournament.

Amazing.

PGA Championship

Believe it or not, Woods didn't win the PGA Championship in a rout. He and Bob May, a journeyman, ended regulation tied at 18 under par at Valhalla Golf Club in Louisville, Kentucky. Woods needed to birdie the final two holes to force the tie.

Woods and May settled the matter in a three-hole playoff. Woods went birdie-par-par; May went par-par-par.

With the victory, Woods became the first player since Denny Shute in 1936–37 to successfully defend his PGA Championship title.

Sports Strategies

As impressive as Tiger Woods's victories were in the U.S. Open and British Open, the combined totals are something else. Keep in mind, these tournaments are supposed to be among the sternest test in golf. He was 31 under par, won by 23 shots, made 43 birdies and 9 bogeys, and averaged 325.5 yards on his tee shots.

The Least You Need to Know

➤ Sam Snead is the all-time leader in PGA Tour wins with 81.

➤ The Ryder Cup is a biennial men's golf team competition between the U.S. and Europe.

➤ The Davis Cup is tennis's equivalent to the Ryder Cup, except that it's played annually.

➤ Prior to 1920, fights that ended with both fighters still standing were recorded as no decisions.

➤ Tiger Woods set scoring records in winning the 2000 U.S. Open and British Open.

Part 5

Frozen Ponds, Big Kicks

For the longest time, the National Hockey League was made up of just six teams—the "Original Six," they were called—and hockey was considered a Canadian game. The National Hockey League now has 30 teams, and only six are located in Canada. The reason the game has spread throughout the United States is Wayne Gretzky, who is hockey to many people. In soccer, the same can be said about Pele. He might be the only soccer player many Americans have ever heard of.

One of the biggest soccer stories to come along in years was authored by the U.S. Women's World Cup team, which captured the attention of the nation with their victory in the 1999 Women's World Cup.

Chapter 18

The Frozen Pond

In This Chapter

➤ The beginning

➤ The early days of the NHL

➤ The Great Gretzky

➤ The defenders

➤ The shooters

➤ Between the pipes

If you like fast-paced games featuring end-to-end action, played by guys who don't mind mixing it up or trying to put an opponent into the third row of seats when the situation calls for it, then ice hockey is for you.

In this chapter, we'll take a look at the origins of the game (and I'll warn you now, the details are rather sketchy), its rise in the United States, and some of the sport's best players.

So strap on your skates, put on your helmet, and make sure your mouthpiece is in place. The puck drops now!

Way Back When

If you're looking for hockey's equivalent of Abner Doubleday (who, as myth has it, invented baseball) or James Naismith (who invented basketball), you better keep looking, because there's no one person who gets credit for inventing the sport.

It's thought that it got its start in Great Britain and France more than 500 years ago. Seems that field hockey, which is played on grass, was a big deal in those parts back then. So when the weather turned cold and the lakes froze, field hockey was adapted to frozen ponds.

Another early version of hockey was called "kolven" and played in Holland in the seventeenth century. The English also had a game called "bandy" that was all the rage in the early 1800s. Kolven and bandy were played on ice with the object being to score a goal.

The Inside Skinny

Many people believe the sport of hockey got its name from the French word *hoquet*, which means shepherd's crook or bent stick. It makes sense, seeing as how hockey sticks are curved.

Two-Minute Warning

When most people think hockey, they think Canada, because that's where the game is most popular and where many of the players in the National Hockey League come from. But in the NHL today, only six of the 30 teams are from Canada. Go figure.

But hockey as we know it was developed in Nova Scotia, where organized games were played during the 1860s. Stones were used to mark the goals, and wooden sticks (which had to be kept below the shoulders) and a wooden puck were used. The rubber hockey puck was invented in 1872. The first organized league, with four teams, was formed in 1895 in Kingston, Ontario.

From that point, the game became wildly popular. Teams from Toronto, Ottawa, and Montreal began playing each other regularly. Lord Stanley of Preston, who happened to be the English Governor General of Canada, was so taken by the sport that he donated a silver bowl with the instructions to award it to the best amateur team in Canada.

All these years later, the Stanley Cup is still around and is given to the winner of the National Hockey League (NHL) playoffs each year. The original Cup was placed in the Hockey Hall of Fame in 1970.

The first pro league, known as the International Pro Hockey League, popped up in 1904, in the U.S., of all places. It was based in the Upper Peninsula of Michigan. But it didn't last, and neither did several other attempts.

It wasn't until 1917 that the National Hockey League was formed. There were five teams—the Montreal Canadiens, the Montreal Wanderers, the Ottawa Senators, the Quebec Bulldogs, and the Toronto Arenas.

In 1926, one of the few pro leagues to last any amount of time, the Pacific Coast Hockey Association (PCHA), met its demise. From 1917 through 1925, the NHL and the PCHA had played for the Stanley Cup. But when the PCHA went under, the NHL accepted five of its teams, doubling in size.

Today, the National Hockey League is made up of 30 teams, which are divided into two conferences, with three divisions each. The Western Conference is made up of the Central, Northwest, and Pacific divisions. The Eastern Conference is made up of the Northeast, Atlantic, and Southeast divisions.

Hockey in the U.S.A.

From 1942 through 1966, the NHL consisted of just six teams, cleverly known as the Original Six. The Boston Bruins, Chicago Blackhawks, Detroit Red Wings, Montreal Canadiens, New York Rangers, and Toronto Maple Leafs probably got sick of each other, for all the times they had to play.

Actually, Boston, Chicago, Detroit, and New York got sick of Montreal and Toronto, because those two teams seemed to win the Stanley Cup every year. The Canadiens won it 10 times during those 24 years and the Maple Leafs nine. Detroit won five Cups and Chicago one. Boston and New York came up empty.

In 1967, the decision was made to expand the NHL in the United States. The league doubled in size by adding the California Seals, Los Angeles Kings, Minnesota North Stars, Philadelphia Flyers, Pittsburgh Penguins, and St. Louis Blues.

From 1970 to '79, the NHL added 10 more teams. After standing pat in the 1980s, nine teams were added over the next decade to bring the total to 30, many of which are located in areas that might surprise you, because they are so un-Canada-like. There are teams in California (three), Florida (two), Georgia, North Carolina, Tennessee, Texas, and Arizona.

And the U.S. teams have done exceptionally well. From 1980 through 2000, U.S.-based teams have

Sports Strategies

The New York Rangers' Stanley Cup futility was one of the most notable streaks in all of sports. The Rangers went 44 years between Cup victories. They won it in 1940, beating Toronto, and then didn't win it again until 1994, when they beat Vancouver. In case you're wondering, the Boston Bruins went from 1941 to 1970 between Cups.

The Inside Skinny

Talk about an identity crisis. The California Seals joined the NHL in 1967. Three months into the first season, they were renamed the Oakland Seals. In 1970, they were renamed the California Golden Seals. In 1975, they were renamed the California Seals. In 1975, they moved to Cleveland and became the Barons. In 1978, the Barons and the Minnesota North Stars merged and kept the name of the latter.

won the Stanley Cup 13 times. The Edmonton Oilers—they're in Canada, in case geography's not your strong suit—won five Cups. The incomparable Wayne Gretzky was the team's leader for the first four.

The Great One

To many people, Wayne Gretzky *is* hockey. Like Michael Jordan, he's one of those rare individuals who transcends sport. Were it not for the impact that Gretzky made on the game and its fans, especially in Los Angeles when he was traded by Edmonton, it's unlikely that the NHL would have as many franchises in nontraditional hockey environments.

Gretzky didn't just play the game, he dominated it with talent and instincts that were otherworldly. The guy was a magician with the puck, blessed with speed, flashy moves, and a sixth sense that almost made it unfair for the other players. He was not only the greatest goal-scorer in NHL history, he was also the greatest passer.

Wayne Gretzky, nicknamed "The Great One," set the standard by which other hockey players are measured.

Photo: Icon Sports Media

His father taught him to skate not long after he learned to walk. Gretzky turned out to be a pretty fast learner. When he was six, he was playing in a league with 10-year-olds; and when he was 10, he was playing against teenagers. You might say he did okay against the teens. During the 1971–72 season, he scored 378 *goals* and had 120 *assists* in 69 games.

By the time he was 18, Gretzky signed a four-year contract worth $875,000 to play for the Indianapolis Racers of the fledgling World Hockey Association (WHA). Eight games into his first season, the Racers sold his contract to the Edmonton Oilers. When the WHA went belly-up in 1979, the Oilers joined the NHL and Gretzky began building his legend.

He led the Oilers to four Stanley Cup championships in five years (1984–85, '87–88). Then, after
the 1988 Cup, the unthinkable happened: Wayne
Gretzky was traded to the Los Angeles Kings. He
never led the Kings to a Stanley Cup championship, but he did get them to the finals in 1993, and
most important, he solidified the support for
hockey on the West Coast.

But mostly, Gretzky will be remembered for the 61
records he holds or shares. Here are the highlights:

➤ Most goals: 894 (1,485 games). Gordie Howe
   is second with 801 in 1,767 games

➤ Most goals, including playoffs: 1,016

➤ Most goals, one season: 92, 1981–82

➤ Most goals, one season, including playoffs:
   100, 1983–84

➤ Most assists: 1,962

➤ Most assists, including playoffs: 2,222

➤ Most assists, one season: 163, 1985–86

➤ Most assists, one season, including playoffs:
   174, 1985–86

➤ Most points: 2,856. Gordie Howe is second
   with 1,850.

➤ Most points, one season: 215, 1985–86

➤ Consecutive 100-point seasons: 13

➤ Most playoff goals: 122

➤ Most playoff assists: 260

➤ Most *Hart Trophies* (most valuable player): 9

➤ Most *Conn Smythe Trophies* (most valuable
   player in the playoffs): 2, tied with four others

Gretzky was traded by the Kings to the St. Louis
Blues in 1996, and after one season, he signed with
the New York Rangers as a free agent. He retired
following the 1998–99 season after a 20-year career.

Usually, the waiting time to enter the Hockey
Hall of Fame is three years. But with Gretzky, an
exception was made. He was inducted immediately.
Who could possibly argue?

The Fundamentals

A **goal** is scored when the entire
puck crosses the goal line and
enters the net. A goal is worth
one point. An **assist** is credited
to a player who helps set up a
goal with a pass. There is a maximum of two assists per goal.
Assists are also worth one point
to the player's scoring total, not
the team's score.

The Fundamentals

The **Hart Trophy** is given to the
player judged to be the most
valuable to his team. It is named
after Cecil Hart, the former coach
of the Montreal Canadiens. The
winner is selected by a vote of
the Pro Hockey Writers Association (PHWA). The **Conn Smythe
Trophy** is given to the most valuable player in the Stanley Cup
playoffs. It is named after Conn
Smythe, former coach, general
manager, and owner of the
Toronto Maple Leafs. It, too, is
voted on by the PHWA.

The Defense Never Rests

It's the responsibility of the *defensemen* to keep the opposition from mounting an attack and also to move the puck up ice and get it to the forwards, whose main job is to do the scoring.

Sports Strategies

In 1998, Wayne Gretzky achieved a milestone that really put his greatness into perspective. Playing for the New York Rangers, the Great One registered 67 assists that season. One of those 67 was the 1,851st of his career, meaning he had more assists than any other player in league history had points. Unbelievable.

The Fundamentals

A **defenseman's** primary responsibility is to slow the opposition's progress toward the offensive zone. Defensemen also move the puck out of their zone and toward the opponent's goal. They usually pass the puck to a forward, whose job it is to create plays and score goals.

So they need to be tough and rugged for the defensive part of their job, while having the skills necessary to skate and handle the puck.

Bobby Orr of the Boston Bruins was unquestionably the best defenseman in NHL history. Eddie Shore, who also played for the Bruins, was arguably the toughest. Plus, Shore did something no other defenseman ever accomplished: He won the Hart Trophy four times.

The Edmonton Express

Eddie Shore's 14-year career in the NHL began in 1929 with the Boston Bruins. He was a terrific defenseman—*The Hockey News* ranked him 10th on its list of the top 100 NHL players—with fine offensive skills.

Actually, it wasn't that he was a speedy skater or an especially deft puck handler. Shore manufactured offense by overpowering anybody who happened to be in his way—hence his nickname, the Edmonton Express.

What Shore was best known for was his fighting. He skated in a low crouch and was almost impossible to knock off stride, but he had no problem knocking his opponents down—and out, if need be.

Shore collected 1,047 penalty minutes during his career and almost an equal number of injuries. He had 978 stitches, 80 cuts, a fractured back, a fractured hip, and a broken collarbone. That's not all. His nose was broken 14 times and his jaw was fractured five times. He almost had his left ear torn off in a fight and each eyeball was split.

I'll bet you can feel his pain, can't you?

One brawl, in particular, still stands out. In 1933, Shore flipped Ace Bailey of the Toronto Maple Leafs into the air. Bailey landed on his head, suffered a fractured skull, and nearly died.

But his penchant for fisticuffs never overshadowed his skill. Shore was the first defenseman ever to win the Hart Trophy as the league's most valuable player. He went on to win the award four times in all. Only Wayne Gretzky and Gordie Howe won it more.

The One and Only

Here's how talented Bobby Orr was: In 1960, when he was 13 years old and playing for a team in Parry Sound, Ontario, the Boston Bruins saw him and decided to sponsor the Parry Sound team, which, in those days, meant Orr was Bruins property.

At 13.

Turns out, they did exactly the right thing, because Bobby Orr is the best defenseman in the history of the NHL. Period. And probably the second-best player after Wayne Gretzky.

Orr had the offensive and playmaking skills of a *center* and because he was so fast, he changed the way the game was played defensively. He made the impossible seem routine.

Orr won the Calder Trophy in 1967, emblematic of the league's rookie of the year. For the next eight years, from 1968 to 1975, he won the Norris Trophy, awarded to the league's best defenseman.

But there was more to Orr than just defense. He is the only defenseman to lead the league in scoring. He did it twice (120 points, 1970; 135 points, 1975). He scored 100 or more points in six straight seasons and won the Hart Trophy as the most valuable player three straight years, starting in 1970.

Unfortunately, knee injuries began to take their toll on Orr. He played only 20 games in 1976, missed all of 1977, and retired six games into the 1978-79 season.

As it was for Gretzky, the three-year waiting period was waived for Orr, who was inducted into the Hockey Hall of Fame in 1979.

The Inside Skinny

Eddie Shore played in an era that emphasized defense and goaltending. Not even the forwards scored that much. Only once did the NHL's top goal scorer during Shore's career have more than 40 goals. That Shore retired with 105 goals, an exceedingly high number for a defenseman, is testament to his all-around ability.

The Fundamentals

In a traditional alignment, the **center** plays between the left wing and the right wing. All are also considered forwards. The center must be able to handle the puck, create plays for his linemates, and be able to shoot the puck and score himself.

He Shoots, He Scores!

The defensemen do most of the dirty work, but the forwards are the guys who often get the glory, because they do the bulk of the scoring.

What's more exciting than to see a player going full-steam ahead with the puck, bearing down on the goalie, and then letting fly with a bullet shot that darn near rips the back of the net to shreds? Now *that's* good fun!

Mr. Hockey

As athletic careers go, Gordie Howe's was nothing short of amazing—for several reasons. First of all, he was an outstanding player. He could score, he was tough, and he was a smooth skater; perhaps the most remarkable thing about him was that he seemed to have played forever.

Howe's career lasted for 32 seasons. He didn't retire until 1980, when he was 52 years old. He spent 25 seasons with the Detroit Red Wings, beginning in 1946 as an 18-year-old.

He led the Red Wings to four Stanley Cup championships (1950, '52, '54–55) and topped the NHL in scoring six times (1951–54, '57, '63). To give you an idea of how good Howe was for how long, he had his career-best season, scoring 103 points, at age 40.

But for all his success in Detroit, the Red Wings were, in Howe's opinion, a little tight with a buck. He was still playing at a high level, but he was only the third-highest paid player on the team. So even though the Red Wings offered to more than double his salary, Howe thought it was too little too late and decided to retire in 1971.

But his retirement didn't last. Two years later, Howe joined the Houston Aeros of the *World Hockey Association,* where he joined two other Howes, his sons, Mark and Marty. Papa Howe spent six years with the Aeros, before retiring again. Although not for good. He returned for one more season in 1979–80 with the Hartford Whalers of the NHL.

Sports Strategies

Bobby Orr hit the jackpot in 1970, when he became the only player in the history of the NHL to win four major individual awards. He won the Hart (most valuable player), the Norris (best defenseman), the Ross (scoring), and the Conn Smythe (most valuable player in the playoffs). To top it off, he also led the Bruins to the Stanley Cup.

The Fundamentals

The **World Hockey Association** debuted in the 1972–73 season to compete with the National Hockey League. The WHA began with 12 teams and lasted seven seasons, disbanding in 1979. The NHL absorbed four WHA teams—the Winnipeg Jets, Edmonton Oilers, Hartford Whalers, and Quebec Nordiques—for the 1979–80 season.

The list of Howe's accomplishments is lengthy. He ranks first all-time in years played (32) and games played (1,767); second all-time in points (1,850) and goals (801); and sixth all-time in assists (1,049).

And how's this for consistency: For 20 consecutive seasons, from 1950 through 1969, Howe ranked among the top five scorers in the league.

That nickname of Mr. Hockey fit to a T.

Super Mario

Mario Lemieux is the total package. You couldn't hope to piece together a hockey player any better than he is. He has size (6' 4", 210 pounds), speed, and a feel for the game that has made him virtually unstoppable.

Lemieux, a center, has spent his entire career with the Pittsburgh Penguins, winning the Calder Trophy as rookie of the year in 1984. He led the league in scoring six times (1988–89, '92–93, '96–97) and was named the Most Valuable Player three times (1988, '92, '96).

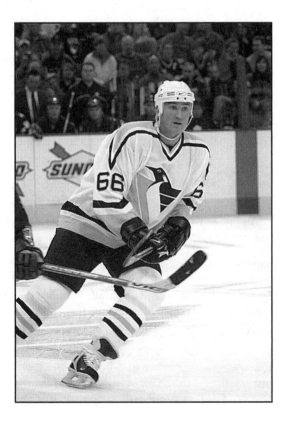

Mario Lemieux, a three-time winner of the NHL's most valuable player award, led the Pittsburgh Penguins to two Stanley Cup championships.

Photo: Icon Sports Media

Early in his career, people wondered if he had leadership qualities to go along with all that talent. Well, Mario showed 'em, leading the Penguins to Stanley Cup championships in 1991 and '92.

Lemieux suffered through numerous injuries throughout his career, including a chronic back problem. In 1993, he was diagnosed with Hodgkin's disease. He took off the 1994–95 season because of his weakened condition and more back trouble, but he returned to win the scoring title in 1996 and '97, after which he retired.

The Inside Skinny

The Pittsburgh Penguins made Mario Lemieux the No. 1 overall draft choice in 1984. Since the NHL began its present draft system in 1969, Lemieux is one of only six players drafted No. 1 who also won the Calder Trophy. The others are Gilbert Perreault, 1970; Denis Potvin, 1973; Bobby Smith, 1978; Dale Hawerchuk, 1981; and Bryan Berard, 1995.

But Lemieux's contribution to hockey in Pittsburgh was far from over. In 1999, when bankruptcy nearly ruined the franchise, Lemieux put together a group of investors and bought the team. He went from player to owner—and then to player again.

After 3¹/₂ years away, Lemieux returned to the ice in December 2000. He scored 35 goals and 41 assists during the season, bringing his career totals to 648 goals and 922 assists. Super Mario indeed!

The Puck Stops Here

Being a goaltender must be the most harrowing job in all of sports. Offhand, I can think of about 437 better ways to make a living than people firing a hard rubber puck at me at speeds of more than 100 mph. And to think, there was a time when these guys didn't even wear masks.

Superstar Goalie, Tragic Figure

According to *The Hockey News,* which ranked the top 100 players in NHL history, Terry Sawchuk is the best goalie of all time. His record proves the point.

Sawchuk is the all-time leader in games played (971) and *shutouts* (103), and is No. 2 in career wins with 447. Patrick Roy of the Colorado Avalanche passed Sawchuk in career wins early in the 2000–01 season.

The Fundamentals

A **shutout** is the goal of every goaltender. It means he has not allowed the opposition to score during a game.

In his first five seasons in the league (1951–55), Sawchuk's goals-against average per game was less than two, which is outstanding. In 1952, while playing for the Detroit Red Wings, he had four playoff shutouts and gave up only five goals in eight games.

Sawchuk played for three teams that won the Stanley Cup—Detroit (1952, '54) and Toronto (1964). He also won the *Vezina Trophy,* awarded to the league's best goalie, three times and shared it once.

Sawchuk, whose career was plagued by numerous injuries, was also beset by personal problems, including drinking and depression. In 1970, he and a teammate from the New York Rangers, Ron Stewart, got into a fight. Sawchuk suffered internal injuries. A blood clot required surgery, which caused a coronary that killed him at age 40.

Masked Man

Jacques Plante, while playing for the Montreal Canadiens in 1959, was the first goalie to wear a mask on a permanent basis. He decided to make this fashion statement after getting hit in the face by a shot from Andy Bathgate of the New York Rangers. Plante, who wore a mask in practice, started wearing it in games.

The mask didn't hinder Plante in the least. He won five straight Vezina Trophies (1956–60) and seven overall. In 1962, he was so good that he won the Hart Trophy as the Most Valuable Player. He won 42, lost 14, and tied 14, with a 2.37 goals-against average.

Plante, who was one of the first goalies to leave the net to pass the puck to a teammate, was third all-time in career wins (434), fourth in shutouts (82), and fifth in goals-against average (2.38).

The Fundamentals

From 1927 to 1980, the **Vezina Trophy** was given to the principal goaltender(s) on the team that gives up the fewest goals during the regular season. The trophy was named after Georges Vezina of the Montreal Canadiens, who died of tuberculosis in 1926. Starting in 1981, the trophy has been given to the outstanding goalie of the year, as selected by the league's general managers.

The Least You Need to Know

➤ Hockey as we know it originated in Nova Scotia in the late nineteenth century.

➤ The National Hockey League was formed in 1917.

➤ Wayne Gretzky is the all-time leader in goals and assists.

➤ Bobby Orr is recognized as the greatest defenseman ever.

➤ Gordie Howe's career lasted for 32 seasons.

➤ Jacques Plante was the first goaltender to wear a mask on a regular basis.

Soccer: The World Game

Soccer is by far the most popular game in the world. Called football everywhere but the United States, the game is like a religion—everywhere but the United States.

The World Cup is the equivalent of the American Super Bowl, and Pele was to soccer what Michael Jordan was to basketball or Tiger Woods is to golf.

The U.S. Women's World Cup team provided the sport with one of its biggest boosts in the United States. The leader of that team, Mia Hamm, gave young girls a role model they could admire—and Gatorade another sports star to sell its product.

Kicking Off

Soccer is so old that it was played before people started recording history. Although there's no definitive date for its creation, historians believe it dates to 217 A.D. during the Roman occupation of England. The games were played without rules and they got pretty wild. Maybe that's where the rowdy crowds at today's games got the idea for how to misbehave.

Soccer as we know it developed its roots in 1863, when the London Football Association came up with the first set of rules and infused order in the sport.

The Inside Skinny

Uruguay was chosen as the host of the first World Cup because it had won the 1924 and 1928 Olympic gold medals, and because it was celebrating its 100th anniversary as a country. The 12 other countries that participated were only too happy to compete, seeing as how Uruguay paid their traveling expenses. The title game, in which Uruguay beat Argentina 4–2, attracted 93,000 fans.

Sports Strategies

The United States hasn't fared all that well in World Cup play. It's fielded a team every year, but only five have qualified for the finals, including the 1994 team that was guaranteed a berth because the U.S. was host of the tournament. The U.S.A.'s overall World Cup record is 4–12–1 in 17 matches. Half of those victories came in 1930.

British sailors get credit for spreading the game's popularity. They brought it to India, South America, and Europe, where it was immediately popular.

In 1904, the Federation Internationale de Football Association, known to this day as FIFA, was formed to oversee tournament play internationally. Four years later, soccer became an Olympic sport.

Among countries winning Olympic medals in soccer, Hungary leads the way with three golds, all since 1952. The United States has never won an Olympic medal of any color in soccer.

The Big Show

The next milestone in the sport's development was the debut of the World Cup in 1930. Teams representing 13 different countries entered the inaugural tournament, which was won by Uruguay.

The driving force behind the competition was Jules Rimet, who served as president of FIFA and the French Soccer Federation. The decision to make Uruguay the site of the first World Cup, rather than Italy, Holland, Spain, or Sweden, didn't sit too well with the European countries because of the travel involved, but eventually teams from outside South America entered.

The field for the first World Cup was made up of Argentina, Belgium, Bolivia, Brazil, Chile, France, Mexico, Paraguay, Peru, Romania, the United States, Uruguay, and Yugoslavia. The Europeans faced a three-week boat trip each way.

Except for 1942 and 1946, the World Cup has been held every four years. There were 138 countries entered in the qualifying round in 1994, with 24 advancing to the finals. In 1998, FIFA increased the number of teams qualifying for the finals to 32, the same number that will qualify for the 2002 Cup.

Brazil has won the most World Cups, four, followed by Italy and West Germany with three each, and Argentina and Uruguay with two each.

The 2002 World Cup will be held in Japan and South Korea, and the 2006 tournament will be held in Germany.

To give you some idea of the worldwide popularity of this event, the 1998 World Cup (France, the host, beat Brazil in the final) was watched by a cumulative global television audience of 37 *billion* viewers—a total that makes the "Survivor" audience seem almost trivial.

One-Name Wonder

He is one of the most recognized, most talented, and most accomplished athletes in all of sport. He is an icon of his game and he is famous the world over.

Surely, you've heard of him: Edson Arantes do Nascimento. What's that? You say that mouthful of a name doesn't ring any bells?

Well, I'll bet his nickname will be instantly familiar. Ever hear of Pele? Of course you have. He's only the most famous, most charismatic player soccer has ever produced. And because of that fame and charisma—and let's not forget his wealth of talent—Pele's also had a major impact on the game internationally.

Pele, arguably the most famous soccer player in history, led his native Brazil to three World Cup titles.

Photo: Icon Sports Media

Humble Beginnings

Pele, born in 1940, grew up in poverty in a small town in Brazil. How poor was he? He was so poor that his first "soccer ball" was either a grapefruit or a stocking stuffed with rags.

Pele finally got his first authentic soccer ball when he was 10, and he practiced it with it constantly. His father, Dondinho, taught him the fundamentals of the game, and by the time he was 15, he transferred from the local soccer club in his town to a big-city club in Santos.

The Inside Skinny

Pele's not sure exactly when, why, or how he came by his nickname (most Brazilian players have them). But he did know that he wasn't fond of it. Not one bit. In fact, he got into fights at school with his class-mates whenever they referred to him as "Pele" and not his given name.

Pele's first job when joining the Santos team was as an errand boy. After all, he was only 15. But it wasn't long before his remarkable talent earned him a place in the lineup. He led Santos to six consecutive championships in his first six seasons, averaging a goal a game.

But like all outstanding athletes, Pele saved his best for his sport's biggest stage, the World Cup.

Simply the Best

Not surprisingly, Pele became the youngest ever to play for a World Cup champion. Of course, to say he merely played would be an understatement. Pele scored twice in the final game as Brazil defeated Sweden 5–2.

A pulled muscle kept Pele out of the 1962 World Cup, which Brazil won. But in 1970, he led Brazil back to the final. He scored once and inspired his country to a 4–1 victory over Italy and an unprecedented third World Cup.

Pele played until 1974, then announced his retirement. But his retirement lasted only 18 months. In 1975, he returned to play soccer in the United States, and in doing so gave the sport a major boost.

Sports Strategies

From the first World Cup in 1930 until Brazil's victory in 1970, the winner of the tournament was presented with the Jules Rimet Trophy, named in honor of FIFA's first president. But Brazil retired the trophy after winning it for the third time in 1970. Since then, the trophy presented to the winner is known as the World Cup.

Pele Comes to New York

The North American Soccer League (NASL), in business since 1968, never was a great success. Teams lost money, and as a result, the NASL lost teams. After the 1974 season, it was obvious that the league needed something spectacular to attract attendances and continue to operate.

And what could be more spectacular than luring Pele out of retirement and having him play in New York?

Nothing, as it turned out. Pele signed a three-year contract for $4.7 million and with his signature, everything changed. Fans turned out in droves and so did the media. Suddenly, soccer games featuring Pele became an event, a happening.

In 1975, Pele played 15 games for the New York Cosmos—six were sold out and 10 set club attendance records. The Cosmos were popular on the road, too, attracting huge crowds wherever they played.

Pele was in magazines; on *The Tonight Show,* chatting it up with Johnny Carson; and at the White House, visiting President Gerald Ford.

The Cosmos moved into Giants Stadium in East Rutherford, New Jersey, in 1977 and, believe it or not, consistently outdrew the New York Mets and the New York Yankees.

Pele led the Cosmos to three straight NASL championships, then retired for good after the 1977 season. His final game attracted 78,000 fans to Giants Stadium.

Overall, Pele played 21 seasons, scored 1,281 goals, and averaged just under one goal a game. Unfortunately for soccer in the United States, at least for the men, things have never been quite the same since Pele left.

The Inside Skinny

In addition to being the ultimate soccer player, Pele also made a lasting contribution as an ambassador for his sport, which is as evident in the United States as anywhere. In 1982, he was presented with FIFA's Gold Medal Award for outstanding service to the game. In 1994, he was appointed Brazil's Minister for Sport, a position he holds today.

The Game in the U.S.

The North American Soccer League met its demise following the 1984 season. The combination of financial mismanagement and the lack of U.S. players on the teams led to the league's death.

It wasn't until 1996, in the wake of the 1994 World Cup held in the United States, that another league was formed. Major League Soccer (MLS) was scheduled to begin in 1995, but difficulty finding investors and sponsors delayed the debut until 1996. The MLS began with 10 teams and expanded to 12 in 1998.

The MLS started off well enough for a new league, but over time its progress leveled off. Case in point: The New York/New Jersey Metro Stars began playing before crowds of close to 50,000 in 1996. By the end of the 1999 season, they were lucky to draw 6,000.

But, like the Energizer battery, it's still going, and it remains the only FIFA-sanctioned outdoor league in the United States.

The Fundamentals

As women's soccer became more established, FIFA pledged in 1986 to stage a women's equivalent to the World Cup. The inaugural **Women's World Cup** was held in 1991 in China. Twelve teams participated, with the United States defeating Norway 2–1 in the final. For the 1999 Women's World Cup, 16 teams qualified for the finals.

Two-Minute Warning

Just because you may never have heard about Mia Hamm prior to the Women's World Cup in 1999, doesn't mean she wasn't making her mark. Hamm played her college soccer at the University of North Carolina, where she was a three-time All-American, scored 103 goals, registered 72 assists, and led the Tar Heels to four straight NCAA championships (1990–93). She also had her No. 19 retired in 1994.

Leading Ladies

When the Men's World Cup was held in the United States in 1994, many soccer enthusiasts hoped, prayed, and crossed their fingers that the event would help the sport's profile skyrocket.

But it never really happened.

Fans attended the games in great numbers, because it was heavily promoted and it was an event, but the U.S. team never really captured the imagination of the nation. As a result, once the World Cup ended, so did the casual fan's interest in soccer.

Five years later, the *Women's World Cup* was held in the United States. There might've been people who expected much the same outcome: enthusiasm for the actual event, followed by waning interest.

Well, nothing could've been further from the truth. The U.S. women's soccer team turned into a phenomenon, the likes of which we've rarely seen.

Several players—among them Mia Hamm, Julie Foudy, and Brandi Chastain—became household names. The players did TV commercials, appeared in print ads, and showed up on *The Late Show with David Letterman*.

By the time the United States reached the Women's World Cup final against China, everyone was in a frenzy. But before we recap the Cup, let's take a look at the game's biggest star.

The Icon

Mia Hamm made a TV commercial for Gatorade, in which she went one-on-one with Michael Jordan. It could've been titled "Battle of the Icons," because what Jordan did for basketball, Hamm did for women's soccer.

Actually, you could make the case that Hamm was more important to her sport, because women's soccer wasn't nearly as well established as was pro basketball.

Hamm is the all-time leader, among men and women, in international scoring with 127 goals. Her 108th goal, which broke the record, occurred against Brazil in May 1999. She was the youngest person ever to play for the U.S. national team (15 years, 140 days in 1987), and she led the U.S. to the 1991 Women's World Cup championship and the U.S. to a gold medal at the 1996 Olympics.

Mia Hamm is the all-time leader among men and women in international scoring.

Photo: Icon Sports Media

At the 2000 Olympics in Sydney, Australia, Hamm and the U.S. team reached the final game, but came home with a silver medal after losing to Norway 3–2.

But the lack of a gold medal has done nothing to stop the growth of women's soccer in the United States. There's even a pro league, the Women's United Soccer Association (WUSA), which debuted in 2001 with eight teams. Hamm is a member of the Washington Freedom and is the focus of the league's promotions.

But without the enthusiasm generated by the Women's World Cup, it's highly unlikely that a women's pro soccer league would've even been discussed, let alone formed.

The Inside Skinny

It wasn't just the fans in the Rose Bowl who were obsessed with the outcome. People across the United States were glued to their televisions. ABC's telecast of the '99 Women's World Cup final generated a 13.3 rating, which was the highest ever for a soccer game and the highest for any domestic sporting event that summer.

The Fundamentals

If a game is tied after regulation and two extra periods, a **shootout** determines the winner. Each team gets five **penalty kicks.** A player stationed 12 yards from the goal goes one-on-one against the keeper. If after the series of five kicks the score is still tied, the process continues until the tie is broken.

A Day to Remember

The U.S. team reached the 1999 Women's World Cup final after a tense 2–0 victory over Brazil. The opponent would be China, which many experts considered the favorite, because of its ability to penetrate and attack.

But the U.S. had something more powerful on its side—a crowd of 90,185 filling the Rose Bowl in Pasadena, California.

The two teams went the entire 90 minutes of regulation play scoreless. Ditto for the two 15-minute overtime periods, which meant the outcome would be decided by a *shootout.*

Talk about drama.

The U.S and China each made their first two *penalty kicks.* Then came the first of two plays that made all the difference.

U.S. goaltender Briana Scurry dove to her left and knocked away a shot by China's Liu Ying, preserving the tie. After the rest of the players scored, making it 4–4, it came down to Brandi Chastain of the United States.

Chastain was a member of the 1991 Women's World Cup championship team and the 1996 Olympic gold medal–winning team, so she was used to pressure. But this was beyond pressure.

Her attempt was a bullet that found its way past the goaltender and into the top corner of the net. It was the most memorable and meaningful goal in the history of U.S. women's soccer. And Chastain celebrated accordingly.

Cover Girl

After Brandi Chastain scored her historic goal, she did something equally historic, and unheard of: She ripped off her shirt and fell to her knees, a euphoric smile covering her face.

(Although there's virtually no way you could've missed the picture, Chastain was wearing a sports bra underneath her game jersey.)

Sports Strategies

Although the teams remained scoreless through regulation and two overtime periods, there was one exceedingly close call in the first overtime. China's Fan Yunjie headed a ball that appeared to get past goalie Briana Scurry. But Kristine Lilly was stationed at the far post of the goal and was able to intercept the would-be game winner before it reached the net.

Chastain, in her famous pose, appeared on the covers of *Time, Newsweek, Sports Illustrated,* and *People.* What were the odds of a women's soccer player gracing the covers of all those national magazines?

Slim to none, but it happened, and because it did women's soccer got a huge boost, and more important, girls got to root for terrific role models and understand that anything was possible.

The Least You Need to Know

➤ Soccer as we know it got its start in London in 1863.

➤ The Federation Internationale de Football Association (FIFA) was formed in 1904.

➤ The first World Cup was played in Uruguay in 1930.

➤ The United States has never reached a men's World Cup final.

➤ Pele is the most famous soccer player of all time.

➤ Mia Hamm is the all-time leader in international scoring.

➤ The United States won the Women's World Cup in 1999.

Ready Class?

Chapter 20

Game Time

In This Chapter

➤ Trivia quiz

➤ Making the grade

➤ Tidbits, facts, and figures

➤ Quotable quotes

➤ Coaching genius

It's quiz time again. The subjects on which you'll be tested are ice hockey and soccer, so hopefully you'll get your kicks with a good grade. (Sorry, I couldn't resist.)

After the quiz, there will be more facts, figures, and tidbits of knowledge to store away; some profound statements; and a look at a coach who might be the best of all time in any sport.

Okay, enough of the preliminaries; it's time for the test!

Twenty Questions

This quiz features questions on hockey and soccer. Good luck!

1. Who was the first hockey player to score 50 goals in one season?
2. Who was the first goaltender to score a goal in a National Hockey League game?

3. Who are the only father and son to each win the Hart Trophy as the NHL's Most Valuable Player?

4. Who is the only hockey player to average two or more goals a game in a single season?

5. Who was the first non–North American player to be inducted into the *Hockey Hall of Fame?*

6. Who has played on the most Stanley Cup championship teams?

7. Who are the only rookies to win the Conn Smythe Trophy as the Most Valuable Player in the Stanley Cup playoffs?

8. Which expansion team was the first to win the Stanley Cup championship?

9. Who was the first hockey player to score 100 points in a season?

10. Who is the only coach to win a college hockey national championship and a Stanley Cup?

The Fundamentals

The **Hockey Hall of Fame,** located in Toronto since 1943, was originally in Kingston, Ontario. Prospective members must be retired three years before being nominated for induction, although that three-year waiting period has been waived 10 times, the last time for Wayne Gretzky in 1999.

11. Who is the NHL's all-time leader in penalty minutes?

12. What is the Lady Byng Trophy?

13. Which team has the most World Cup victories of all time?

14. Who is the World Cup career leader in goals?

15. Who is the Women's World Cup career leader in goals?

16. Who are the only two players to play and coach for winning World Cup teams?

17. What is the largest soccer stadium in the world?

18. What is the most goals scored in a World Cup final?

19. Which team has appeared in the most World Cup finals?

20. What was the championship game of the North American Soccer League known as?

Twenty Answers

Let's see if you got a kick—that's a soccer pun—out of this quiz.

1. Maurice "The Rocket" Richard scored 50 goals during the 1944–45 season. He beat the previous single-season record by five.

2. Technically, it was Billy Smith of the New York Islanders on November 28, 1979. But he wasn't actually aiming for the opposition's goal. He was the last player to touch the puck before Colorado's Rob Ramage accidentally put the puck in his own net.

   Ron Hextall of the Philadelphia Flyers was the first goalie to score a goal by actually shooting the puck into the opponent's net. He did it on December 8, 1987.

3. Bobby Hull and his son, Brett, are the only two father-and-son winners of the Hart Trophy, awarded to the NHL's Most Valuable Player. Bobby, playing for the Chicago Blackhawks, won it in 1965 and '66; Brett, playing for the St. Louis Blues, won it in 1991.

4. In 1917–18, Joe Malone of the Montreal Canadiens scored 44 goals in a 20-game season. That computes to an average of 2.2 goals a game.

5. Vladislav Tretiak, a Russian goalie, who led his team to gold medals in three Winter Olympics, was inducted in 1989.

6. Henri Richard, brother of Maurice Richard, played for 11 Stanley Cup championship teams while with the Montreal Canadiens.

7. Interestingly, they're both goaltenders and they both won playing for the Montreal Canadiens—Ken Dryden in 1971 and Patrick Roy in 1986.

8. The Philadelphia Flyers, who entered the league in 1967 and were known as the "Broad Street Bullies," beat the Boston Bruins in six games to win the Stanley Cup in 1974.

9. Phil Esposito of the Boston Bruins scored 126 points, on 49 goals and 77 assists, in the 1969–70 season. He was the first player to do it twice, scoring 152 (76 goals, 76 assists) in 1970–71.

10. Bob Johnson won the NCAA title three times with the University of Wisconsin (1977, '81, '83). He then led the Pittsburgh Penguins to the 1991 Stanley Cup.

Sports Strategies

To put Joe Malone's 2.2 goals-a-game average in perspective, Wayne Gretzky, the all-time leader in goals, averaged 1.7 goals a game. Had Malone maintained his pace over the 80-game season played today, he would've scored 172 goals, or 80 more than Gretzky's record of 92.

Two-Minute Warning

Remember, assists in hockey do not affect the score of the game in any way. Only goals count in the score. Assists, worth one point each, are a statistical measure for players only and count toward their individual point totals.

The Fundamentals

Penalty minutes are assessed when players commit such infractions as roughing, slashing with the stick, coming up high with a stick, interference, and tripping. Players are sent off the ice and into a penalty box for two, five, or ten minutes. For serious infractions, players can be disqualified for the rest of the game.

Sports Strategies

The Lady Byng Trophy has been awarded since 1925. During that time, only two defensemen have won it—Bill Quackenbush of the Detroit Red Wings in 1949 and Red Kelly, also of the Red Wings, in 1951, '53–54, and '61. Both are members of the Hockey Hall of Fame.

11. Dave "Tiger" Williams leads the NHL in career *penalty minutes* with 3,966 over his 14-year career (1975-88). That computes to more than 66 games.

12. The Lady Byng Trophy is awarded annually to the player "adjudged to have exhibited the best type of sportsmanship and gentlemanly conduct combined with a high standard of playing ability." It is named after Lady Evelyn Byng, wife of former Canadian Governor General Baron Byng. Frank Boucher of the New York Rangers, who played in the 1920s and '30s, has won the trophy the most times with seven.

13. Brazil, which has won the World Cup four times, leads in all-time victories with 53. Germany is second with 45, followed by Italy (38), Argentina (29), and France (21).

14. Gerd Muller of West Germany scored 14 career goals in World Cup competition. He competed in the 1970 and 1974 tournaments.

15. Michelle Akers of the United States scored 12 goals in Women's World Cup competition, including 10 in the 1991 tournament.

16. Mario Zegalo of Brazil won World Cup titles as a player in 1958 and 1962 and as a coach in 1970. Franz Beckenbauer of West Germany won the World Cup as a player in 1974 and as a coach in 1990.

17. The Maracana in Rio de Janeiro has held 200,000 spectators.

18. Brazil beat Sweden 5–2 in the 1958 final, held in Stockholm.

19. Brazil and West Germany (Germany these days) have appeared in six finals each. Brazil won four, Germany three.

20. The North American Soccer League's title game was called the Soccer Bowl.

Bet You Didn't Know ...

➤ Hockey rules in the nineteenth century provided for three ways to decide the end of a hockey game: when one team scored three goals, when the men had to return to the barracks (these rules applied to military men in Nova Scotia who played to keep in shape while waiting for invasion), and when a player fell through the ice and was in danger of drowning.

➤ Jean Beliveau of the Montreal Canadiens was the first hockey player to appear on the cover of *Sports Illustrated,* in 1956.

➤ Mark Recchi is the only player to take *penalty shots* in the same season for two different teams—Montreal and Philadelphia in 1995.

➤ The Sutter family has produced a record six NHL players. Brothers Brian, Darryl, Duane, Brent, Rich, and Ron all played in the NHL, starting in 1976. In 1982, all six were in the league at the same time.

➤ The Stanley Cup weighs 32 pounds and stands $35\frac{1}{2}$ inches tall.

➤ From 1962 through 1988, a span of 27 seasons, only six teams won the Stanley Cup—Toronto (1962–64, '67), Montreal (1965–66, '68–69, '71, '73, '76–79), Boston (1970, '72), Philadelphia (1974–75), the New York Islanders (1980–83), and Edmonton (1984–88).

The Fundamentals

A **penalty shot** in hockey is awarded to an offensive player who, on a breakaway, is illegally checked or impeded. The puck is placed at the center of the ice, and the player has a free try to score on the opposing goaltender. There are no other players on the ice except the shooter and the goalie.

➤ The longest hockey game ever played took place in the 1936 Stanley Cup semifinals. Detroit beat the Montreal Maroons 1–0 in the sixth overtime period. The elapsed time was 176 minutes, 30 seconds, or nearly the equivalent of three regulation games.

➤ Overtime periods for NHL regular-season games were reinstated in 1983, at five minutes, rather than the 20 minutes that had been played before 1942, when they were discontinued because of wartime restrictions.

➤ Pat Burns has won the Jack Adams Award, given to the NHL Coach of the Year, three times with three different teams—Montreal in 1989, Toronto in 1993, and Boston in 1998.

➤ In the 1928–29 season, George Hainsworth, a goalie for the Montreal Canadiens, registered 22 shutouts in 44 games. He won the first three Vezina Trophies awarded (1927–29).

➤ Bernie Parent of the Philadelphia Flyers holds the record for most wins by a goaltender in one season. In 1973–74, he posted 47 victories in helping the Flyers win the Stanley Cup.

Sports Strategies

NHL games consist of three 20-minute periods, followed by a five-minute overtime period if the game is tied at the end of regulation. If the teams remain tied after the five-minute overtime, that's how the result is recorded. In Stanley Cup play, however, if the game is tied at the end of regulation, teams continue to play 20-minute periods until a goal is scored.

A regulation tie signifies any game tied after regulation, but lost in overtime. They are worth one point to the losing team. A tie is any game in which neither team scores in the five-minute overtime. Each team gets one point.

➤ Darryl Sittler of the Toronto Maple Leafs holds the record for the most points in a game with 10. He had six goals and four assists against Boston in February 1976.

➤ The United States went 44 years between World Cup victories. The U.S. beat England 1–0 in 1950, then didn't win another game until beating Columbia 2–1 in 1994.

➤ The United States set a World Cup attendance record in 1994, when nearly 3.6 million fans attended the tournament games.

➤ St. Louis University has won the most NCAA men's Division I soccer titles with 10. Indiana University, University of San Francisco, and University of Virginia are tied for second with five each.

➤ The University of North Carolina has dominated the NCAA women's Division I soccer tournament. Since the tournament's inception in 1982, the Tar Heels have reached the final every year but one (1995) and won the championship 16 times, through 2001.

➤ Oleg Salenko of Russia holds the record for most goals in one World Cup game—5, against Cameroon in 1994.

➤ Of the 16 World Cup tournaments held, Brazil is the only country to compete in each one. Germany has appeared in all but one.

Say What?

Let's see what hockey and soccer players have to say about their sports.

➤ Lester Pearson, former prime minister of Canada: "This fastest of games (hockey) has become almost as much of a national symbol as the maple leaf."

➤ Wayne Gretzky, responding to a newspaper article that underestimated his ability: "When we were in Toronto earlier in the year, someone wrote that I wouldn't be in the top 10. When I read something like that, it gives me the drive to do what they say I can't do."

➤ Eric Lindros, Philadelphia Flyers center: "It's not necessarily the amount of time you spend at practice that counts; it's what you put into practice."

➤ Bobby Hull, the 10th leading goal scorer in NHL history, on players in 1974 making too much money: "Why should a guy with a half-million dollar contract want to have blood dripping down his face? Or sweat? Or play with bruises? Hell, they won't even play with bruised feelings now."

➤ Fred Shero, former coach of the Philadelphia Flyers: "If they want pretty skating, let 'em go to the Ice Capades."

➤ Shero, on coaching: "When you're a coach, you're miserable. When you're not a coach, you're more miserable."

➤ Derek Sanderson, former Boston Bruins center: "A hockey player must have three things planted in his head: hate, greed, and jealousy. He must hate the other guy, he must be greedy for the puck, and he must be jealous when he loses."

➤ Bill Barber, former Philadelphia Flyer and Hall of Fame member, on losing his teeth: "I was 14 when I lost them. The main thing was, we won that game, so I was the happiest. You hate to lose your teeth and the game, too."

➤ Johnny Bower, former Toronto Maple Leafs goaltender, on why he decided to become a goalie: "I just made up my mind that I was going to lose my teeth and have my face cut to pieces."

➤ Michelle Akers, member of the 1991 and 1999 U.S. Women's World Cup championship teams, on her injury-plagued career: "People

The Inside Skinny

The University of North Carolina women's soccer team, coached by Anson Dorrance, has usually had little trouble winning the NCAA championship. It has won 11 of its 16 titles by shutout. The combined score in the 16 title games is 53–4. In his 19 seasons, Dorrance has an overall record of 487–22–11.

Sports Strategies

Michelle Akers, a mainstay of the U.S. women's national soccer team from 1985 until her retirement in 2000, has overcome illness and numerous injuries. She has undergone more than 10 knee surgeries and suffers from Chronic Fatigue and Immune Dysfunction Syndrome, which also causes migraines, insomnia, and loss of balance and short-term memory. Still, she is one of only four players to score more than 100 goals in international competition.

are sick of seeing me get hurt, but that's who I am. I take big risks. Sometimes I fall flat on my face, but I also get some mountaintop moments."

➤ Pele, world-renowned soccer player, on what the game means to him: "(Soccer) is like a religion to me. I worship the ball, and I treat it like a god. Too many players think of a (soccer ball) as something to kick. They should be taught to caress it and to treat it like a precious gem."

➤ Mia Hamm, member of the 1991 and 1999 U.S. Women's World Cup championship teams, on the future of the Women's United Soccer League: "This will be the world's premier league for women's soccer. One of the things we realized and have known for a while is how deep the player pool is. The level of competition is going to be extremely high."

➤ Julie Foudy, member of the 1999 U.S. Women's World Cup championship team, on the impact of the team's victory: "I grew up watching Magic Johnson and Kareem Abdul-Jabbar, men I could never emulate. Girls need role models."

Bowman's the Best

You could make a pretty strong case that Scotty Bowman, the winningest coach in NHL history, should also be considered as the most successful coach of any team in any sport.

The Inside Skinny

Scotty Bowman is one of only two coaches in the four major sports to win championships with three different teams—Montreal, Pittsburgh, and Detroit. Guy Chamberlain, a former NFL coach, won titles with Canton, Cleveland, and Frankford (Pennsylvania) in the 1920s.

No matter where he's been—and he's been around—he has been a winner. And he's been at his best when it counts the most—the Stanley Cup playoffs.

The 2001–02 season will be Bowman's 30th as an NHL head coach. He has won 1,400 of his 2,389 games, including playoffs, and he has led teams to the Stanley Cup championship eight times, tying him with legendary former Montreal Canadiens coach Toe Blake.

Only twice in Bowman's first 29 seasons—1986–87 with the Buffalo Sabres—did his team fail to make the playoffs. His eight Stanley Cup titles came with three different teams—Montreal (1973, '76–79), Pittsburgh (1992), and Detroit (1997–98).

Bowman lost his first three appearances in the Stanley Cup finals—1968–70, while coaching the expansion St. Louis Blues. But ever since, he's been undefeated.

Said Guy Lafleur, who played for Bowman during his stint in Montreal: "I never saw anyone outcoach him."

Bowman's record backs up Lafleur's claim.

Scotty Bowman has stood the test of time, winning Stanley Cup championships from the 1970s to the 1990s.

Photo: Icon Sports Media

The Least You Need to Know

➤ Maurice "The Rocket" Richard was the first player in NHL history to score 50 goals in one season.

➤ Ron Hextall of the Philadelphia Flyers was the first goaltender to shoot a puck into the opponent's net.

➤ Henri Richard of the Montreal Canadiens played on the most Stanley Cup–winning teams, 11.

➤ Brazil has won four World Cup championships, the most of any nation.

➤ The 1999 U.S. Women's World Cup championship team gave a huge boost to women's soccer.

Part 6

The Olympic Spirit

Once every four years, we go crazy for the Olympics. TV networks pay exorbitant fees for the television rights, advertisers fall over themselves to associate their products with the Games, and we make their efforts worthwhile by tuning in.

In almost every case the Olympics, Summer and Winter, are defined by the performances of the athletes—Carl Lewis winning four gold medals in 1984; Mark Spitz winning seven in 1972; Mary Lou Retton scoring a perfect 10 on a vault in 1984; Peggy Fleming turning in a flawless figure skating performance in 1968; the U.S. Hockey team doing the improbable by beating the Russians in 1980.

Sometimes it's not the spectacular, but the unfortunate that gets our attention. And if you were a member of the 1972 U.S. Basketball team, there was nothing more unfortunate than the last three seconds of the gold medal game against Russia.

Fun in the Summertime

In This Chapter

➤ Ancient history

➤ Track and field

➤ Swimming

➤ Basketball

➤ Gymnastics

Every four years, the eyes of the world turn to whichever city is hosting the Summer Olympics. And for two weeks, those eyes stay glued to the Games as viewers watch sports that don't even create blips on the radar screen any other time. Be honest, would you watch fencing if it weren't part of the Olympics?

But that's the power and the appeal of the Olympics. Advertisers shell out big bucks to be a part of the festivities, and so does the network that televises them.

The Olympics have produced great athletes, remarkable performances, and even a bit of controversy—like the gold medal in men's basketball that the United States should've won, but didn't.

Let the Games Begin!

The Olympics began in 796 B.C.E. as a religious festival. And things were going along quite nicely until Theodosius I, a Roman emperor and killjoy, put an end to them, as he stopped all pagan festivals in 393 A.D. The Olympics, you see, celebrated Zeus, a Greek god.

It wasn't until 1894 that the Games were revived, thanks to Baron Pierre de Coubertin, a French educator. De Coubertin was giving a speech to international sports leaders at the Sorbonne in Paris. He came up with the idea of reviving the Games on an international scale. The rest, as they say, is history.

The modern Olympics were born. The first Games were held in Athens, Greece, in 1896. Nearly 250 athletes from 14 countries competed.

Americans won gold medals in nine of the 12 track and field events, but Greece won the most medals with 47. Except for the war years—1916, 1940, and 1944—the Olympics have been held every four years since 1896. The 2004 Summer Games will take place in Athens, Greece.

Sports Strategies

Over the years, American athletes have dominated the Olympics. The U.S. has won 2,116 medals, more than double the number won by Russia, No. 2 on the list (1,010). That ratio also holds for the number of gold medals won. The U.S. has 872 gold medals. Russia is second with 395.

Runners and Jumpers

The Olympics have been a showcase for track and field stars since their inception, and what a show some of those stars have put on, using a variety of talents—speed, strength, endurance, all-round athleticism, or all of the above.

And sometimes, the performances go far beyond winning a medal, as in the case of Jesse Owens, whose showing in the 1936 Games made a powerful political statement.

The Inside Skinny

Jesse Owens, the son of an Alabama sharecropper, moved to Cleveland when he was 9 years old. He took to running by necessity, because his family was too poor to afford any athletic equipment. As a senior at Cleveland East Technical High School, he ran the 100-yard dash in 9.4 seconds, tying the scholastic world record.

Making a Statement

The Olympic Games of 1936, held in Berlin, were referred to as the Nazi Olympics, because of Adolf Hitler's prediction of Aryan supremacy. Hitler didn't give the United States and its "African auxiliaries," as he called them, a chance.

But Jesse Owens, an African American and one of those "African auxiliaries," showed Hitler a thing or two. Did he ever!

The first event in which Owens competed in Berlin was the 100-meter dash. And sure enough, Hitler was watching and expecting a victory by one of his runners.

Jesse Owens won four gold medals at the 1936 Olympics in Berlin, but the impact of his perform-ance went beyond sports.

Photo: ArtToday

Owens, running in Lane 1, used a late surge to not only win the race, but set an Olympic record of 10.3 seconds.

And that was only the beginning.

Owens went on to win three more gold medals—for the long jump, the 200 meters, and the 400-meter relay. In the long jump he set an Olympic record at 26 feet, 5$\frac{1}{2}$ inches; he finished the 200 meters in 20.7 seconds, another Olympic record; and as a member of the 400-meter relay team, he helped set a world record of 39.8 seconds.

Owens was the first man to win four gold medals in one Olympic Games, a distinc-tion he would enjoy until 1984, when Carl Lewis won four golds.

Owens was named the Associated Press Male Athlete of the Year, but he didn't win the Sullivan Award, given to the year's outstanding amateur athlete. That went to Glenn Morris, the Olympic decathlon champion, who was white.

Because he was African American, Owens was never invited to the White House to meet the president, nor was he allowed past the front door of the Waldorf-Astoria in New York for a reception in his honor.

Four in '84

If Carl Lewis isn't the greatest all-round athlete in Olympic history, he certainly de-serves a spot high on the list.

It's not just that Lewis won medals, it's that he won them in four different Olympics. And had the United States not boycotted the 1980 Games, he would've made it five.

Lewis's first Olympics were the 1984 Games in Los Angeles. It was there that he equaled Jesse Owens's milestone performance of winning four gold medals. He won his medals in the same events as Owens did—the 100-meter dash, the 200 meters, the long jump, and as a member of the 400-meter relay team.

Sports Strategies

The 1980 Summer Olympics, held in Moscow, were boycotted by the United States and 63 other countries in protest of the Soviet Union's invasion of Afghanistan. President Jimmy Carter made the highly controversial decision.

Two-Minute Warning

Carl Lewis did not have an easy time of it growing up, mainly because he grew too fast. He was an undersized kid until he experienced a growth spurt when he was 15 years old. The spurt was so severe that he needed to use crutches for about a month while his body adjusted to the sudden change in size.

At the 1988 Games at Seoul, South Korea, Lewis won gold in the 100 meters and the long jump, and a silver in the 200 meters. When the 100 meters was completed, it appeared Lewis had won the silver, finishing second to Ben Johnson of Canada. But Johnson tested positive for steroids, an illegal performance-enhancing drug, and Lewis was awarded the gold. He ran a world-record 9.92 seconds.

By the time the 1992 Games rolled around, Lewis seemed to be past his prime. He failed to qualify for the 100 and 200 meters, but he did earn a spot on the 400-meter relay. He rose to the occasion, winning gold medals in the long jump and anchoring the 400-meter relay team to a gold medal in world-record time (37.40).

The last medal won by Lewis came at the 1996 Games in Atlanta, where he won another gold medal in the long jump. That brought his total gold medals to nine, one short of the all-time record set by Ray Ewry, a U.S. track and field athlete in the early twentieth century.

As you might expect, Lewis won a slew of awards, including the 1981 Sullivan Award as the outstanding amateur athlete, and the 1983 and 1984 Associated Press Male Athlete of the Year Award.

Out of the Blue

When Bob Beamon entered the 1968 Olympics in Mexico City, he was a favorite to win a medal in the long jump. But no one had an inkling that he'd make history.

On Beamon's first jump of the finals, he experienced a jump that he said "felt like a regular jump." It was anything but. Beamon soared through the air, going so far that he hurled himself out of the back of the jumping pit.

Chapter 21 ➤ *Fun in the Summertime*

The world record at the time was 27 feet, $4^3/_4$ inches. Beamon had leaped an astounding 29 feet, $2^1/_2$ inches. He had taken a record that had been improved upon just $8^1/_2$ inches in the previous 33 years and obliterated it.

Wrote Coles Phinizy in *Sports Illustrated:* "(Beamon) had taken off into thin air in the year 1968 and landed somewhere in the next century."

Beamon's remarkable leap was a once-and-done thing. He never jumped farther than 27 feet for the rest of his career. But that doesn't take away from the time he did.

Superwoman

Jackie Joyner-Kersee is the total package—arguably America's greatest all-around female athlete, and blessed with style and charisma.

Joyner-Kersee first showed an interest in track and field at age 9. She and her friends made a makeshift jumping pit out of potato chip bags for her to jump into. When she watched long jump competition from the 1976 Summer Olympics, she vowed she would someday make the team.

In high school, she played volleyball and basketball as well as competing in track and field. She went to UCLA on a basketball scholarship and started for four years. She also was a champion long jumper.

Because she was so athletic, her coach, Bob Kersee (who would eventually become her husband), suggested she practice multiple events.

It turned out to be great advice, because Jackie Joyner-Kersee excelled in the *heptathlon,* a series of seven events. At the time, the heptathlon was a little-known event, but starting in 1982, Joyner-Kersee brought it to prominence.

At the 1984 Olympic trials, Joyner-Kersee broke the American record by scoring 6,659 points. At the Games, she fell five points short of the gold medal and won the silver. She blamed her poor mental approach for falling short and vowed it would never happen again.

Sports Strategies

Bob Beamon's record stood for 23 years. Everyone assumed that if anyone broke the record, it would be Carl Lewis, the four-time Olympic gold medalist. But at the 1991 World Championships in Tokyo, Mike Powell of the United States jumped 29 feet, $4^1/_2$ inches to beat Beamon's mark by two inches. As of this writing, Powell's record still stood.

The Fundamentals

The **heptathlon** is an event for women that consists of seven events—200-meter dash, high jump, long jump, javelin, shot put, 100-meter hurdles, and 800-meter run. Points based on the finish in each individual event are totaled. The competitor with the most points wins.

231

Joyner-Kersee kept her promise. At the 1986 Goodwill Games in Moscow, she was the first woman to exceed 7,000 points, setting a world record of 7,148 points. A few weeks later at the U.S. Olympic Sports Festival, she accumulated 7,158 points.

Joyner-Kersee won the gold medal in the heptathlon at the 1988 and 1992 Olympics, the gold medal in the long jump in 1988, and the bronze medal in the long jump in 1992. In 1996, she withdrew from the heptathlon because of injury, but still managed one more bronze in the long jump.

And she did it in dramatic fashion. Entering her last jump, Joyner-Kersee ranked sixth among the eight in the finals. But on her last jump in Olympic competition, she soared 22 feet, $11^3/_4$ inches to earn the bronze by one inch.

Jackie Joyner-Kersee closed out her career in style—which is exactly what you'd expect.

Splish, Splash

Swimming and diving are among the highlights of any Olympic Games. The speed of the swimmers and the graceful athleticism of the divers make for must-see TV.

Swimmers Mark Spitz and Matt Biondi, with 11 medals each, are the all-time leading medal winners among U.S. men. For the women, Jenny Thompson leads with 10, followed by Dara Torres with nine and Shirley Babashoff with eight.

The U.S. also has excelled in diving, having produced Greg Louganis, the most accomplished diver in Olympic history.

Golden Obsession

Mark Spitz entered the 1968 Olympics in Montreal predicting greatness. He claimed he would come home with six gold medals. Instead he won two, both in relays.

By the time the 1972 Games rolled around, Spitz had worked long and hard to make up for his disappointing showing four years earlier and to please his father, Arnold, who was a taskmaster of the highest order.

At the 1972 Games in Munich, Spitz did the unthinkable: He entered seven events, won seven gold medals, and set seven world records. No one had ever won more gold medals in a single Olympics.

The Inside Skinny

Arnold Spitz, Mark's father, was as demanding as a drill sergeant. His motto was, "Swimming isn't important, winning is." Once before a race, he told his son: "There are eight guys in that pool for the race, but only one is a winner. The others are bums." Obviously, Arnold Spitz wasn't one to mince words.

Spitz won the 100- and 200-meter butterfly, as well as the 100- and 200-meter freestyle, and was a member of the winning 400- and 800-meter freestyle and 400-meter medley relay teams.

Overall, Spitz won 26 national championships and set 23 world and 35 American records.

The Best Ever

If you tried to construct the perfect diver, you'd come up with Greg Louganis, who was a blend of athleticism, strength, and grace—hence, the comparisons to Nureyev, the great Russian ballet dancer.

Louganis won a silver medal at the 1976 Olympics and couldn't compete at the 1980 Games because of the United States' boycott, but made history at the 1984 Olympics in Los Angeles. He became the first diver ever to surpass the 700-point mark and the first to win the platform and springboard events at the same Games since 1928.

Louganis won two more gold medals at the 1988 Games in Seoul, South Korea. But not without some anxious moments.

While qualifying in the springboard competition, he hit his head on the board. The cut required five stitches, but Louganis was able to return some 20 hours later and win the gold medal.

Louganis compiled quite a resumé during his career, which ended with the 1988 Games. He won forty-seven national titles, six world championships, three NCAA championships, and five Olympic medals, four of them gold.

Sports Strategies

Greg Louganis made his mark at competitions other than the Olympics. At the 1982 World Championships, he became the first diver ever to receive a perfect 10 score from all seven judges at a major international event.

The Inside Skinny

The U.S. Olympic basketball teams were always made up of the best college players, who had never played together before. The opposing countries sent teams that, while not technically professionals, played together year-round. After the U.S. won the bronze medal at the 1988 Games, the decision was made to allow NBA players to participate.

Hooping It Up

Olympic basketball has been dominated by the United States. Only twice since the game became an Olympic sport in 1936 has the U.S. failed to bring home the gold, including 1972, when America got robbed.

But in 1992, when professionals were allowed to play for the U.S. team, the Red, White, and Blue made it clear which nation reigned supreme in basketball.

Sports Strategies

Prior to the game against the Soviet Union, the United States had no trouble with any of its opponents. In the eight games before the gold medal game, the U.S. won by an average of 32.5 points. The closest game was seven points, against Brazil; the most lopsided was 66 points against Japan.

The Inside Skinny

The Dream Team attracted attention worldwide—not just from the fans and the media, but from the opposition as well. Players from other teams sought out Dream Team members for autographs. One member of the opposition, being guarded by Magic Johnson, waved to a teammate on the bench with a camera, making sure a picture was taken with both players in the shot.

The Gold Medal That Wasn't

The United States had won seven straight gold medals and 63 straight games in Olympic basketball competition, entering the 1972 Olympics in Munich. It looked as if they would extend both streaks.

Doug Collins, who went on to become a fine NBA player and coach, made two foul shots with three seconds left to give the U.S. a 50–49 lead over Russia in the gold medal game.

The Russians inbounded the ball, but referee Renato Righetto of Brazil stopped play with one second on the clock. It was decided that the Soviet coach, Vladimir Kondrashkin, had called a timeout, after which the ball was inbounded with three seconds left. The Russians missed a desperation shot and the Americans began to celebrate—prematurely, as it turned out.

Kondrashkin protested that the clock had been reset incorrectly. So the Soviets got a third chance to replay the final three seconds. And the third time proved to be the charm, as the Russians got the ball to its star player, Alexander Belov, who made the basket for a 51–50 win.

The U.S. filed an official protest, which was denied. Then the U.S. came up with a protest of its own: The team voted unanimously to refuse its silver medals.

Dream Team Rules

The second time the United States failed to win the basketball gold medal was 1988, when it could do no better than bronze. That marked the last time the team was made up of college players. Starting in 1992, NBA players were allowed to compete, and the result was the Dream Team, called the greatest collection of talent ever assembled in any sport.

The team included Michael Jordan, Magic Johnson, Larry Bird, Charles Barkley, David Robinson, Patrick Ewing, Karl Malone, Scottie Pippen, Chris Mullen, Clyde Drexler, and John Stockton.

The games weren't the least bit competitive, but no one was complaining, because this was an event—a happening unlikely to be duplicated.

The U.S. won their games by an average of 44 points, and defeated Croatia for the gold medal 117–85.

Flipping for Gold

You watch these gymnasts fly around the mat, hurl themselves into midair, and flip every which way, and you can't help but wonder how it's possible to do such things.

But they not only do it, they make it look as effortless as walking across the street.

No gymnasts made it look as effortless as Olga Korbut and Mary Lou Retton—or made more of an impact on the sport.

The Revolutionary

She stood just 4' 11" tall and weighed all of 80 pounds, but in spite of her small stature, Olga Korbut turned in a heavyweight performance at the 1972 Olympics in Munich.

Korbut, subbing for an injured teammate, changed gymnastics forever with her athletic, acrobatic routines and her cheery demeanor.

Her winning smile made her a huge favorite with the fans, and the joy she displayed while she performed was something never before seen.

Korbut won three individual medals at the 1972 Olympics—gold in the floor exercise and balance beam, and silver in the uneven bars. She also helped Russia win the team gold medal.

And even though she relinquished the spotlight to Nadia Comeneci of Romania at the 1976 Olympics, Korbut still managed to win a silver on the balance beam.

The Inside Skinny

After the 1976 Olympics, Olga Korbut retired and became a coach in Minsk, Russia, located near Chernobyl, site of a 1987 nuclear reactor explosion. Korbut developed a thyroid condition from the radiation poisoning. But she turned a negative into a positive by using her celebrity to help raise funds for the victims of the accident.

Star Power

Mary Lou Retton didn't have the classic build of most female gymnasts. She was boxier and more compact than usual. But it didn't keep her from becoming a star of the 1984 Olympics and an icon in her sport.

Retton made a name for herself with one vault. That's all it took.

Romania's Ekaterina Szabo, the reigning world champion in the all-around competition, held a .05 lead over Retton entering the final event, the vault. By the time Retton completed her attempt, the gold was hers.

Talk about rising to the occasion! Retton's vault earned a perfect 10 from every judge.

From that vault forward, life was never the same for Retton, who exuded charisma and was adored by the public. She was named the Associated Press Female Athlete of the Year in 1984; appeared on the cover of *Sports Illustrated* with hurdler Edwin Moses, sharing the Sportsman of the Year award; and even got herself on a Wheaties box.

In addition to all that, Retton also had staying power. Nine years after her golden vault, a national poll ranked her and figure skater Dorothy Hamill as the two most popular female athletes in the United States.

The Least You Need to Know

➤ Baron Pierre de Coubertin is credited with bringing about the modern Olympics.

➤ Jesse Owens made a political statement with his four gold medals in the 1936 Games.

➤ Jackie Joyner–Kersee is renowned as one of America's greatest Olympic athletes.

➤ Swimmer Mark Spitz won a record seven gold medals at the 1972 Olympics.

➤ The U.S. lost the basketball gold medal in 1972 on a controversial call.

➤ The 1992 Dream Team is regarded as the greatest team ever assembled in any sport.

➤ Mary Lou Retton scored a perfect 10 from all judges with her vault in the all-around competition at the 1984 Games.

Chapter 22

Chills, Thrills, and Spills

In This Chapter

➤ Beginning of the Winter Games

➤ Figure skaters

➤ Speed skaters

➤ Hockey

➤ Skiers

Although not as old as the Summer Olympics, the Winter Games have become exceedingly popular. Whether it be the grace and artistry of the figure skaters or the no-fear attitude of the downhill skiers, the Winter Olympics provide plenty of action.

In addition to learning about some of the most successful skaters and skiers in Winter Olympics history, we'll also take a look at one of the most stunning upsets, not just in Olympic history, but in sports history. I'll give you a hint: "Do you believe in miracles? Yes!"

Let the (Winter) Games Begin!

The Winter Olympics took a while to get started, although not for lack of effort. The first thought of staging the Winter Games occurred in 1908, when figure skating was still part of the Summer Olympics.

The organizers of the 1916 Games planned to start a Skiing Olympics, but the outbreak of World War I in 1914 canceled the Games, which didn't resume until 1920.

It wasn't until 1924 that the International Olympic Committee sanctioned what was then called "International Winter Sports Week." It featured skiing, speed skating, figure skating, ice hockey, and bobsledding.

Eventually, International Winter Sports Week, which you have to admit is a bit of a mouthful, became known as the Winter Olympics.

From 1924 through 1992, except for 1940 and 1944, when the Games were canceled because of World War II, the Winter Games were held every four years. That cycle was broken in 1994, when the Games were staged in Lillehammer, France, two years after the previous Winter Olympics. The schedule was changed to keep the Winter and Summer Games from taking place in the same year, and now they alternate every two years.

Sports Strategies

The United States has played host to three Winter Olympics—1932 in Lake Placid, New York; 1960 in Squaw Valley, Idaho; and 1980 in Lake Placid. The 2002 Winter Games, the XIX Olympiad, will be held in Salt Lake City, Utah, February 8–24.

Compulsory Figures

Without a doubt, figure skating, especially women's figure skating, is among the highlights of every Winter Olympics.

The television ratings for figure skating usually go through the roof, and over the years, figure skaters, especially women's figure skaters, have emerged as the Games' biggest stars.

Starting with Sonja Henie of Norway, who won an unprecedented three gold medals (1928, '32, '36) and continuing through Tenley Albright, Carol Heiss, and Peggy Fleming of the U.S., the skaters kept getting more athletic.

On the men's side, Dick Button of the U.S., who went on to become a popular television commentator for ABC Sports, won two gold medals (1948, '52). By the way, he's the last male figure skater to win multiple gold medals. But it's the women who take center stage when it comes to figure skating, so let's look at the careers of some of the greats.

An Ice Skating Icon

In addition to dominating the sport, Peggy Fleming changed figure skating, much like Sonja Henie did in her day. Fleming introduced athleticism and combined it with a certain artistic elegance. The resulting style made her one of the most popular skaters of all time. She executed difficult jumps and combinations of jumps, and she was also blessed with an exceptional sense of music and dance.

Fleming began skating when she was nine, and her father, a press operator at a newspaper, took a part-time job to help pay for training, rink fees, and travel expenses.

Fleming finished sixth at the 1964 Winter Olympics, and then in 1965, at age 15, started a run of five straight U.S. Championships and was the youngest ever to win a U.S. title.

Fleming's biggest moment came in the 1968 Games at Grenoble, France. Skating in outfits her mother made for her, she won the gold medal—the only gold won by an American athlete in 1968—and helped raise the profile of figure skating to unprecedented levels.

Fleming, who won three consecutive World Championships, starting in 1968, appeared in ice shows and on television specials after she retired. She also worked as a commentator for ABC Sports.

America's Sweetheart

There was something about Dorothy Hamill that endeared her to the American public in a big way. Part of it was her talent on the ice, and part of it was her personal style and charisma. She was attractive in an All-American girl sort of way, and her popularity was so great that girls all over the country imitated her hairstyle—a "wedge" cut that became all the rage.

Hamill was a stronger, more athletic skater than Peggy Fleming, and she and her coach, Carlo Fassi (who had also coached Fleming), worked to emphasize her jumping ability. They also went so far as to create a new move, dubbed the *Hamill Camel*.

Hamill made her mark initially by winning three straight U.S. Championships, beginning in 1974. A spectacular performance at the 1976 Olympics at Innsbruck, Austria, earned Hamill the gold medal.

After the Olympics, Hamill turned pro and joined the Ice Capades, signing a seven-figure deal. She left the Ice Capades in 1984 and went on to win the World Figure Skating Championship four years in a row (1984–87).

The Inside Skinny

Peggy Fleming was long retired when she made headlines again, although this time not for figure skating. In 1999, Fleming was back in the spotlight, this time as a breast cancer survivor. She appeared on TV and radio shows, telling her story, stressing the need for mammograms and inspiring everyone with her courage.

The Fundamentals

The **Hamill Camel,** created by Dorothy Hamill and her coach, Carlo Fassi, is a camel spin into a sit spin. A camel spin is done on one leg with the nonskating leg extended in the air parallel to the ice. A sit spin is just what it sounds like—a spin done while crouching like a catcher in baseball.

But Hamill wasn't finished with the Ice Capades. With the ice show teetering on the brink of bankruptcy in 1994, Hamill rode to the rescue. Oh, she didn't just make a donation; she bought the entire troupe and kept it going.

That was another gold medal performance.

Beating the Odds

When Scott Hamilton was just a toddler, you would've never bet on him to become a figure skating champion. Hamilton suffered from a serious disease called Schwachman's syndrome. It is a rare intestinal condition that prevents the body from absorbing nutrients.

Sports Strategies

Scott Hamilton overcame his personal difficulties with hard work and lots of practice. But another key to his development into an Olympic gold medalist was the coaching change he made in 1980, switching from Carlo Fassi, who coached Peggy Fleming and Dorothy Hamill, to Don Laws, who instituted a more rigorous training program. A year later, Hamilton won his first World Championship.

Hamilton had to be kept alive by feeding tubes, but eventually he got stronger and he even began to skate. The exercise helped his condition improve.

Still, Hamilton wasn't very big or strong, and his prospects of becoming a champion were slim. But he was a tireless worker and his practice paid off. At the 1981 World Championships, Hamilton registered his first perfect score and won the gold medal, his first of four straight. He also won three straight U.S. titles.

But his big moment came at the 1984 Olympics in Sarajevo, Yugoslavia, where he won the gold medal.

For Hamilton, the gold medal wasn't an end, it was a beginning. He turned pro after the Olympics and founded and coproduced Stars on Ice, a showcase for many of the best skaters in the world.

Much like Peggy Fleming, who is a breast cancer survivor, Hamilton had to overcome cancer. In 1997, he was diagnosed with testicular cancer. He also went public with his condition, hoping to help make men aware of the importance of self-examination and early detection. Not surprisingly, given his history, Hamilton was back on the ice in less than a year.

On Your Mark ...

Speed skating requires precisely what the name implies—speed. Duh! Skaters compete head-to-head on an oval track—one on the outside lane, the other on the inside lane. So that one skater doesn't have the advantage of the inside lane throughout, at the halfway point the skaters cross over and change lanes.

Bonnie Blair and Eric Heiden, both of the United States, are among the best speed skaters in Olympic history. Let's find out why.

Doing What Comes Naturally

When Bonnie Blair says skating is second nature to her, as effortless as walking, believe her. Born into a skating family, she began entering races at the ripe old age of four. By the time she was seven, she won the Illinois State championship.

At age 16, Blair failed to make the 1980 Olympic team, but she qualified for the 1984 Games and finished eighth in the 500 meters. It was a respectable showing for her first time out, but the best was yet to come.

Blair decided she was too lazy and stepped up her training regimen to include weight training, running, biking, and roller skating. The result was lots of time spent in the winner's circle.

Blair was the U.S. sprint champion from 1985 to 1990, and in 1986 she set the world record in the 500 meters. She won gold in the 500 meters, setting a world record, and bronze in the 1,000 meters at the 1988 Olympics.

But that was just a warm-up for the 1992 and 1994 Games, where she won the 500 and the 1,000 meters at each Olympics and became the first U.S. athlete to win the same event in three straight Olympics.

Blair is the most decorated athlete, man or woman, in U.S. Winter Olympic history with six medals (five gold, one bronze).

But Blair wasn't finished. In 1994 and 1995, she won the 500 and the 1,000 meters at the World Cup and at the World Sprint Championships.

Eric the Great

What Eric Heiden accomplished at the 1980 Winter Olympics in Lake Placid will likely never be duplicated. You could say he dominated the speed skating competition, but that wouldn't do justice to Heiden's performance, which was domination squared.

The Fundamentals

Speed skating is contested at five different distances for men and women. The men race at 500, 1,000, 1,500, 5,000, and 10,000 meters. The women race at 500, 1,000, 1,500, 3,000, and 5,000 meters.

The Inside Skinny

Bonnie Blair earned more than just victories as the result of dominating her sport. She also got the perks associated with stardom—her face on the Kellogg's Corn Flakes box, a street named for her in her hometown of Champaign, Illinois, and a vanity license plate (GOLD X5).

The Inside Skinny

The night before the 10,000-meter race, Eric Heiden spent hours tossing and turning in bed before finally falling asleep. And he overslept, giving himself almost no time to eat breakfast or perform his usual warm-up. But it didn't matter a bit. Heiden not only won the 10,000 meters, he broke the world record by a whopping 6 seconds.

Sports Strategies

There was good reason the United States ice hockey team was given no chance against the powerful Soviets, recognized as the best team in the world. In an exhibition prior to the Olympics, the Soviets and the U.S. faced off at Madison Square Garden in New York City. The Soviets didn't have too much trouble with the American amateurs. The final score—10–3.

Heiden entered each of the five distances (500, 1,000, 1,500, 5,000, 10,000) and came away with five—count 'em—five gold medals. No one has ever won more gold medals in a single Winter Olympics.

Bill Rodgers, one of America's great marathoners, compared Heiden's feat to a runner winning a gold medal at every distance, from the 400 meters to the 10,000.

Heiden had the chance to cash in on his Olympic gold rush by endorsing a slew of products, but he accepted only a few, preferring not to sell himself the way Mark Spitz and Bruce Jenner, an Olympic decathlon champ, did.

After he retired from speed skating, he took up cycling and won the 1985 U.S. Pro Cycling Championship. These days, Heiden is a practicing orthopedist in California.

Miracle on Ice

Conventional wisdom made it crystal clear that the United States hockey team had absolutely no chance—zero, zip, nada—of beating the Soviet Union in the semifinals of the 1980 Olympic ice hockey tournament.

The Soviets were the equivalent of a professional team, playing together regularly throughout the year. The Americans, on the other hand, were a collection of college players and amateurs put together expressly for the Olympics. Professionals from the National Hockey League weren't eligible for Olympic competition back then, and even if they had been, the game hadn't developed to the point that there were a lot of highly talented American-born professionals.

So the odds against the Americans beating the Soviets and advancing to the gold medal game were long.

Thankfully, the odds don't always play out and conventional wisdom isn't always foolproof.

The U.S. fell behind to the Soviets 2–0, but Mark Johnson scored in the final second of the first period to cut the deficit in half. The goal by Johnson also caused Soviet coach Viktor Tikhonov to remove goaltender Vladislav Tretiak, who was nothing short of a legend, and replace him with Vladimir Myshkin, who was nowhere near as experienced.

The Soviets took a 3–2 lead in the second period, but the U.S. tied it at 3–3 in the third on another goal by Johnson. By this time the fans in the jam-packed arena were beside themselves, sensing the possibility of an upset.

They got their wish when Mike Eruzione, the U.S. team captain, whose heart and soul typified the Americans, scored the game-winner.

United States 4, Soviets 3.

And as time ran out, Al Michaels, who called the game on ABC Sports, came up with one of the most memorable calls in broadcasting history: "Do you believe in miracles? *Yes!*"

Of course, there was still the small matter of the gold medal game to worry about. Having expended so much energy to beat the Soviets, who knew how much the Americans would have left in the tank? Turns out, they had enough. The U.S. scored three goals in the third period to defeat Finland 4–2 and bring home the gold.

You bet we believe in miracles.

Two-Minute Warning

You might think that Mike Eruzione, the captain of the U.S. Olympic hockey team in 1980, was a superstar player who went on to a fine career in the National Hockey League. Well, you'd be wrong on both counts. Eruzione wasn't a great player, but his heart, enthusiasm, and work ethic did wonders for the U.S. team, which won the gold medal.

Downhill Racers

There may be nothing more thrilling than the sight of an alpine skier tearing down the mountain, trying to beat the clock. They go so fast and seemingly so recklessly that you wonder how in the world they remain upright. In this section, we'll learn about three skiers who have done it better than most.

Hitting a Triple

Jean-Claude Killy of France is one of the most famous names in Olympic skiing. From 1966 through the 1968 Olympics in Grenoble, France, he just about owned the sport.

In the 1966–67 season, he won every downhill race he entered, as well as the World Cup, which is awarded for consistency in a series of international races. He won his second World Cup the following season.

But it was at the 1968 Olympics where he made the biggest news. Killy won gold medals in the *downhill,* the *slalom,* and the *giant slalom,* making him only the second skier in Olympic history to accomplish the triple.

There was one bit of controversy in Killy's victory in the slalom. Austria's Karl Schranz, who was Killy's main competition, claimed an unidentified man came onto the course during his second run.

The Fundamentals

In Alpine skiing, the **downhill** is the longest, highest-speed race with the fewest turns. The **giant slalom** is shorter and has lower speed and more gates, which the skiers have to zigzag around, than a downhill, but is longer and faster than a **slalom.**

Sports Strategies

Jean-Claude Killy made his mark in Olympic history in ways other than careening down the mountainside and winning gold medals. He served as co-president of the 1992 Games held in Albertville, France.

So Schranz was allowed to take another run, and he ended up with a better time than Killy. But Killy was awarded the gold because Schranz missed two gates on the first run. Of course, Schranz insisted the reason he missed the gates was because of the man on the course. No matter, the Jury of Appeal ruled in Killy's favor and the triple was his.

By the way, the other skier to win the downhill, slalom, and giant slalom was Anton Sailer of Austria in 1956.

The Daredevil

Besides being recognized as one of the greatest down-hill skiers of all time, which he is, Franz Klammer of Austria is also known as the star of one of the most exciting, most unbelievable, and most replayed ski runs in Olympic history.

If you've seen it, you know what I'm talking about. If you haven't seen it, keep your fingers crossed that you get the chance.

At the 1976 Games, Klammer was the favorite in the downhill; he had won the first of four straight World Cup championships in 1975. But entering his final Olympic run, he trailed Bernhard Russi of Switzerland by a mere fraction of a second.

What Klammer managed on that final run has to be seen to be believed. He barreled down the mountain at break-neck speed. Sometimes he was literally flying through the air; other times he looked as if he were on the verge of soaring off the course.

But he made it to the finish line, miraculously, and won the gold medal by a third of a second.

Picabo, We See You

The first thing that got our attention was her name, Picabo, pronounced *peek-a-boo*. I kid you not. Her parents, who described themselves as "classic flower children," named her for a town in Idaho. Picabo is the Native American word for "shining waters."

Picabo Street fought back from serious injury to win a gold medal in super giant slalom at the 1998 Winter Olympics.

Photo: Icon Sports Media

Street, a bit of a tomboy growing up, began skiing when her elementary school started a weekly program. In 1988, at age 16, she was a member of the U.S. Ski Team, but in 1990 she was thrown off the team because she was out of shape.

But Street eventually got herself physically fit, rejoined the team in 1991, and at the 1994 Olympics in Lillehammer, Norway, won the silver medal in the downhill.

In 1995 and 1996, she was the women's World Cup downhill champion. In 1996, she suffered a serious knee injury, tearing her anterior cruciate ligament, which sidelined her for six months.

But she persevered to recover, and at the 1998 Games in Nagano, Japan, Street returned to win the gold medal in the super giant slalom.

The Inside Skinny

The first three years of Picabo Street's life she went nameless. Her birth certificate listed her only as "Baby Girl." Her parents, Stubby and Dee Street, traveled extensively, and when they ended up in Mexico, authorities there required a name on Baby Girl's passport. That's when they flashed back to the small town in Idaho and came up with Picabo.

The Least You Need to Know

➤ The first Winter Olympics were held in 1924.

➤ Peggy Fleming and Dorothy Hamill brought athleticism to figure skating.

➤ Bonnie Blair is the most decorated American Winter Olympic athlete, male or female.

➤ Eric Heiden won five gold medals in the 1980 Olympics.

➤ The U.S. hockey team pulled one of the most stunning upsets in Olympic history in 1980, beating the Soviets.

➤ Jean-Claude Killy became the second skier to win three events at one Olympics in 1968.

Game Time

By this time, you should be getting used to the drill. This is the chapter in which you'll be tested and you'll get the answers. You'll also be given your fill of interesting facts and figures, as well as memorable quotes.

In the last section of the chapter, we'll take a look at two of the most inspiring stories in sports history—Lance Armstrong and Greg LeMond. They haven't made their names in the Olympics, although cycling is an Olympic sport, but what they've overcome to become champions is inspiring stuff.

Twenty Questions

This Olympic-themed quiz should test your knowledge. On your mark, get set, let's go!

1. Which four U.S. Olympic men's basketball coaches won a gold medal and an NCAA Championship?

2. Who coached the U.S. men in the 1988 Games when they won the bronze medal?

3. In what year did tennis return as an Olympic sport?

4. Who was the first coach of the U.S. women's Olympic basketball team?

5. Who is the only man to win the 200 and 400 meters in the same Olympics?

6. What U.S. woman holds the record for winning the most silver medals?

7. What Hall of Fame golfer won two Olympic gold medals in track and field?

8. Which competitor in the *steeplechase* ran one extra lap, but still managed to win the gold medal?

9. What two women are tied for the most career gold medals in Olympic diving?

10. Who was the first American woman to win three gold medals in one Olympics?

11. What Olympic gold medal winner became a movie star after he was finished competing?

12. Who is the youngest woman to win a Winter Olympics gold medal?

13. Who coached the U.S. hockey team to the 1980 gold medal?

14. Which country has won the most medals in Winter Olympics history?

15. What man has won the most Winter Olympics medals?

16. Who was the first American to win an Olympic medal in skiing?

17. What female skater won the most gold medals in pairs figure skating?

18. Where is the site of the 2004 Summer Olympics?

19. Which individual won the most medals at the 2000 Summer Olympics?

20. Who holds the record for most track and field gold medals in a single Olympics?

The Fundamentals

The **steeplechase** is an Olympic event in which runners negotiate a series of walls and water-filled trenches. The men's 3,000-meter steeplechase has 28 walls and seven water jumps. Over the years, the distances have varied from as few as 2,500 meters to as many as 3,460 meters.

Twenty Answers

Well, did you get a gold, silver, or bronze medal for your performance in the quiz? Let's find out.

1. The four coaches to win Olympic gold and NCAA tournament titles are: Pete Newell (gold medal, 1960; NCAA title, 1959, University of California), Hank Iba (gold, 1964, '68; NCAA 1945–46, Oklahoma A&M), Dean Smith (gold, 1976; NCAA 1982, '93, North Carolina), and Bob Knight (gold, 1984; NCAA, 1976, '81, '87, Indiana).

2. John Thompson of Georgetown University coached the U.S. men's basketball team to a bronze medal in 1988.

3. Tennis returned as an Olympic sport in 1988. It had been part of the Games from 1896 through 1924, then was discontinued.

4. Pat Summitt of the University of Tennessee coached the U.S. women's basketball team to a gold medal in 1984.

5. Michael Johnson is the only man to win the 200 and 400 meters in the same Olympics. He did it in the 1996 Games in Atlanta, setting an Olympic record in the 400 (43.49 seconds) and a world record in the 200 (19.32 seconds).

6. Shirley Babashoff, a U.S. swimmer who competed in the 1972 and 1976 Olympics, is the all-time leader with six silver medals.

7. Babe Didrikson, one of the pioneers of the LPGA Tour, won gold medals at the 1932 Olympics in the 80-meter hurdles (11.7 seconds) and the javelin (143 feet, 4 inches).

8. In 1932, Volmari Iso-Hollo of Finland ran one extra lap due to a counter's mistake, but still won the gold medal, finishing in 10:33.4. Iso-Hollo also won in 1936.

9. Pat McCormick of the U.S. and Fu Mingxia of China won four each. In 1952 and 1956, McCormick won the springboard and the platform. In 1996 and 2000, Mingxia won the springboard, and in 1992 and 1996, she won the platform.

10. Wilma Rudolph of the U.S. won three gold medals in the 1960 Olympics—the 100 meters and 200 meters, and as a member of the 400-meter relay team.

11. Johnny Weissmuller, who won six Olympic medals (five gold, one bronze in swimming), achieved even more fame as the star of Tarzan movies.

12. Tara Lipinski, a U.S. figure skater, won the gold medal in 1998 at 15 years, 256 days.

Sports Strategies

Since tennis returned to the Games in 1988, only three U.S. players have won multiple gold medals. Gigi Fernandez and Mary Joe Fernandez (no relation) won the women's doubles in 1992 and 1996. Venus Williams won the singles and the doubles, with sister Serena, in 2000.

The Inside Skinny

Babe Didrikson also entered the high jump in the 1932 Olympics. She and Jean Shiley of the U.S. tied for the best jump at 5 feet, 5¼ inches, but Shiley was awarded the gold and Didrikson the silver, because Didrikson used a style of jumping that caused her head to clear the bar before her body, which apparently the judges didn't approve of.

13. Herb Brooks, who coached the University of Minnesota to three NCAA championships and also coached four teams in the National Hockey League, led the U.S. team to the 1980 gold medal.

14. Norway is the all-time leader in medals won with 239 (83 gold, 87 silver, 69 bronze).

15. Bjorn Dahlie of Norway has won 12 medals (eight gold, four silver) in cross-country skiing.

16. Billy Kidd, the first great American male skier, won a silver medal in the slalom and a bronze in the Alpine combined (total time of downhill and slalom) in the 1964 Games.

Sports Strategies

The U.S. hasn't been a dominant force in the Winter Olympics. It ranks third all-time in medals won with 159 (59 gold, 59 silver, 41 bronze). The Soviet Union with 194 (78 gold, 57 silver, 59 bronze) is second to Norway.

17. Irina Rodnina of the Soviet Union won three gold medals in pairs figure skating—in 1972 with Alexei Ulanov and in 1976 and 1980 with Aleksandr Zaitsev.

18. The 2004 Summer Olympics will be held in Athens, Greece.

19. Alexei Nemov, a Russian gymnast, led with six medals (two gold, one silver, three bronze). Among women, Marion Jones, a U.S. track and field athlete, and Dara Torres, a U.S. swimmer, won five each. Jones won three gold and two bronze; Torres won two gold and three bronze.

20. Fanny Blankers-Koen of the Netherlands won four gold medals in the 1948 Summer Olympics.

The Inside Skinny

The only athlete to win medals in the Winter and Summer Olympics in the same year was Crista Luding-Rothenburger of East Germany in 1988. She won a gold medal in speed skating and a bronze in cycling.

Bet You Didn't Know ...

➤ There were 15 world records set or tied at the 2000 Summer Olympics in Sydney, Australia. The Australians led with five; the U.S. was next with four.

➤ Germany was barred from competing in the 1924 and 1948 Winter and Summer Olympics, because it had been an aggressor nation in World War I and World War II.

➤ Eddie Eagan of the United States is the only person to win gold medals at the Winter and Summer Olympics. He won the light heavyweight boxing title in 1920 and was a member of the winning four-man bobsled team in 1932.

➤ Ed Sanders of the United States won the gold medal in the super heavyweight division in 1952 when his opponent, Ingemar Johansson, was disqualified in the second round for not trying.

➤ Bradford Cooper of Australia finished second to Rick DeMont of the United States in the 1972 400-meter freestyle, but DeMont was disqualified, because he failed the post-race drug test. His asthma medicine was on the International Olympic Committee's list of banned substances.

The Fundamentals

The **marathon** is one of the most grueling events in track and field. The official distance of a marathon is 26 miles and 385 yards, or 42,195 meters. But from 1896 through 1920, the Olympic distances varied from as few as 40,000 meters to as many as 42,750 meters.

➤ Ray Ewry, the all-time leader in gold medals won with 12, won them all prior to 1912, in the standing high jump, standing long jump, and standing triple jump. All three of those events have been discontinued.

➤ Johnny Hayes of the United States was named the winner of the 1908 *marathon*, when Dorando Pietri of Italy, the apparent winner, was disqualified for being helped across the finish line.

➤ Stella Walsh of Poland won the women's 100 meters at the 1932 Games in 11.9 seconds. So you're thinking, of course someone named Stella won the *women's* 100 meters. But an autopsy performed on Walsh in 1980 revealed she was a man.

➤ Irving Jaffee of the United States won the 1928 10,000-meters speed skating gold medal in an unofficial time of 18:36.5. The time was unofficial because the event was called off prior to completion because of thawing ice.

➤ Bob Seagren of the United States, who won the gold medal in the pole vault at the 1968 Olympics, had a good chance to repeat in 1972. Seagren used a carbon pole and set a world record at the Olympic Trials. But shortly before the Games began, the carbon pole was banned by the International Amateur Athletic Association, and Seagren was forced to use an unfamiliar pole. He won the silver.

➤ Wyomia Tyus and Gail Devers of the United States are the only women to win the 100 meters in consecutive Olympics (1964 and '68 for Tyus; 1992 and '96 for Devers).

➤ Emil Zatopek of Czechoslovakia, one of the greatest distance runners of all time, completed an unprecedented triple at the 1952 Olympics by winning the 5,000 and 10,000 meters and the marathon, which he ran for the first time. He also set Olympic records in each event.

The Fundamentals

The **decathlon** is a men's competition consisting of 10 events—100-meter sprint, long jump, shot put, high jump, 400-meter sprint, 110-meter hurdles, discus, pole vault, javelin, and 1,500-meter run.

Sports Strategies

Edwin Moses lost to Harald Schmid of Germany on August 26, 1977, in a 400-meter hurdles race. Two weeks later, he defeated Schmid, which was the first victory of his 122-race winning streak that stretched until June 4, 1987, when he lost to Danny Harris in Madrid, Spain. Three months later, Moses came back to win the World Championships.

Say What?

The Olympians have their say about their sports, their achievements, and what it takes to excel.

➤ Bob Mathias of the United States, two-time gold medal winner in the *decathlon* (1948, '52): "We shall never know how many truly superior athletes in this country missed their opportunity for Olympic greatness, because they did not have the wherewithal to make the most of their God-given, natural athletic talents."

➤ Al Oerter of the United States, four-time gold medalist in the discus (1956, '60, '64, '68): "I was never the best discus thrower at any of those Olympics. I was just the best prepared."

➤ Wilma Rudolph of the United States, three-time gold medalist at the 1960 Olympics: "Believe me, the reward is not so great without the struggle. I have spent a lifetime trying to share what it has meant to be a woman first in the world of sports so that the other young women have a chance to reach their dreams."

➤ Pete Cava, member of the U.S. Track and Field Federation, on nine-time gold medalist Carl Lewis: "He was the Babe Ruth and Michael Jordan of our sport."

➤ Bill Rodgers, great American marathoner, on Eric Heiden's five-gold medal speed skating performance at the 1980 Winter Olympics: "He gave the most dominant performance in the history of mankind in an Olympic competition and he got robbed by a lucky hockey team (the gold medal–winning U.S. team that beat the Russians). What he did in 1980 was one of a kind and we'll probably never see it again."

➤ Eric Heiden, on his five gold medals in the 1980 Winter Olympics: "Heck, gold medals? What can you do with them? I'd rather get a nice warm-up suit. That's something I can use. Gold medals just sit there."

➤ Edwin Moses, gold medal–winning U.S. hurdler, on his 122-race winning streak: "I'm hoping that my streak will stand for a long time. That it will be my mark on the sport, my legacy."

➤ Greg Louganis, who won four Olympic gold medals in diving, on his decision to make public his homosexuality: "Being gay and being in sports isn't supposed to mix. I think I proved that wrong."

➤ Jackie Joyner-Kersee, a three-time Summer Olympics gold medal winner, on the impact of female athletes: "All we ever wanted was to be respected for what we were trying to do. I think that's what's happening now. Now people are accepting us and saying that it's okay."

➤ Former U.S. speed skating coach Mike Crowe, on five-time gold medal winner Bonnie Blair: "She's smooth, graceful—it's almost like she's floating over the ice."

➤ Michelle Kwan, U.S. silver medalist in figure skating: "Any skater dreams of being the world champion. It would be a dream come true."

➤ Jesse Owens, winner of four gold medals in the 1936 Summer Olympics, on his technique: "I let my feet spend as little time on the ground as possible. From the air, fast down, and from the ground, fast up."

➤ Picabo Street, U.S. skier and Olympic gold medalist, on her determination: "When someone tells me there is only one way to do things, it always lights a fire under my butt. My instant reaction is, 'I'm gonna prove you wrong.'"

➤ Emil Zatopek, who won gold medals in the 5,000 and 10,000 meters and the marathon in the 1952 Summer Olympics: "You can't climb up to the second floor without a ladder. When you set your aim too high and don't fulfill it, then your enthusiasm turns to bitterness. Try for a goal that's reasonable, and then gradually raise it. That's the only way to get to the top."

Two-Minute Warning

You might think Emil Zatopek was an accomplished long-distance runner when he managed to win the 5,000 and 10,000 meters and the marathon in the 1952 Summer Olympics. But his marathon run in '52 was his first attempt at the distance.

The Fundamentals

The **Tour de France,** held annually, is the world's premier cycling race. It is contested over four weeks and runs throughout France, sometimes passing into neighboring countries. The race is run in stages. The cyclist with the lowest combined time after all the stages is the winner. The 2000 Tour de France was made up of 20 stages and covered 2,276 miles.

Sports Strategies

Greg LeMond and Lance Armstrong are the only Americans to have won the Tour de France. There have been four 5-time winners—Jacques Anquetil, France; Bernard Hinault, France; Miguel Indurin, Spain; and Eddy Merckx, Belgium. Indurin won his five Tours consecutively (1991–95).

Profiles in Courage

Lance Armstrong and Greg LeMond made their names by winning the *Tour de France,* cycling's version of the Olympics, only the Tour is held annually, and is one of the most grueling events in the world. But it's not just that they won the Tour de France—it was what each overcame to do so.

Armstrong and LeMond each demonstrated perseverance that is reserved for champions. They dealt with life-threatening conditions and overcame them.

Winning the Tour de France is tough for guys who have been 100 percent healthy. Armstrong and LeMond weren't. But still, they managed to not only win, but inspire.

The First

Greg LeMond won the Tour de France in 1986, when he became the first American and the first non-European ever to win cycling's most prestigious event.

And make no mistake about it, it was a monumental achievement. But not nearly as monumental as the second time he won it.

Less than a year after his 1986 victory in the Tour, LeMond was hunting with relatives and was accidentally shot in the back. Two pellets lodged in the lining of his heart, his right lung collapsed, he lost 75 percent of his blood supply, and there was some concern he might suffer spinal damage.

Undaunted, LeMond promised he would be back racing in the Tour de France. But let's face it, no one really expected him to fulfill his vow. Well, shame on the doubters, because in 1989, LeMond entered the Tour and entering the final stage of the race he was in second place. He trailed the leader, Laurent Fignon, by 50 seconds, an almost insurmountable deficit.

But LeMond won the final stage of the Tour and defeated Fignon by eight seconds, the narrowest finish in the event's 85-year history.

LeMond wasn't finished. In 1990, he won the Tour de France for a third time, and was named Sportsman of the Year by *Sports Illustrated*.

But as remarkable as LeMond's comeback was, Lance Armstrong's might have been more amazing.

Beating the Big "C"

After a successful amateur career, Lance Armstrong turned pro in 1992 and a year later, he won 10 titles, including the World Championship and the U.S. Pro Championship. His future appeared bright until he was diagnosed with testicular cancer in 1996.

And as if that wasn't bad enough, the cancer had spread to his stomach, lungs, and brain. After three surgeries in three weeks, his chances for recovery were no better than 50-50.

Lance Armstrong battled back from cancer to win the Tour de France in 1999 and 2000.

Photo: Diane Staskowski

Part of his treatment included doses of an aggressive form of chemotherapy. His hair fell out, he was nauseated, and he lost 15 pounds. But the chemo began to work, Armstrong began to recover, and a year later, he was proclaimed cancer-free.

Armstrong returned to racing in 1998, and in 1999, against all odds, he won the Tour de France and the admiration of fans the world over.

And as if that wasn't enough of a statement, Armstrong made a louder one in each of the next two years. He won the Tour de France in 2000 and 2001, the latter in a dominating performance. He took over the lead and separated himself from the field in the grueling mountain stages.

His winning streak is at three and counting. Many experts have called Armstrong unbeatable and predicted that he will rewrite the Tour de France history books. Four riders—Jacques Anquetil, Bernard Hinault, Miguel Indurain, and Eddy Merckx—have won the Tour a record five times. Don't be surprised if Armstrong makes it to six.

The Inside Skinny

Lance Armstrong is using his celebrity to help others. He established the Lance Armstrong Foundation to benefit cancer research and promote awareness and early detection. He also became a spokesman for testicular cancer as well as other forms of cancer, appearing in television commercials and print ads.

The Least You Need to Know

➤ Pete Newell, Hank Iba, Dean Smith, and Bob Knight are the only coaches to win an Olympic gold medal in basketball and an NCAA championship.

➤ Michael Johnson is the only man to win the 200 and 400 meters in the same Olympics.

➤ Tara Lipinski is the youngest athlete to win a gold medal at the Winter Olympics.

➤ Wyomia Tyus and Gail Devers are the only women to win the 100 meters in consecutive Olympics.

➤ Greg LeMond was the first American and non-European to win the Tour de France.

Part 7
Speed Thrills

Every Memorial Day weekend, nearly 500,000 fans fill the stands at the Indianapolis Motor Speedway to watch the Indianapolis 500, known as the Greatest Spectacle in Racing. Over the years, some of the greatest names in racing—Mario Andretti, A.J. Foyt, Rick Mears, and Al Unser—have made their mark at Indy.

NASCAR's version of the Greatest Spectacle in Racing is the Great American Race, also known as the Daytona 500, which has defined the careers of such drivers as Richard Petty, Jeff Gordon, and the late Dale Earnhardt.

In contrast to Indy car racing and stock car racing, where left turns are all the rage, drag racing and Formula One couldn't be more different. Drag racing requires no turns, just a flat-out run down a quarter-mile track; Formula One racing is all about turns as drivers have to maneuver their way around a road course.

Time to buckle up!

Chapter 24

The Greatest Spectacle in Racing

In This Chapter

➤ On track

➤ Rite of spring

➤ Traditionally speaking

➤ The drivers

➤ The ugly split

The Indianapolis 500—like the Super Bowl, like the World Series, like the Kentucky Derby—is one of those events that everyone at least takes note of.

You may not be a racing fan, but chances are you're aware that Memorial Day weekend means another running of the Indianapolis 500.

They don't call it the Greatest Spectacle in Racing for nothing. The combination of more than 400,000 people filling the stands and 33 cars flying around the track at speeds of more than 200 mph makes its nickname the perfect fit.

Laying the Foundation

Before there could be an Indianapolis 500, there had to be a racetrack to hold it on. The land for the Indianapolis Motor Speedway—four adjoining 80-acre tracts of farmland—was purchased by four local businessmen during the winter of 1908–09. The $2^1/_2$-mile track opened in 1909 and the first Indy 500 was held in 1911.

But we're getting a bit ahead of ourselves, because there was one major renovation that occurred before the first 500 was held. The original track was made of crushed rock and tar, but it became obvious that it wasn't strong enough to take the wear and tear that the race cars could dish out.

So in September 1909, the track was resurfaced and made of brick. The entire job took 63 days and required some 3.2 million bricks.

But the bricks didn't last. Starting in 1936, they were gradually replaced by asphalt. The turns were paved by 1938, and the backstretch was done in 1939. Over the next several years, the patching continued, until 1955, when the entire track was covered in asphalt, except for several hundred yards of the main straightaway, which remained brick to preserve the tradition.

The Inside Skinny

The Indianapolis Motor Speedway is, not surprisingly, known as the Brickyard, because of the decision to replace the original surface of crushed rock and tar with bricks in 1909. It is one of the most recognizable nicknames in all of sports. Most of the bricks were from companies located in Indiana. More than 140,000 bricks were laid on one day alone.

It Happens Every Spring

The first Indianapolis 500—200 laps around the $2^1/_2$-mile track—was held on Memorial Day, 1911, but it didn't exactly go off without a hitch. Ralph Mulford was given the checkered flag, a signal that he was the race winner, but just to be sure, Ol' Ralph ran three extra laps to guarantee he ran 500 miles.

Unfortunately for Ralph, while he was tooling around the track, Ray Harroun was being presented with the winner's trophy. Ralph lodged a protest, but it fell on deaf ears, and Harroun made history as the Indy 500's first winner.

The average speed of that first race was 74.602 mph. The average speed of the 2001 race, won by Helio Castroneves, was 153.601.

Now there's some added horsepower.

It wasn't until 1925 that the average speed climbed above 100 mph. Peter DePaolo did the trick, averaging 101.127 mph. The 150-mph barrier was broken in 1965 by Jim Clark (150.686); Mark Donohue cleared the 160 mph mark in 1972 (162.962); Bobby Rahal edged past 170 mph in 1986 (170.722); and Arie Luyendyk set the all-time average speed mark in 1990 (185.981).

Speeds have gone down because of safety measures and some speeds are slower because of the number of caution laps run during a race.

Besides the speed of the Indy 500, there's also the spectacle. More than 500,000 fans fill the track annually, all waiting for the call that starts it all: "Gentlemen, start your engines."

Two-Minute Warning

If you're wondering why the average speeds are so much lower than the qualifying speeds, which routinely top 220 mph, here's the answer. The average race speed includes laps run under the caution flag, which is waved when there is an accident. Drivers slow down for these laps, which count toward the total, thus bringing down the overall average speed. On a caution lap, a pace car comes onto the track and the cars must follow behind it and hold their positions. They are not allowed to pass.

Of course, there have been occasions when the call has been, "Gentlemen and lady, start your engines." Three females—Janet Guthrie, Lyn St. James, and Sarah Fisher, who ran in 2001—have driven in the Indy 500. Guthrie, the first woman to run in the Indy 500, was in the field in 1977, 1978, and 1979. St. James made the field seven times in the '90s.

Brickyard Traditions

As you might imagine, an event such as the Indianapolis 500 is steeped in tradition.

We've already mentioned one: the call of "Gentlemen, start your engines." Hearing it is part of what the Indy 500 is all about.

So are these traditions:

➤ Prior to the start of the race, Jim Nabors, who used to be Gomer Pyle on TV, sings "Back Home Again in Indiana." He first did it in 1973 and has done it every year since the early '90s.

➤ After the race, the winner, upon climbing out of his car, takes a gulp from a bottle of milk. It was started in 1936, when Louis Meyer won, and the winner has done it every year since 1956.

➤ The Borg-Warner Trophy is presented to the winning driver.

The Inside Skinny

The milk-drinking tradition started with Louis Meyer's win in 1936. He heeded his mother's advice that drinking buttermilk would be refreshing on a hot day. From 1947 through 1955, the milk-drinking stopped, because the Dairy Industry stopped offering $500 as an inducement. In 1956, the money began flowing again and so did the milk. The American Dairy Association gives $5,000 to the winning driver for taking a swig.

The trophy, first awarded in 1936, is made of sterling silver and is on display at the Indianapolis Motor Speedway Hall of Fame.

The original trophy stood four feet high and was perched on a marble base. Each winner gets his likeness embossed on the trophy. The original had space for 70 drivers. In 1986, a new base was made to allow for more drivers. Those spaces will be filled in 2003.

Stars of the Show

Because the Indianapolis 500 is an event of such magnitude, the drivers who have excelled in the race are among auto racing's biggest stars.

Only three drivers have won the race four times—A.J. Foyt, Rick Mears, and Al Unser. We'll also learn about a driver who's only won it once—Mario Andretti—but who is nevertheless an icon of his sport.

A.J.

Speaking of icons, there is none bigger than A.J. Foyt, who is synonymous with auto racing in general and the Indianapolis 500 in particular.

The first thing you have to know about A.J. Foyt is that he was just as ornery as he was talented. And he was very talented.

His driving style was no-nonsense and hard-charging, and he was never afraid to speak his mind. There was no mincing words for A.J. Foyt.

Two-Minute Warning

A.J. Foyt, because he was so outspoken and so competitive, had a tendency to get into altercations—sometimes with his competitors, and on occasion with his own crew.

One of the most famous incidents occurred at Texas Motor Speedway in 1997, when he slapped Arie Luyendyk in Victory Lane after a scoring dispute. Foyt, a team owner, thought his driver, Billy Boat, won the race; but a failure in the scoring and timing systems took place and Luyendyk was the actual winner. Which didn't sit well with Foyt, who let Luyendyk have it.

Foyt's father summed it up best when asked to describe his son's personality: "Talking to A.J. when he's angry is like dancing with a chainsaw."

Foyt, who began his career as a teenager in Houston, Texas, where he raced roadsters, motorcycles, and midget cars, dropped out of high school to race full-time.

He won his first Indianapolis 500 in 1961. His average speed was a record 139.130 mph. He also won in 1964, 1967, and 1977.

Winning the Indy 500 four times isn't Foyt's only notable accomplishment at the Brickyard. Check these out:

➤ Foyt is the only driver to have run in the Indy 500 for 35 consecutive years (1957–92).

➤ Foyt completed 4,909 laps around Indianapolis Motor Speedway. That's a total of 12,272.5 miles and is the equivalent of five trips from New York City to San Francisco.

➤ Foyt earned more than $2.6 million in the Indy 500.

Foyt also has made his mark on *Indy car* racing beyond Indianapolis Motor Speedway.

Foyt is the all-time leader in Indy car victories with 67 (15 more than Mario Andretti, who ranks second) and Indy car season championships with seven (three more than No. 2 Andretti). His last Indy car victory came in 1981 at Pocono International Speedway in Long Pond, Pennsylvania.

He attempted one last hurrah at Indianapolis, entering the 1993 Indy 500, but then retired on the opening day of qualifying, ending a career that may never be eclipsed.

Calm, Cool, Collected

Aside from his abundant talent behind the wheel, if there's one thing Rick Mears was noted for it was his low-key demeanor. Nothing seemed to rattle him, which can be a critical characteristic when you're flying around the track at speeds of more than 200 mph.

Mears got his start by racing motorcycles, but he soon switched to a dune buggy that had been built by his dad, a former race car driver himself, to calm his mother's fears.

The Fundamentals

Indy cars—also known as Champ Cars, also known as open-wheel racers—are cars that sit very low to the ground; their wheels are not covered by fenders. The engines are located in the rear and the drivers sit in a cockpit, which is not covered.

The Fundamentals

The **Formula One** racing circuit is contested mainly in Europe, although there are races in Australia, South America, Japan, and the United States. The cars are much like Indy cars, with open wheels and built low to the ground, but the racetracks are road courses, with the drivers having to wend their way through a series of turns.

After being named U.S. Auto Club Rookie of the Year in 1976, Mears was hired by Roger Penske, one of the most successful team owners in the sport, to fill in for Mario Andretti, who was pursuing the *Formula One* championship in Europe.

A year later, Mears joined Penske as a full-time driver, and their partnership resulted in four Indianapolis 500 victories.

Mears was co-Rookie of the Year at the Indianapolis 500 in 1978 and won his first Indy 500 in 1979. His second Indy 500 win came in 1984, and there was a time that many thought it might be his last. In September 1984, Mears crashed during practice near Montreal, severely injuring both feet and ankles. It was feared he might never walk again, but after several surgeries and a long rehab, Mears returned to racing in 1985.

His third Indy 500 victory came in 1988 and his fourth in 1991. Another accident, this one in May 1992 during practice for the Indy 500 at the Indianapolis Motor Speedway, caused him to miss most of the rest of the season, which turned out to be his last. He announced his retirement at Penske's annual Christmas party.

Mears ranks seventh all-time with 29 Indy car victories. He won the Indy car season championship three times and was the first driver to earn more than $10 million in Indy car racing.

Sports Strategies

Bobby Unser, Al Unser's older brother, is a three-time winner of the Indianapolis 500 and a two-time Indy car season champ. Bobby and Al are the only brothers to win the Indy 500. Bobby's 35 Indy car wins rank fifth all-time. Al Unser Jr. has won the Indianapolis 500 twice and has 31 career Indy car wins to rank sixth all-time. He has won the Indy car season championship twice.

Throughout his career, Mears was known for being a team player, so it figures that since his retirement, he's been an adviser to Penske Racing, imparting his wealth of knowledge to today's drivers.

Family Matters

There is no greater racing family than the Unsers, and Al Unser, younger brother of Bobby and father of Al Jr., ranks among the best drivers of all time.

Unser won his first Indianapolis 500 in 1970, when he dominated the season with 10 victories and the season championship.

In 1971, Unser became just the fourth driver to successfully defend his Indy 500 championship. He also won the 500 in 1978 and in 1987.

The 1987 victory was unexpected, because Unser wasn't even scheduled to enter the race. But fate has a funny way of altering conventional wisdom.

Al Unser won the Indianapolis 500 four times and the Indy car season championship three times.

Photo: Reading Eagle Co.

Unser filled in for Danny Ongais, who drove for Penske Racing, one of the elite teams in the sport. When Ongais suffered an injury and couldn't drive, Roger Penske, the team owner, turned to Unser, who formerly drove for Penske Racing. Unser ended up in Victory Lane, taking the traditional swig of milk and surprising everyone—probably even himself.

As of this writing, Unser ranks fourth all-time in Indy car victories with 39. He won the Indy car season championship three times.

Mario

He's one of those rare athletes who are recognizable just by the mention of their first name. When you're talking motor sports and the name "Mario" comes up, you know immediately the subject of the conversation.

Mario Andretti, besides being one of the most versatile and most successful drivers of all time, is also near the top of a short list of the most popular.

Everyone, it seems, loves Mario.

The Fundamentals

NASCAR, which stands for National Association for Stock Car Auto Racing, is the most popular of the racing circuits. It's also the fastest-growing sport in the United States. Stock cars on the NASCAR circuit are vehicles made by Chevrolet, Pontiac, Dodge, and so on. They look much like the ones you see on the street, but they have a few more horses under the hood.

The Fundamentals

The **pole** goes to the fastest qualifier. It is the best spot on the starting grid, in the front row and closest to the inside of the track. The rest of the qualifiers earn spots based on their qualifying times. At the Indianapolis 500, there are three cars in each row. NASCAR usually starts with two cars in each row.

You name it, he's won it. On racing's three major circuits—Indy car, *NASCAR*, and Formula One—Andretti has managed to win the most significant events.

Said legendary team owner Roger Penske: "Mario is the best all-around driver I've ever had. He's a racer's racer—completely dedicated, single-minded, and passionately competitive."

Here's the proof:

➤ In 1967, Andretti won NASCAR's crown jewel, the Daytona 500.

➤ In 1978, he became only the second American to win the Formula One championship. Phil Hill in 1961 was the first.

➤ He won four Indy car season championships.

➤ He won the 1969 Indianapolis 500.

And he won the 1969 Indy 500 against all odds. He arrived at Indianapolis Motor Speedway with one of the best cars, but a crash in practice forced him to use a backup car. He didn't win the *pole,* but he qualified for the front row.

Andretti fell back early in the race, but worked his way toward the front. He won the 500 in record time, finishing with an average speed of 156.867 mph.

In 1981, it appeared that Andretti lost the Indy 500 to Bobby Unser. However, Unser's victory was overturned; he was penalized for passing under a caution flag. That made Andretti the winner.

But Andretti's "victory" stood for only four months. Roger Penske, for whom Unser drove, appealed the decision and Unser was eventually declared the winner.

Andretti's remarkable career lasted 36 years, and he is the only person to be named Driver of the Year in three different decades (1967, 1978, 1984).

How's that for staying power?

Andretti's 52 Indy car victories rank second all-time to A.J. Foyt.

Why Can't We All Just Get Along?

In 1995, there was a divorce in the Indy car racing world. As you probably know, breakups are never cut and dried. They always tend to get complicated. So bear with me while I explain what happened to Indy car racing.

Up until the late 1970s, Indy car racing was governed by the U.S. Auto Club (USAC). But some of the more prominent owners were dissatisfied with the way the circuit was headed, so they broke away to form Championship Auto Racing Teams (CART).

CART ran its own circuit of races that featured the best drivers. So from CART's standpoint, things were hunky-dory. But then in the mid-'90s, a fellow named Tony George decided to form a rival circuit—the Indy Racing League (IRL).

George also owned the Indianapolis Motor Speedway, which turned out to be bad news for CART, because 25 of the 33 starting spots in the Indianapolis 500 were reserved for IRL drivers. George attempted to attract CART teams to the IRL with those eight spots up for grabs, but his ploy didn't work.

The CART drivers didn't show up, and the Indianapolis 500 lost some of its luster, because the best and the most well-known drivers weren't competing.

Although through the 2001 race there was no resolution to the conflict, some CART teams have begun racing in the Indy 500. In 2000, Juan Montoya, a CART driver, won the race; in 2001, Helio Castroneves, Gil de Ferran, Michael Andretti (Mario's son), Jimmy Vasser, and Bruno Junqueira—all CART drivers—finished 1-2-3-4-5.

I'll bet the IRL folks were just thrilled with those results.

Sports Strategies

The Indy car circuit has been run under three different organizations. From 1909 through 1955, the American Automobile Association ran the show. The U.S. Auto Club took over in 1956 and continued until 1978, the year Championship Auto Racing Teams (CART) broke away. With the inauguration of the Indy Racing League (IRL) in 1995, CART and IRL run separate schedules and crown different season champs.

The Least You Need to Know

➤ The first Indianapolis 500 was run in 1911.

➤ Ray Harroun won the inaugural race.

➤ It's tradition that the Indy 500 winner celebrate by drinking milk in Victory Lane.

➤ A.J. Foyt, Rick Mears, and Al Unser have won the Indy 500 four times each.

➤ Mario Andretti has won the Indy 500, the Daytona 500, and the Formula One championship, the only driver to do so.

➤ A split between CART and the IRL has cost the Indianapolis 500 some of its luster.

Chapter 25

Good
Ol' Boys

In This Chapter

➤ The Super Bowl of NASCAR

➤ The Guys Who Ruled the Road Then

➤ The Guys Who Rule the Road Now

➤ Passing of a Legend

At one time, stock car racing was thought to be a sport whose fans resided only in the southeast quadrant of the country. Boy, has that changed. Over the last several years, NASCAR racing has become one of the most popular forms of racing in the United States.

And the reason for that popularity is the fans' faithful allegiance to their favorite drivers. We'll look at some of the drivers—past and present—who have helped make NASCAR's appeal much more mainstream.

But first, we'll check out the Daytona 500, NASCAR's biggest race.

The Great American Race

Imagine, for a moment, the National Football League playing its Super Bowl before the regular season, or Major League Baseball starting, instead of ending, with the World Series.

First, it would be impossible to know who the best teams were before the regular season played out, so it couldn't be done; and second, even if it could, what sense would it possibly make to stage the marquee event on the schedule at the beginning?

The Fundamentals

The **Winston Cup** is a series of more than 30 races, with points awarded for each race. Drivers earn points for where they finish and laps led. A race winner, for example, earns 175 points. The points accumulate throughout the season. The driver with the most points at season's end is the Winston Cup champion.

Two-Minute Warning

Lest you think NASCAR racing began with the Daytona 500, it didn't. NASCAR was founded by Bill France Sr. in 1947, with the first sanctioned stock car race being held in 1948. The first series of races took place in 1949. The oldest of the 500-mile races on the schedule, the Southern 500, held in Darlington, South Carolina, was run for the first time in 1950.

Well, the obvious answer is it would make no sense. None whatsoever.

Except in the case of the Daytona 500, known as the Great American Race.

The Daytona 500 is, by far, the most prestigious, the most well-known, and the most anticipated event on the NASCAR schedule. It's also the one race that drivers want to win more than any other, because, like a major championship in golf or tennis, it's an event that can define a career.

Believe it or not, the Daytona 500 is the *first* event on the NASCAR *Winston Cup* schedule. And it hasn't hurt the sport in the least.

Although racing at Daytona International Speedway in Daytona Beach, Florida, dates back to 1936, the Daytona 500 was first run in 1959. The race is 200 laps around the $2^1/_2$ mile high-banked oval.

The inaugural race was won by Lee Petty, at an average speed of 135.521 mph. The record for winning average speed was 177.602 mph, by Buddy Baker in 1980.

The winners of the race read like a Who's Who of NASCAR racing—Richard Petty, Cale Yarborough, Bobby Allison, Darrell Waltrip, Dale Earnhardt, Dale Jarrett, and Jeff Gordon, to name a few.

While all Daytona 500s are important to stock car fans, none was more important to the sport as a whole than the 1979 race. At that time, NASCAR racing was pretty much considered a regional sport. It wasn't on network television for that very reason.

But the folks at CBS Sports decided to take a gamble in 1979 and air the race live nationally for the first time.

Luckily for CBS and NASCAR, a snowstorm blanketed the heavily populated Northeast and forced residents to stay inside. Many of those residents happened upon CBS's coverage of the Daytona 500. Maybe they tuned in on purpose or maybe they found it by accident, but whatever the reason, the important thing was they didn't tune out.

What those viewers saw was one of the most exciting races in Daytona 500 history. Donnie Allison and Cale Yarborough were running 1-2 on the final lap, when Yarborough tried to pass Allison, forcing both to crash. Richard Petty, in the right place at the right time, won the race. Yarborough and Allison, who was eventually joined by brother Bobby, ended up duking it out in the infield grass.

Talk about great television. The ratings soared, the Daytona 500 has been televised ever since, and NASCAR proved itself to be a sport for the masses.

That has never been more evident than during the 2001 season. Fox Sports, which telecast the first half of the 2001 season, saw the ratings rise an astounding 26 percent over 2000, proving this isn't your father's NASCAR anymore.

The Old Guard

When you think about the pioneers of NASCAR, the guys whose accomplishments helped lay the foundation for the surge in popularity that's taking place today, one name comes to mind: Richard Petty, also known as the King, and for good reason.

Petty's combination of charisma, humility, and immense talent behind the wheel helped put stock car racing on the map in places other than the South.

And you couldn't talk about Petty without mentioning his fiercest rival, David Pearson. Petty and Pearson rank 1-2 in all-time NASCAR victories, and their memorable battles are a big part of the history of the sport.

Sports Strategies

Richard Petty's popularity was more than just something people talked about. He's got the hardware to prove it. Nine times— 1962, '64, '68, '70, and '74–78— Petty was voted the Most Popular Driver on the NASCAR circuit.

The King

At the tender age of 12, Richard Petty was part of his father Lee's pit crew. But that was as involved as he would get. His daddy refused to allow him to compete before he was 21. It took Richard all of 10 days after his 21st birthday to enter his first race. He finished sixth.

One of the valuable lessons Petty learned at a young age was the importance of being, as he put it, "smooth," not "flashy." He drove aggressively, but he was always under control.

Petty was named NASCAR's Rookie of the Year in 1959, and he went on to validate his promise in a big way. He owns just about every record kept. Think I'm kidding? Take a look:

The Inside Skinny

In 1964, Richard Petty won the Daytona 500 and eight other races. His competitors, jealous fellows that they were, claimed Petty's engines were too big. Weary of the pettiness, Petty spent most of the 1965 season as a drag racer, but returned to NASCAR full-time in 1966, after a crash in Georgia in a drag race killed an eight-year-old boy. Petty's car went off the track and into the crowd.

Sports Strategies

Richard Petty is the most famous member of a longtime racing family. Before Richard, there was his father, Lee, who won the first Daytona 500 in 1959. Richard's son, Kyle, continues to drive on the NASCAR circuit. Kyle's son, Adam, an up-and-coming driver, was killed in a crash at New Hampshire Motor Speedway in July 2000, just a few months after Lee passed away.

➤ Most career victories: 200

➤ Most races started: 1,177

➤ Most consecutive wins: 10 in 1967

➤ Most runner-up finishes: 155

➤ Most top 10 finishes: 356

➤ Most poles: 127

➤ Most Winston Cup championships: 7 (tied with Dale Earnhardt)

➤ Most Daytona 500 victories: 7

Petty dominated Daytona like no one before or since. His seven victories—in 1964, '66, '71, '73–74, '79, and '81—are three more than anyone else. The 1979 victory came after having more than 40 percent of his stomach removed, due to ulcers, the previous year.

In 1967, the Daytona 500 was just about the only race he didn't win. Petty had one of the great seasons in history, winning 27 of 48 races, including 10 straight.

That was also the year he won the second of his record-tying seven Winston Cup championships, the others coming in 1964, 1971–72, '74–75, and '79. He also finished second in 1976 and '77.

Petty, known for his trademark cowboy hat, wrap-around shades, and his familiar No. 43 car, won his last race at the 1984 Firecracker 400. He retired in 1992.

Of course, had Petty not been so dominant, the real hero of NASCAR might've been David Pearson, Petty's chief rival.

Chasing the King

David Pearson had the misfortune—bad timing, actually—of being a contemporary of Richard Petty. What rotten luck.

Pearson compiled a glittering resumé, but as impressive as it was, it still didn't stack up to the King's—although he certainly had his share of moments.

Take 1966, for example; Pearson won 14 races in 42 starts and finished in the top 10 another 18 times. If you think that was good, 1968 was even better—16 wins in 48 races, with 22 top-10 finishes.

Pearson won three Winston Cup championships, and in 1976 he won the Daytona 500. He also won, numerous times, NASCAR's most significant races—the Winston 500, the Coca-Cola 600, and the Southern 500, known as the Crown Jewels of the sport. He has three victories in the Winston 500, three victories in the Coca-Cola 600, and three victories in the Southern 500.

But it's his rivalry with Petty that he's most remembered for.

From 1963 through June 1967, Petty and Pearson finished first and second to each other 63 times. Pearson won 33 of those battles, but overall, he lost the war. His 105 career NASCAR victories are a distant second to Petty's 200. But, hey, finishing second to a "King" isn't all that bad.

The Inside Skinny

In addition to being successful at finding his way to Victory Lane, David Pearson was also consistent. He was on the pole in one of every five races he entered, and he had a winning percentage of 18.29 percent, both of which are NASCAR records as of this writing. He is one of only four drivers to win three of the Crown Jewels in one year (1976).

The Heir Apparent

Jeff Gordon was named NASCAR Rookie of the Year in 1993. Two years later, at age 25, he won his first Winston Cup championship, the youngest ever to do so.

Jeff Gordon is a three-time winner of the Winston Cup championship.

Photo: RJR Sports Marketing

Obviously, he was a fast learner. And he has continued to learn—and excel on the NASCAR circuit. His record in the latter half of the 1990s is nothing short of remarkable.

From 1995 through 1998, Gordon was king of the hill. He won 40 races during those four seasons, including his first Daytona 500 victory in 1997. In 1998 he won an astounding 13 races, including four in a row.

Sports Strategies

Jeff Gordon hasn't been an all-or-nothing driver. During his four seasons of domination, during which he won 40 races, he also demonstrated a great deal of consistency. Over those four seasons, he finished in the top 10 in 90 of his 158 races.

The Fundamentals

The **pit crew** is what makes racing a team sport. It's the pit crew's job to change the tires, fill the gas tank, clean the windshield, make air pressure adjustments, and so on, whenever the driver makes a stop during a race. The quicker the pit crew finishes, the quicker the driver is back out on the track. A good pit stop these days is completed in less than 15 seconds.

After winning the Winston Cup championship in 1995, Gordon finished second to Terry Labonte in 1996. But it didn't take long for him to get back on top. He won back-to-back Winston Cup titles in 1997 and 1998.

Gordon's remarkable success did not endear him to many NASCAR fans, who resented not only his domination, but the ease with which he appeared to dominate.

Gordon is the driver who many fans love to hate, because he's too polished, too perfect, and it's perceived that things come too easily for him. But as he is fond of saying, the louder the boos, the more success he's enjoying.

Hitting a Pothole

For a while, it seemed as if Jeff Gordon would never lose a race; he was that dominant. But in 1999, the crew chief of his race team, Ray Evernham, left to form his own team with Dodge.

Gordon, known as the Rainbow Warrior because of his brightly colored No. 24 car, suddenly hit the skids, relatively speaking. He won his second Daytona 500 in 1999, but the consistency that had been his hallmark was missing, and he finished sixth in Winston Cup points, his lowest finish since 1994.

Now, winning the Daytona 500 and registering a sixth-place finish in the Winston Cup points standings would have any other driver celebrating a terrific season. But Gordon had set his standards so high that 1999 was quite the comedown.

But if he thought things tailed off in 1999, they got worse in 2000—again, relatively speaking.

As if his crew chief leaving wasn't bad enough, Gordon lost many members of his famed *pit crew*, the Rainbow Warriors, so named because Gordon's car had a rainbow design at the time. They left because they got a better offer from Dale Jarrett, another Winston Cup star.

Gordon won only three times in 2000 and dropped to ninth in the Winston Cup points standings, meaning there were no boos to serve as music to his ears. But it wouldn't be long before the boo birds would be back in business.

The Return to Form

At about the midway point of the 2001 season, it was obvious that Jeff Gordon was back where he was accustomed to being—leading the Winston Cup points race.

Through the first 15 events of the season, Gordon had three wins, four second-place finishes, a third, a fourth, and a fifth. The three wins gave him 55 in his career; he's tied with Lee Petty for seventh all-time.

Gordon went through one six-race stretch with two wins and four seconds. There's that consistency Gordon was famous for. Well, apparently, he still is. It just took him some time to adjust to a new crew chief and a new pit crew.

The Intimidator

Without a doubt, the saddest day in the history of NASCAR racing occurred on February 18, 2001. That's the day Dale Earnhardt, the Intimidator, was killed in a crash on the final lap of the Daytona 500.

Dale Earnhardt, seven-time Winston Cup champion, was killed in a crash on the final lap of the 2001 Daytona 500.

Photo: RJR Sports Marketing

Earnhardt, driving his trademark black No. 3 car, hit the wall at about 180 mph and was pronounced dead shortly thereafter.

The shock of his death and the void it left will not dissipate anytime soon— Earnhardt was that popular and that important to his sport.

The Legacy

Dale Earnhardt was an athlete who transcended his sport. Even if you didn't know the first thing about auto racing, there was a very good chance that you knew Dale Earnhardt.

It's not stretching the point to suggest that Earnhardt brought more fans to the sport than any driver since Richard Petty.

Earnhardt, the Man in Black, had a distinctive personality. His hard-charging, uncompromising, never-give-an-inch style endeared him to his legion of fans and angered those who rooted for other drivers.

The Inside Skinny

Dale Earnhardt was as talented a businessman as he was a driver, which is saying something. In addition to his own car, he ran a three–car race team under the umbrella of Dale Earnhardt Enterprises. Also running for Earnhardt were Steve Park, Michael Waltrip, and Earnhardt's son, Dale Jr. Earnhardt was also a master at marketing himself. He ran one of the most successful souvenir businesses in all of racing.

Cautious, he wasn't. Beware the driver who stood between Earnhardt and the spot he wanted on the track. If Earnhardt couldn't pass, he'd bump, tap, or brush the other car to earn better track position.

He wasn't called the Intimidator for nothing.

Earnhardt's tactics weren't dirty; they were aggressive. As the saying goes, "That's racin'," and Earnhardt did it better than just about anyone else.

The Record

If you took a poll to find out who the best driver in NASCAR history was, it's likely that Richard Petty would finish first. It's also likely that Dale Earnhardt would finish a close second.

Bobby Allison, who ranks third all-time in NASCAR victories with 84, said of Earnhardt: "Earnhardt made due with what he had; he made his equipment better. Some drivers today start to complain about conditions and their foot gets lighter on the gas pedal. Earnhardt just went out and raced harder."

Oh, did he race hard.

Earnhardt won his first race in 1979 at Bristol Motor Speedway in Bristol, Tennessee, and was named Rookie of the Year. A year later, he claimed his first Winston Cup championship.

He went on to win six more—1986–87, '90–91, and '93–94—giving him seven and tying him for the most Winston Cup championships with Petty.

Earnhardt won 76 races during his career to rank sixth all-time. He also is the all-time money winner in NASCAR history with more than $41.6 million in earnings.

But the most significant race Earnhardt ever won was one of his last—the 1998 Daytona 500.

That one of the very best drivers in NASCAR history hadn't won the circuit's most important race didn't seem quite right. But when he finally did win, the overwhelming reaction from fans and fellow competitors was proof of what a popular victory it was.

Two-Minute Warning

There was more to Dale Earnhardt's victory in the 1998 Daytona 500 than just winning NASCAR's biggest race, although that would've been quite enough. But the win came in Earnhardt's 20th Daytona 500 start and in NASCAR's 50th anniversary season. It also ended a 59-race winless streak.

The Least You Need to Know

➤ The Daytona 500 is the most important race on the NASCAR schedule.

➤ Richard Petty is the all-time leader in NASCAR victories with 200.

➤ David Pearson, Petty's chief rival, is second in wins with 105.

➤ NASCAR racing is the fastest-growing sport in America.

➤ Jeff Gordon won three Winston Cup championships in four seasons.

➤ Dale Earnhardt was killed in a last-lap crash at the 2001 Daytona 500.

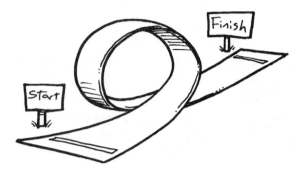

Chapter 26

The Short and Winding Roads

In This Chapter

➤ Hardly a drag

➤ Finished in a flash

➤ Roundabout

➤ Expert navigators

Drag racing and Formula One racing couldn't be more different. A drag race is over literally in seconds, which figures, seeing as how the track is only a quarter-mile long and the cars are powered by 6,000-horsepower nitromethane-burning engines. Imagine how those cars could get you through traffic!

Formula One races are contested on road courses, which consist of a series of turns and straightaways. The drivers have to maneuver their way around the course and be on their toes at all times. The turns are sharp and the competition is intense.

In both cases, hold on for the ride.

Drag Racing 101

First things first. Here's a primer to familiarize yourself with the sport of drag racing.

A drag race is an acceleration contest between two cars, racing side by side from a standing start down a straight, quarter-mile track.

Now, that sounds simple enough, and it is. But here's where it gets a tad more complicated: The winner is the first to cross the finish line—no, that's not the complicated part—but the winner isn't necessarily the driver with the quickest time or the fastest speed.

Now you're confused, right?

Well, here's how it works. A set of lights, which is called a Christmas Tree, is used to start each race. First, three amber lights flash simultaneously; 0.4 of a second later, a green light flashes, signifying the start of the race.

Sometimes a driver can win a race, even though he has a slower elapsed time and speed than his opponent, because his reaction time to the green light on the Christmas Tree was greater than the opponent's performance advantage on the track.

Drivers' performances are measured in elapsed time and speed. Elapsed time, also known as E.T., is the total time to go from the starting line to the finish line. The speed is how fast the car went.

The Fundamentals

Top Fuel dragsters are the quickest accelerating of all dragsters. They are powered by supercharged, custom-built, 500-cubic-inch engines mounted behind the driver. **Funny Cars** are short-wheelbased cars with a fiberglass replica of a production car body. The engines are mounted in the front of the car. **Pro Stock** cars most closely resemble cars you would see on the street, but feature extensive engine modification, sophisticated chassis and suspension development, and a 500-cubic-inch engine.

So if you're checking out the drag racing results in the newspaper and you see that a driver won a race with a 4.523/326.44, it means his elapsed time was 4.523 seconds at a speed of 326.44 mph.

There are three main classes in drag racing—*Top Fuel*, for the fastest and most powerful cars; *Funny Cars*, which have fiberglass bodies; and *Pro Stock Cars*, which look like cars you might see in a new car showroom.

The top level of professional drag racing is conducted by the National Hot Rod Association (NHRA). The NHRA holds more than 20 national events across the country, with the competitors at each event accumulating points based on their finishes. At the end of the season, the driver with the most points wins the championship.

The NHRA was founded by Wally Parks in 1951. He was an avid hot-rodder, who became the editor of *Hot Rod* magazine. Using the magazine as a forum, he created the NHRA, as he claims, to bring "order from chaos" and to institute safety rules and performance standards.

The NHRA's first official event took place in 1953 at a parking lot at the Los Angeles County Fairgrounds in Pomona, California. Today, the circuit plays to full houses throughout the U.S. and has all of its races televised.

Quarter-Mile Rush

Drag racing has produced some colorful characters with some descriptive nicknames. Let's see, there's "Big Daddy" Don Garlits, Don "the Snake" Prudhomme, "Grumpy" Bill Jenkins, and Tom "Mongoose" McEwen.

It's also produced some great champions. We'll look at four—Shirley Muldowney (who broke more than speed barriers on her way to the top), the Snake, John Force, and Big Daddy.

Proving She Belongs

It probably won't come as a big surprise that when Shirley Muldowney broke into drag racing in the early 1970s, the men in the sport—which is to say everyone—didn't exactly welcome her with open arms. It was more like a collective cold shoulder. But it wasn't long before Shirley, a real sporting pioneer, proved to them that she belonged.

Did she ever.

Muldowney, who began racing in the NHRA's Top Fuel division in 1973, won her first national event title in 1976. Now, I'm sure darn near every one of her male colleagues would've bet their favorite wrenches that the victory was nothing more than a fluke, a one-time, never-to-be-seen-again occurrence that would be soon forgotten.

Yeah, right. In 1977, Muldowney won the NHRA season points championship. And for those guys who thought *that* might've been another fluke, they soon came to the conclusion that Muldowney was the real deal. She won the Top Fuel title in 1980 and again in 1982.

Tragedy struck in 1984, when Muldowney was involved in a near-fatal crash. Traveling about 250 mph during a race in Montreal, Muldowney's dragster had a front-tire failure. She suffered broken bones in all 10 fingers, a broken pelvis, and serious injuries to her legs. The bones in her left leg needed to be fused, leaving it an inch shorter than her right.

Two-Minute Warning

The history of drag racing and the NHRA is pretty simple. But the origin of the term drag racing is open to debate. Some think it came from a challenge like, "Drag your car out of the garage and race me." Others think it referred to the "main drag," as in the city street that kids pretended was a racetrack. Still others think it had something to do with "dragging the gears," accomplished by holding the transmission in gear for longer than normal. You can take your pick.

Sports Strategies

If you're thinking that Shirley Muldowney's story would make a great movie, well, it's already been done. In 1983, *Heart Like a Wheel* was released. It chronicled Muldowney's life and career in drag racing. Starring Bonnie Bedelia in the title role, it's available at your local video store.

In all, Muldowney went under the knife five times for major surgery. Her recovery took 18 months and many wondered if she'd ever walk again, let alone get back behind the wheel.

But Shirley Muldowney was nothing if not tough and determined. She returned to the track in 1986, was voted Comeback Driver of the Year by the American Auto Racing Writers and Broadcasters of America, and went on to finish in the top 10 in points through the 1990 season, when she curtailed her schedule.

The Inside Skinny

Shirley Muldowney's accolades haven't been bestowed only by motor sports organizations. In 1998, the New York State Senate named her one of 30 Women of Distinction, in conjunction with a Women's History Month exhibition. Among others named were Eleanor Roosevelt and Susan B. Anthony.

Muldowney raced occasionally during the '90s, but in 2000, she returned to race in the NHRA's most prestigious event: the U.S. National in Indianapolis. She qualified for the 16-car finals, but was defeated in the first round.

Muldowney won 18 NHRA national events and was inducted into the Motorsports Hall of Fame in 1990. The First Lady of Racing, as she's called, certainly earned her spot.

The Snake

Don Prudhomme got his nickname, the Snake, because he was so quick off the starting line. As soon as that green light flashed, he was gone.

But more than his rapid reaction time and his ability to get to the finish line first, Prudhomme helped put the NHRA on the map with fans. He was charismatic and had a certain flair about him.

The other thing that helped raise the NHRA's profile was his rivalry with Tom McEwen, who was nicknamed the Mongoose. Get it? The Snake vs. the Mongoose? Their battles helped bring not only attention from the fans, but from the media as well.

Prudhomme started his NHRA career in 1965, driving in the Top Fuel division. He registered 14 Top Fuel victories, but he didn't last in the division.

Sports Strategies

Since 1975, the Funny Car division has been dominated by four drivers—Don Prudhomme won four straight titles (1975–78), Raymond Beadle three straight (1979–81), Kenny Bernstein four straight (1985–88), and John Force 10 in 11 years (1990–2000).

In 1973, Prudhomme switched to Funny Cars, and for the competition it was no laughing matter, because Funny Cars is the division in which he made his greatest mark on the sport.

Prudhomme won the Funny Car season championship four straight years, beginning in 1975. He won six national events in 1975 and seven in 1976.

Overall, Prudhomme registered 35 Funny Car career victories, which ranks second all-time to John Force, who's first with 97. Add his 14 Top Fuel victories and he has 49 total wins, which ranked him sixth all-time in the pro categories midway through 2001.

Force to Be Reckoned With

John Force is arguably the most popular drag racer on the NHRA circuit. The fans love him because he's a down-to-earth, regular guy. He exudes charisma, he's a veritable quote machine, he makes himself available to the fans and the media, and he just seems to be having the time of his life. The NHRA is lucky that the Force is with it.

Oh, there's one other thing that I forgot to mention: The guy can drive.

Nobody in racing has dominated a division the way Force has ruled the Funny Car division. Since 1990, he's won 10 season championships. That's more titles than any other driver in any division has ever won.

John Force is one of the most popular and the most successful Funny Car drivers in NHRA history.

Photo: Reading Eagle Co.

The only year in that stretch that Force didn't finish on top was 1992. Force winning the Funny Car division is as inevitable as the Boston Red Sox or the Chicago Cubs not winning the World Series.

In 1996, he won an astounding 13 events, a single-season record. He has won at least one race every year since 1987, when he registered his first victory.

Midway through 2001, Force had 97 Funny Car national event victories. He not only leads the Funny Car division, which you'd expect, but he's also the winningest driver in NHRA history in all divisions. The runner-up, Bob Glidden, is a dozen behind.

Force isn't just a force in drag racing, either. In 1996, in balloting by the national motor sports media, he was named Driver of the Year, the first drag racer to receive that honor.

Sports Strategies

Although John Force is the most dominant driver in the history of the NHRA, Bob Glidden, who raced in the Pro Stock division, runs a close second. Glidden won nine Pro Stock season titles, one fewer than Force, including five in a row from 1985 through 1989. Glidden leads the Pro Stock division with 85 career national event victories.

The Inside Skinny

When Don Garlits retired, he left the track but not the sport. After his competitive days had ended, he was credited with several important technical innovations, including the development of the Top Fuel dragster with its engine in the rear, which protected the driver from fire and flying debris, and the fire-resistant racing suit.

Big Daddy

I've saved perhaps the most significant figure in drag racing history for last. "Big Daddy" Don Garlits is known as the Father of Drag Racing. After all, were it not for him, who knows if Muldowney, Prudhomme, Force, and the other stars of the NHRA would've been able to accomplish what they did as quickly as they did.

Garlits was a pioneer when it came to going fast. In 1964, Garlits, driving a Top Fuel dragster, was the first to accelerate from a standing start to 200 mph on the quarter-mile track. But he had been achieving milestones for years before hitting 200 mph. Garlits was the first to exceed 170 mph (1957), 180 mph (1958), 200 mph (1964), 240 mph (1968), 250 mph (1975), and 270 mph (1986).

It figures that if Big Daddy was going so fast, he was winning his share of titles. He won 35 career NHRA Top Fuel national event titles. He also won three NHRA season championships—1975, 1985, and 1986, when he was 52 years old.

It also figures that this legendary figure was a charter member of the Motorsports Hall of Fame in 1989.

Formula One

Formula One racing has never made the impact in the United States that it has in Europe, where it is a huge deal and the drivers are as popular as NASCAR drivers are in this country.

Formula One races are run on road courses, with lots of turns, not oval tracks, which require drivers to make only left turns. Lots and lots of left turns. The Formula

One cars are single-seat vehicles and built very low to the ground, which allows them to be maneuvered more adroitly on the tricky course.

Kings of the Road

Alain Prost, Ayrton Senna, and Jackie Stewart were three of the most successful drivers in Formula One history. Between them they won 10 World Championships and nearly 120 races.

And if you're old enough, you might remember Jackie Stewart for another reason besides his driving. See if it comes to you before I tell you.

Prost vs. Senna

Alain Prost is the winningest driver in Formula One history with 51 victories in 199 races. To save you the trouble of doing the math, that means he won about one of every four events he entered.

Prost was first offered a Formula One ride in 1979, but he turned it down, because he didn't think he was prepared enough to run at the highest level of racing.

So he waited until 1980 to join the Formula One circuit and until 1985 for his first victory. He also won his first World Championship in 1985 and his second in 1986. Three years later, Prost won his third world title. He was also runner-up four times.

But then he hit a dry spell, which coincided with the emergence of Ayrton Senna, who had won the 1988 World Championship. He and Prost developed a fierce rivalry.

Senna won the 1990 and 1991 World Championships, taking the spotlight away from Prost, who many people assumed was washed up, finished, yesterday's news.

Prost even sat out the 1992 season after having been fired by the Ferrari team in 1991. But in 1993, Prost returned to the track, driving for Williams-Renault ... driving very well for Williams-Renault. He won the 1993 World Championship and retired the following season.

Senna won 41 races in his career, second all-time to Prost. He is the all-time leader in pole positions with 65, nearly double the number of Prost and Jim Clark, who are tied for second with 33.

The Inside Skinny

As a child, Ayrton Senna wasn't much of an athlete. He was uncoordinated and awkward. But he loved cars, so his father gave him a one-horsepower kart, which Senna fell in love with. It made all the difference in his personality, making him much more focused and confident. It also made him a better student, because poor grades would've resulted in losing his driving privileges.

Prost and Senna are also the two most consistent racers in Formula One history. They rank 1-2 in *podium finishes;* Prost has 106, Senna 80.

The Fundamentals

A **podium finish** is either first, second, or third. It's called a podium finish for obvious reasons: After the race, the top three drivers step up onto a podium, with the winning driver in the middle, positioned higher than the other two.

Senna's days as a Formula One force were cut tragically short. He was killed in a crash in Imola, Italy, in May 1994. He was 34 years old.

Jackie Stewart

Jackie Stewart is probably the most well-known Formula One racer in the United States, not so much because he was a talented and accomplished driver, but because he worked for many years as a television commentator for ABC Sports. In his lilting Scottish brogue, Stewart brought his considerable racing insights to the American television public.

But his main claim to fame was as a Formula One driver. He joined the circuit full-time in 1965 and won the first of his three World Championships in 1969, when he won seven of the 14 races he entered. His other World Championships came in 1971, when he was honored with the Order of the British Empire, and 1973.

The 1973 world title was a bit of a surprise, because Stewart considered retiring in 1972, due to a bleeding ulcer. But he came back, for what turned out to be his last hurrah. He retired at the end of the 1973 season.

Stewart won 27 races in just 99 starts in his career, and registered 43 podium finishes. In addition to his driving, Stewart also made his mark on the Formula One circuit by being a vigilant crusader for safety improvements.

The Least You Need to Know

➤ Drag racing is contested on a quarter-mile track.

➤ The three main classes in drag racing are Top Fuel, Funny Car, and Pro Stock.

➤ "Big Daddy" Don Garlits is known as the Father of Drag Racing.

➤ John Force is the winningest driver in NHRA history.

➤ Formula One racing is much more popular in Europe than the United States.

➤ Alain Prost is the winningest driver in Formula One history.

Game Time

Well, we've reached the end of the line; the end of the book, too. Your final quiz will be all about cars and the people who drive them so fast.

We'll also take a look at another type of racing—horse racing—including the Triple Crown and the greatest horse of them all, Secretariat. So buckle your seat belt or get up in the saddle, whichever you choose, and let's take our final exam!

Twenty Questions

OK, this is your last quiz. This one will deal with fast cars and fast drivers. But you can take your time.

1. Who is the youngest driver ever to win the Winston Cup championship?

2. What is a superspeedway?

3. Besides the Daytona 500, what other race is held annually at Daytona International Speedway?

4. Who is the oldest driver to win a NASCAR race?

5. What two drivers are tied for the most consecutive wins at one racetrack?

6. What is the closest margin of victory in a Winston Cup point race?

7. How many NASCAR Rookies of the Year have gone on to win the Winston Cup championship?

8. Who holds the record for most consecutive races started?

9. Who started the most races without a win?

10. Which NASCAR race featured the most lead changes?

11. Which brothers have combined for the most NASCAR wins?

12. What was notable about the 1994 Brickyard 400?

13. What is Happy Hour?

14. Who are the two pairs of father-son winners of the Indianapolis 500 Rookie of the Year award?

15. Who holds the record for the fastest speed ever recorded in drag racing?

16. Who holds the record for most Top Fuel victories?

17. Who won the most Formula One World Championships?

18. Who has the most Indy car victories without having won the Indianapolis 500?

19. Who is the all-time leader in poles won at the Indianapolis 500?

20. Who won the inaugural U.S. Grand Prix, the first Formula One race in the U.S. since 1989?

Sports Strategies

Tony Stewart, the 1999 NASCAR Rookie of the Year, had the most successful season of anyone who's ever won the award. He won three races, claimed two poles, finished in the top 10 a whopping 21 times, and earned more than $3.1 million.

The Fundamentals

A **superspeedway** is a racetrack that is a mile or more in distance. A short track is less than a mile in distance, and an intermediate track is at least one mile, but less than two miles.

Twenty Answers

Let's see if you got enough correct answers to earn a spot in Victory Lane.

1. Jeff Gordon is the youngest driver ever to win the Winston Cup championship. He was 24 years old when he won it in 1995.

2. A *superspeedway* is any racetrack of a mile or more in distance.

3. The Pepsi 400 is held annually in July at Daytona International Speedway. It used to be called the Firecracker 400.

4. Harry Gant was 52 years, 219 days when he won the Pepsi 400 at Michigan International Speedway on August 16, 1992.

5. Richard Petty won seven consecutive races at Richmond Fairgrounds Raceway (1970–73). Darrell Waltrip won seven in a row at Bristol International Raceway (1981–84).

6. In 1992, Alan Kulwicki won the Winston Cup championship by 10 points over Bill Elliott.

7. Five Rookies of the Year have gone on to win Winston Cup championships—Richard Petty (1959, seven Winston Cup titles), David Pearson (1960, three titles), Dale Earnhardt (1979, seven titles), Alan Kulwicki (1986, one title), and Jeff Gordon (1993, three titles).

8. Terry Labonte holds the record for most consecutive races started, with 655 (1979–2000). The streak ended on August 5, 2000, when Labonte wasn't in the field at the Brickyard 400, because he was injured.

9. J.D. McDuffie started 653 races between 1963 and 1991 without a victory.

10. The 1984 Winston 500 at Talladega Superspeedway had 75 lead changes. The 1984 Talladega 500 is next with 68, followed by the 1978 Talladega 500 with 67.

11. The Allison brothers—Bobby and Donnie—combined for 94 NASCAR victories. Bobby was responsible for 84.

12. The 1994 Brickyard 400 was the first race other than the Indianapolis 500 to be run at Indianapolis Motor Speedway. In 2000, the U.S. Grand Prix, a Formula One race, was also added to the schedule at the Indianapolis Motor Speedway, which was adapted to run a Formula One race.

13. Happy Hour is a slang term that refers to the last official practice session held before an event. It usually takes place the day before the event.

14. Mario and Michael Andretti were named the Indianapolis 500 Rookie of the Year in 1969 and 1984, respectively. Bill and Billy Vukovich III won it in 1968 and 1988.

15. Mike Dunn, a Top Fuel driver, recorded the fastest speed in NHRA history, going 331.61 mph on March 23, 2001, in Houston.

The Inside Skinny

Bobby Allison also shared a distinction with his son, Davey. They were one of only two father-son tandems to finish 1-2 in a NASCAR race. The Allisons did it in the 1988 Daytona 500, won by Bobby. The Pettys, Lee and Richard, did it twice, the first time in 1959 in Atlanta and again in 1960 in Pittsburgh.

16. Joe Amato is the all-time leader in Top Fuel victories with 52.

17. Juan-Manuel Fangio of Argentina won five World Championships (1951, '54–57).

18. Midway through the 2001 season, Michael Andretti ranked fourth all-time in career Indy car victories with 40, but he had not won the Indianapolis 500.

19. Rick Mears sat on the pole for the Indianapolis 500 a record six times (1979, '83, '86, '88–89, '91).

20. Michael Schumacher, the 2000 winner of the World Championship, won the U.S. Grand Prix held at Indianapolis Motor Speedway.

Sports Strategies

Of Rick Mears' record-tying four Indianapolis 500 victories, three came when he sat on the pole—1979, 1988, and 1991. In his other Indy 500 win, in 1984, he started from the third position.

Sports Strategies

Dale Jarrett's father, Ned, was one of the pioneers of stock car racing. Ned was a two-time Grand National champion (now Winston Cup), winning in 1961 and 1965. His 50 career victories tie him for 10th all time. Ned also had a distinguished career as a broadcaster.

Bet You Didn't Know ...

➤ Terry and Bobby Labonte are the only brothers to win the Winston Cup championship. Terry won it in 1984 and 1996; Bobby won it in 2000.

➤ Jeff Gordon's first appearance in a NASCAR race was in the last race of the 1992 season, which also happened to be the final race of Richard Petty's career.

➤ Bill Elliott enjoyed one of the greatest seasons in NASCAR history in 1985. He won 11 races, including the Daytona 500, the Winston 500, and the Southern 500. Because he won those three 500-mile races, he earned a $1 million bonus.

➤ Dale Jarrett, the 1999 Winston Cup champion, is a scratch golfer, and likely would've attempted a career in professional golf had he not gotten involved in racing.

➤ Joe Gibbs, former Super Bowl–winning coach of the Washington Redskins, has been a successful NASCAR team owner since 1992. Dale Jarrett, Bobby Labonte, and Tony Stewart have driven for Gibbs.

➤ From 1988 through 2000, Mark Martin has never finished lower than eighth in the Winston Cup points standings. He's been in the top 3 six times.

Bill Elliott dominated the 1985 NASCAR season by winning 11 races.

Photo: Reading Eagle Co.

➤ Tony Stewart and John Andretti have each run the Indianapolis 500 during the day and the Coca-Cola 600 at night on the same date. Andretti did it in 1994; Stewart did it in 1999 and 2001.

➤ With Michael Waltrip's victory in the 2001 Daytona 500, he broke a career-long winless streak that had reached 462 races.

➤ In the modern era of NASCAR racing, which started in 1972, the longest consecutive-race winning streak has been four, accomplished by seven drivers—Cale Yarborough, 1976; Darrell Waltrip, 1981; Dale Earnhardt, 1987; Harry Gant, 1991; Bill Elliott, 1992; Mark Martin, 1993; and Jeff Gordon, 1998.

➤ Bill Elliott has just about owned the award that goes annually to NASCAR's most popular driver. Since 1984, he has won it every year but two—1989 and 1990, when Darrell Waltrip was the winner.

➤ Thirteen times NASCAR races have been won by drivers who started in 30th position or lower—Johnny Mantz, 43rd, 1950, Southern 500; Jeff Burton, 38th, 1999, Jiffy Lube 500; Bill Elliott, 38th, 1988, Firecracker 400; Bobby Labonte, 37th, 2000, Southern 500; Labonte, 37th, 1999, NAPA 500; Kyle Petty, 37th, 1995, Miller 500; Jeff Gordon, 36th, 2000, DieHard 500; Dale Earnhardt, 35th, 2000, Cracker Barrel 500; Rusty Wallace, 33rd, 1993, Slick 50 300; Bobby Allison, 33rd, 1978, Daytona 500; Benny Parson, 32nd, 1975, Daytona 500; Earnhardt, 31st, 1980, Atlanta 500; and Neil Bonnett, 30th, 1988, Goodwrench 500.

➤ Bobby Isaac holds the record for most NASCAR poles won in one season with 20 in 1969.

The Inside Skinny

David Pearson had a knack for winning poles at Charlotte Motor Speedway, which is now called Lowe's Motor Speedway. He holds the record for most consecutive seasons with at least one pole, 20; most consecutive poles won at one track, 11 at Charlotte Motor Speedway; and the most poles at one track, 14 at Charlotte.

Two-Minute Warning

That 1916 race wasn't the only Indianapolis 500 that was shorter than 500 miles. Several races have been shortened by rain. The 1926 race was shortened to 400 miles, the 1950 race to 345 miles, the 1973 race to 332.5 miles, the 1975 race to 435 miles, and the 1976 race to 255 miles.

➤ Only four drivers have won NASCAR's Crown Jewels (Daytona 500, Coca-Cola 600, and Southern 500) in the same year—Lee Roy Yarbrough, 1969; David Pearson, 1976; Bill Elliott, 1985; and Jeff Gordon, 1997.

➤ Only four drivers have won the Formula One World Championship and the Indianapolis 500. Graham Hill won the World Championship in 1962 and '68 and the Indy 500 in 1966; Jim Clark won the World Championship in 1963 and '65 and the Indy 500 in 1965; Mario Andretti won the World Championship in 1978 and the Indy 500 in 1969; and Emerson Fittipaldi won the World Championship in 1972 and '74 and the Indy 500 in 1989 and '93.

➤ The Rookie of the Year award given annually at the Indianapolis 500 does not necessarily go to the highest-finishing first-year driver. The award is determined by a vote of the media. For instance, in 1966 Graham Hill, a rookie, won the race, but the Rookie of the Year award went to Jackie Stewart, who was leading with 10 laps to go when he lost oil pressure and finished sixth.

➤ No winner of the Indianapolis 500 has started deeper in the field than Ray Harroun and Louis Meyer. They each started 28th, Harroun in 1911 and Meyer in 1936. More recently, Johnny Rutherford won from the 25th spot in 1974 and Al Unser won from 20th in 1987.

➤ The 1916 Indianapolis 500 was scheduled for only 300 miles; race officials feared a shortage of cars because of the war in Europe.

➤ Nigel Mansell left the Formula One circuit in 1993 (after winning the 1992 World Championship) to run Indy cars, and he did pretty well. He was voted the Indianapolis 500 Rookie of the Year and he won the season point championship, becoming the first rookie to do so.

➤ The nitromethane-powered engines of Top Fuel dragsters produce more than 6,000 horsepower, which is about 43 times that of an average street car.

➤ A Top Fuel dragster leaves the starting line with about the same force that a space shuttle leaves the launch pad.

➤ A Top Fuel dragster can accelerate from 0 to 100 mph in less than 0.8 seconds.

Say What?

Here are some quotable quotes from guys who probably can't talk too much while they're driving.

➤ Al Unser, on A.J. Foyt: "There has never been a driver with such an absolute urge to excel, the absolute necessity to win."

➤ Mario Andretti: "No one ever taught me how to drive. I've been driving all my life. When I got to the big time, I asked guys things, but no one would help me much. So I watched guys and I drove. I learned by doing."

➤ Stirling Moss, British race car driver, on concentration: "It is necessary to relax your muscles when you can. Relaxing your brain is fatal."

➤ Moss, on danger: "To achieve anything in this game, you must be prepared to dabble on the boundary of disaster."

➤ Richard Petty: "I've had the good fortune to grow up with the sport and have my daddy (Lee) to watch and learn from. Then I raced with some of the greats and they taught me a lot. And maybe I taught them a few things, too."

➤ Petty, on his choice of careers: "My daddy was a race driver, so I became a race driver. If he'd been a grocer, I might have been a grocer."

➤ A race fan, describing Jeff Gordon: "He's too slick, too smart, too preppy, he doesn't even look like a race car driver."

➤ A.J. Foyt: "I feel safer on a racetrack with the traffic going in the same direction and good drivers behind the wheel than I do on Houston expressways."

➤ Jim Murray, legendary sportswriter, on the Indianapolis 500: "It's not so much a sporting event as a deathwatch. They hold it, fittingly, on Memorial Day."

Sports Strategies

Stirling Moss might be one of the best Formula One drivers never to win a World Championship. Moss, a legend in his native Great Britain, won 16 Formula One events and was runner-up for the World Championship four times.

The Fundamentals

The **Triple Crown** is a series of three races held annually each spring. The Kentucky Derby (1¼ miles) is held the first weekend in May at Churchill Downs in Louisville, Kentucky. The Preakness Stakes (1³/₁₆ miles) follows two weeks later at Pimlico Race Course in Baltimore. The Belmont Stakes (1½ miles) is run three weeks after the Preakness at Belmont Park in New York.

Sports Strategies

Secretariat set the Belmont Stakes record, finishing in 2:24, which still stands as a world record for 1½ miles on a dirt track. He broke the previous Belmont Stakes record, set by Gallant Man in 1957, by 2³/₁₅ seconds, the equivalent of 13 lengths.

➤ Janet Guthrie, the first woman to drive in the Indianapolis 500, on whether strength is a requirement for a driver: "You drive the car, you don't carry it."

➤ Jackie Stewart: "In my sport, the quick are too often listed among the dead."

➤ Shirley Muldowney: "I want to be the fastest woman in the world—in a manner of speaking."

And They're Off!

Horse racing at the highest level is all about the *Triple Crown*—the Kentucky Derby, the Preakness, and the Belmont Stakes. These three races can determine a horse's place in history.

There have been 11 Triple Crown winners—Sir Barton in 1919, Gallant Fox in 1930, Omaha in 1935, War Admiral in 1937, Whirlaway in 1941, Count Fleet in 1943, Assault in 1946, Citation in 1948, Secretariat in 1973, Seattle Slew in 1977, and Affirmed in 1978.

"Big Red"

Secretariat was nicknamed Big Red, but Big Deal also would've fit, because in 1973, he became a bona fide celebrity.

In becoming the first Triple Crown winner in 25 years, Secretariat staked a claim of being the best horse of all time.

Secretariat won the Kentucky Derby in a world-record time of 1:59²/₅ seconds. Had it not been for a malfunctioning clock, he would've set a record in the Preakness. As it was, he was two-fifths of a second off the record.

But it was at the Belmont Stakes that Secretariat did the unthinkable. He won by an astounding 31 lengths. The margin was so great that CBS's cameras could barely get Secretariat and the second-place horse, Twice a Prince, in the same shot.

Secretariat made the covers of *Time, Newsweek,* and *Sports Illustrated* the same week. When ESPN announced its list of the 50 greatest athletes of all time, Secretariat made the cut (the only nonhuman to do so).

The Shoe

Bill Shoemaker, one of the most accomplished jockeys of all time, had a way with horses, many of which he rode into the winner's circle.

Wrote William Nack in *Sports Illustrated:* "Watching Shoemaker ride was like watching Gene Kelly dance or Gauguin paint. It was art. You had the feeling he could win the Kentucky Derby on a Brahma Bull."

Shoemaker won 11 Triple Crown races, 10 national money titles, and 1,009 stakes races during his 42-year career. He was the all-time winningest jockey until 1999, when Laffit Pincay surpassed him.

Two races in Shoemaker's career stand out—one he won, and one he should've won.

In the 1957 Kentucky Derby, Shoemaker was leading the race on Gallant Man when he misjudged the finish line, stood up on his mount, and lost a race that was his to win.

The 1986 Kentucky Derby was a much happier occasion. Shoemaker rode Ferdinand, an 18-to-1 shot, to a victory. At age 54, Shoemaker was the oldest jockey ever to win the Derby.

Shoemaker retired in 1990. He finished fourth on his 40,352nd—and final—mount.

Two-Minute Warning

You might think that a jockey of Bill Shoemaker's talent should never make a mistake as fundamental as misjudging the finish line. But according to fellow jockey Eddie Arcaro, who won 17 Triple Crown races, it wasn't entirely Shoemaker's fault. Arcaro said Shoemaker mistook a furlong post for the finish line, because the track was lengthened that year. The remedy was to put lines on the fence to show the finish.

The Least You Need to Know

➤ Jeff Gordon is the youngest winner of the Winston Cup championship.

➤ The Brickyard 400, a NASCAR race, was the first race other than the Indy 500 to be run at Indianapolis Motor Speedway.

➤ John Force is the winningest driver in NHRA history.

➤ Only four drivers have won NASCAR's Crown Jewels in the same season.

➤ Only four drivers have won the Formula One World Championship and the Indianapolis 500.

➤ In 1973, Secretariat became the first Triple Crown winner in 25 years.

Glossary

ace   In golf, a hole in one; in tennis, an outright winning serve that the receiver doesn't touch.

All-America Football Conference   Professional league with 14 teams that merged with the NFL following the 1949 season.

all-purpose yardage   Total of a player's rushing, receiving, and punt and/or kickoff return yardage.

American Basketball Association   Began play in 1967 with 10 teams. It used a red, white, and blue ball and the three-point basket. The ABA lasted nine seasons before going under.

American Professional Football Association   Formed in 1920, but changed its name to the National Football League in 1922.

assist   In hockey and basketball, the pass that immediately precedes a goal or a field goal, respectively; in hockey, a maximum of two assists are awarded per goal. In basketball, only one assist is awarded. In baseball, an assist is awarded when a fielder throws out a runner.

Atlantic Coast Conference   Also known as the ACC; one of the nation's foremost collegiate basketball leagues. Formed in 1954, it is made up of Clemson, Duke, Florida State, Georgia Tech, Maryland, North Carolina, North Carolina State, Virginia, and Wake Forest.

backhand   In tennis, a stroke hit from the side of the body opposite the racket hand.

backstroke   In swimming, a stroke in which the swimmer must stay on his back, except during turns.

balk   In baseball, an illegal move by a pitcher with a runner on base. When a balk is committed, the runner or runners advance one base.

ballhandler   In basketball, the player who directs the play, usually the point guard.

bank shot   In basketball, a ball that hits the backboard before falling through the hoop.

bantamweight   In boxing, a division with a 118-pound weight limit.

baseline   In tennis, the back line of the court, joining the sidelines. A baseliner is a player who stays near the baseline.

batting average   In baseball, the number of hits divided by the number of at bats.

birdie   In golf, completing a hole in one-under par.

blitz   In football, when the defensive team sends several players to try to sack the quarterback.

bogey   In golf, completing a hole in one-over par.

breaststroke   In swimming, a stroke that requires simultaneous movements of the arms on the same horizontal plane. The hands are pushed forward from the breast on or under the surface of the water. The kick is a simultaneous thrust of the legs.

bunker   In golf, a hazard filled with sand.

butterfly   In swimming, a stroke that features the simultaneous overhead stroke of the arms, combined with a dolphin kick.

camel spin   In figure skating, a spin done on one leg with the nonskating leg extended in the air parallel to the ice.

center   In football, the offensive lineman that snaps the ball to the quarterback; in basketball, usually the tallest player on the team, who plays close to the basket. In hockey, the player who is stationed between the left and right wings.

changeup   A pitch thrown with the same arm speed as a fastball. The pitcher holds it between the ring finger and index finger, which keeps him from throwing it as hard. It's used to throw off hitters' timing.

check, checking   In hockey, any defensive or guarding tactic.

college player draft   A system that allows the worst professional teams in baseball, football, basketball, and hockey to select the best players from the college and amateur ranks.

complete game   When a pitcher starts a game and lasts until the outcome is decided.

compulsory figures   In figure skating, required moves performed by all skaters. No longer a part of competitions.

Conn Smythe Trophy   Given to the most valuable player in the Stanley Cup play-offs.

cruiserweight   In boxing, a division with a 190-pound limit.

curveball   A pitch that curves on its way to the plate.

Davis Cup   Tennis team competition for men that began in 1900 and is still played today. Four-man teams represent their countries, playing two singles the first day, a doubles match the second, and two singles the third day, with the opponents reversed. All matches are best-of-five sets.

decathlon   In men's track and field, it consists of 10 events—100-meter sprint, long jump, shot put, high jump, 400-meter sprint, 110-meter hurdles, discus, pole vault, javelin, and 1,500-meter run.

decision   In boxing, a bout decided by the scoring of ringside judges.

default   In tennis, the termination of a match other than by completing it, either by a walkover (the match is never begun, because a participant either concedes or doesn't show up) or retirement (a player is unable to continue due to illness or injury).

defensemen   In hockey, two players who make up a team's defensive unit.

designated hitter   Adopted by the American League in 1973 in an effort to generate more offense. Instead of the pitcher batting, another player bats, but does not play in the field. The rule began as a three-year experiment and continues to this day. Also referred to as the DH.

double bogey   In golf, completing a hole in two-over par.

double-double   In basketball, reaching double digits in two statistical categories.

double eagle   In golf, completing a hole in three-under par.

double play   In baseball, when two players of the batting team are put out on the same play as a result of continuous action by the defense.

downhill   In Alpine skiing, the longest, highest-speed race with the fewest turns.

draw   In boxing, a bout that results in neither fighter being declared the winner.

drop shot   In tennis, a softly hit shot intended to barely clear the net.

eagle   In golf, completing a hole in two-under par.

earned run average   In baseball, the average number of earned runs scored on a pitcher per nine innings. It is calculated by taking the number of earned runs scored on the pitcher, divided by the total number of innings pitched and multiplied by nine.

extra point   In football, a placekick from the two-yard line after a touchdown, also known as a point-after touchdown (PAT).

299

face off In hockey, the act of starting a play by dropping the puck between the sticks of two players, one from each team.

fastball Usually the prime weapon in a pitcher's aresenal. It can reach speeds of more than 90 mph.

fast break In basketball, after a rebound, the offense moves the ball quickly upcourt in order to score before the defense is in position.

field goal In basketball, a shot worth two points if it goes through the basket or three points if it goes into the basket from beyond the three-point line; in football, a placekick worth three points if it goes through the goal posts.

first down In football, the first chance out of four that the offense has to gain 10 yards. If it gains 10 yards within four plays, the team gets another first down.

forecheck In hockey, to closely guard an opponent; usually done by forwards trying to regain control of the puck.

forehand In tennis, a stroke hit from the same side of the body as the racket hand.

Formula One A racing circuit contested mainly in Europe, although there are races in Australia, South America, Japan, and the United States. The cars are much like Indy cars, with open wheels and built low to the ground, but the racetracks are road courses, with the drivers having to wend their way through a series of turns.

forward In basketball, players who are bigger than guards, smaller than the center, and usually play near the basket; in hockey, the center, the left wing, and the right wing—the players who usually make up the attacking line.

free agent A player whose contract expires, allowing him to negotiate and sign a contract with another team.

free skate In figure skating, the free skate counts for 66.7 percent of a skater's final score. It does not have required elements. The skater chooses his or her own music and choreography.

freestyle In swimming, the stroke is characterized by alternate overhead motions of the arms and a flutter kick.

Funny Car In drag racing, short-wheelbased cars with a fiberglass replica of a production car body. The engines are mounted in the front of the car.

giant slalom In alpine skiing, a course that is shorter and lower speed and containing more gates than a downhill, but longer and faster than a slalom.

Gold Glove Awarded annually to the best-fielding baseball player at each position. The winners are determined by a vote of the Major League coaches and managers.

Grand Slam In tennis and golf, the rare feat of winning each of the four major championships in the same year. The Australian, French, Wimbledon, and U.S. championships make up the tennis Grand Slam. The Masters, U.S. Open, British Open, and

PGA Championship make up the golf Grand Slam. The Nabisco Championship, the U.S. Women's Open, the LPGA Championship, and the Women's British Open make up the women's golf Grand Slam. In baseball, a home run with the bases loaded.

goals-against average   In hockey, a measure of a goaltender's effectiveness, calculated by dividing the number of goals scored against him by the number of minutes played.

groundstroke   In tennis, a stroke made after the ball has bounced.

guards   In basketball, usually the smallest players on the court, who are responsible for setting up plays, scoring, and making passes; in football, the offensive linemen on either side of the center.

halfback option pass   A play in which the halfback takes a handoff from the quarterback and has the option to throw a pass or, if no receivers are open, to run.

Hamill Camel   A figure-skating move, created by Dorothy Hamill and her coach, Carlo Fassi, in which the skater progresses from a camel spin directly into a sit spin. A camel spin is done on one leg with the nonskating leg extended in the air parallel to the ice. A sit spin is just what it sounds like—a spin done while crouching like a catcher in baseball.

Hart Trophy   Given to the NHL player judged to be the most valuable to his team.

hat trick   In hockey, three goals in one game scored by the same player.

heavyweight   In boxing, the division with no weight maximum.

Heisman Trophy   Given to the most outstanding college football player in the nation. Named for John Heisman, who spent 36 years as a college football coach (1892–1927) and who was also the president of the Downtown Athletic Club (DAC).

heptathlon   In women's track and field, it consists of seven events—100-meter hurdles, high jump, shot put, 200-meter sprint, long jump, javelin, and 800-meter run.

Hockey Hall of Fame   Located in Toronto since 1943, the hall was originally in Kingston, Ontario.

hole in one   In golf, a ball that goes into the hole from a tee shot.

hook   In boxing, a punch thrown from wide out, into the body or face, with the arm bent at a right angle; in basketball, a one-handed overhead shot made with the back arm when the body is turned sideways to the basket.

hook and ladder   A play in football in which the quarterback has to complete the pass to one of his receivers. That receiver then laterals the ball to a teammate, who is running alongside or slightly behind. This is considered a gimmick play and is rarely used.

individual medley   In swimming, it features all four competitive strokes—butterfly, backstroke, breaststroke, and freestyle.

301

Indy cars   Also known as Champ Cars and open-wheel racers; cars that sit very low to the ground, their wheels not covered by fenders. The engines are located in the rear and the drivers sit in a cockpit, which is not covered.

interception   In football, a pass picked off by a defender.

intermediate track   A racetrack at least one mile, but less than two miles, in distance.

jab   In boxing, a short punch into the body or face.

junior middleweight   In boxing, a division with a 154-pound limit. Also known as a super welterweight.

junior welterweight   In boxing, a division with a 140-pound limit. Also known as a super lightweight.

light heavyweight   In boxing, a division with a 175-pound limit.

lightweight   In boxing, a division with a 135-pound limit.

line of scrimmage   In football, an imaginary line that no player may cross before the ball is snapped.

linebacker   In football, defensive players who are positioned behind the defensive linemen.

long program   In figure skating, a slang expression for the free skate.

major championship   In golf and tennis, the four events in each sport that are the most important.

majority decision   In boxing, a bout in which two judges favor one fighter and the third scores a draw.

marathon   In track and field, a race of 26 miles, 385 yards.

match play   In golf, a form of competition where holes are won, lost, or halved. The winner has won the most holes.

medal play   In golf, a form of competition where strokes are recorded. The winner has the fewest number of strokes. Also known as stroke play.

medalist   In golf, the lowest tournament qualifying score.

medley relay   In swimming, each stroke—butterfly, backstroke, breaststroke, and freestyle—by four different swimmers.

middleweight   In boxing, a division with a 160-pound limit.

mixed doubles   In tennis, doubles with a male and female on each side.

National Invitation Tournament   The first postseason basketball tournament, begun in 1938. Until 1977, the 32-team tourney was played entirely in Madison

Square Garden in New York. But in 1977, the games were moved to on-campus sites, with the semifinals and final being played in the Garden.

NASCAR   National Association for Stock Car Auto Racing; is the most popular of the racing circuits. Stock cars on the NASCAR circuit are vehicles made by Chevrolet, Pontiac, Dodge, and so on. They look much like the ones you see on the street, but they have a few more horses under the hood.

National League   Formed in 1876, was made up of eight teams—Chicago White Stockings, St. Louis Brown Stockings, Cincinnati Reds, Louisville Grays, Boston Red Caps, Hartford Dark Blues, New York Mutuals, and Philadelphia Athletics. The National League is referred to as the Senior Circuit.

no-hitter   In baseball, a game in which the pitcher does not allow a hit. Players who reach base on errors or walks do not affect a no-hitter.

Open era   In tennis, it began in 1968, when professionals and amateurs were allowed to compete in the same tournaments. Prior to the Open era, professionals were prohibited from entering any of the four Grand Slam events.

own goal   In soccer, a goal resulting from a member of the defensive team accidentally putting the ball into his or her own net.

par   In golf, the number of shots needed to complete a hole, figuring two to reach the green, plus two putts. The pars for each individual hole are added to get the course's par.

passing shot   In tennis, a shot that is driven beyond the reach of an opponent at the net.

penalty killing   In hockey, the act of preventing a team with a power play from scoring.

penalty minutes   Assessed when players commit such infractions as roughing, slashing with the stick, coming up high with a stick, interference, and tripping. Players are sent off the ice and into a penalty box for two, five, or ten minutes. For serious infractions, players can be disqualified for the rest of the game.

penalty shot   Awarded to an offensive player who, on a breakaway, is illegally checked or impeded. The puck is placed at the center of the ice, and the player has a free try to score on the opposing goaltender. There are no other players on the ice except the shooter and the goalie.

perfect game   In baseball, a pitcher retiring all 27 batters he faces; in bowling, 12 strikes in a row, also known as a 300 game.

pinch-hitter   In baseball, a batter substituted for another batter. The original batter cannot return to the game.

pinch-runner   In baseball, a player substituted for a base runner. The original runner cannot return to the game.

pit crew   The workers who change the tires, fill the gas tank, clean the windshield, make air pressure adjustments, and so on, whenever the driver makes a stop during a race. The quicker the pit crew finishes, the quicker the driver is back out on the track. A good pit stop these days is completed in less than 15 seconds.

pocket   In football, the area behind the offensive line, where the quarterback is protected by his blockers.

podium finish   In Formula One racing, a first, second, or third place. It's called a podium finish because the top three drivers step up onto a podium, with the winning driver in the middle, positioned higher than the other two.

point guard   In basketball, the player whose job it is to call plays, orchestrate the play, and act as a coach on the floor.

pole   In auto racing, the best position on the starting grid, earned by the driver with the fastest qualifying time.

power-play goal   In hockey, a goal scored with one or more members of the opposing team in the penalty box.

pro-am   In golf, a tournament in which pros are paired with amateur partners.

Pro Stock   In drag racing, cars that most closely resemble cars you would see on the street, but featuring extensive engine modification, sophisticated chassis and suspension development, and a 500-cubic inch engine.

qualifying   In auto racing, preliminary sessions in which cars' starting positions are determined, based on their speed.

relief pitcher   In baseball, any pitcher who enters a game subsequent to the starter.

reserve clause   Written into the standard player's contract in 1887. It mandated that a player remain with his team for his entire career, unless the team decided to trade him, release him, or sell his contract to another team.

Royal & Ancient Golf Club   Located in St. Andrews, Scotland, it is the governing body for golf worldwide, except for the United States and Mexico.

runs batted in   In baseball, the number of runners able to score, including the batter, as a result of the batter's at-bat. For example, if a batter hits a home run with two men on base, he is credited with three runs batted in. Runs batted in are not credited because of errors. Also referred to as RBI.

rush   In hockey, moving the puck toward the opponent's goal; in football, a running attempt.

Ryder Cup   Began as an unofficial golf match between players from the United States and England. Samuel Ryder, who was a British seed merchant, enjoyed the competition so much, he donated the Ryder Cup to be given to the winning team. The first Ryder Cup was played in 1927. The U.S. holds a 24–7–2 lead in the series, which is now contested against Europe.

sack   In football, tackling the quarterback behind the line of scrimmage.

sacrifice   In baseball, a bunt on which the batter is put out, while another runner advances.

safety   In football, being tackled in or having the ball go out of bounds from your own end zone. The defensive team receives two points and the ball. Also, a defensive back whose primary job is to cover pass receivers.

save   In baseball, when a relief pitcher maintains a lead for his team until the game is over; in hockey, the act of a goalie stopping a shot.

secondary   In football, a reference to the defensive backs.

serve-and-volley   In tennis, a style of play where the server rushes the net after serving to get in position to volley.

shootout   If a soccer game is tied after regulation and two extra periods, a shootout determines the winner. Each team gets five penalty kicks. A player stationed 12 yards from the goal goes one-on-one against the keeper. If after the series of five kicks the score is still tied, the process continues until the tie is broken.

short game   In golf, those techniques used on and around the green, including chipping, pitching, and putting.

short program   In figure skating, the two-minute, 40-second program that consists of eight required elements, set to music of the skater's choice.

short track   A racetrack of less than a mile in distance.

short-handed goal   In hockey, a goal scored when one or more of the opposing players are in the penalty box.

shutout   A game in which a pitcher pitches a complete game and doesn't allow any runs. In hockey, a game in which the goaltender allows no goals.

skyhook   In basketball, a hook shot released above the level of the basket; popularized by Kareem Abdul-Jabbar.

slap shot   In hockey, a shot in which the stick is raised above the shoulder on the backswing and then driven with considerable velocity into the puck.

slugging percentage   In baseball, a measure of a batter's ability to hit for extra bases. It is calculated by dividing the total number of bases reached safely by the total number of times at bat.

Solheim Cup   The women's version of the Ryder Cup. It began in 1990 and was named after Karsten Solheim, the inventor of Ping golf clubs.

Southeastern Conference   A renowned college football and basketball conference, formed in 1932; made up of 12 teams split into two divisions. Florida, Georgia, Kentucky, South Carolina, Tennessee, and Vanderbilt are in the East. Alabama, Arkansas, Auburn, Louisiana State, Mississippi, and Mississippi State are in the West.

special teams In football, players who participate in kickoffs, punts, and field goals.

speed skating Contested at five different distances for men and women. The men race at 500, 1,000, 1,500, 5,000, and 10,000 meters. The women race at 500, 1,000, 1,500, 3,000, and 5,000 meters.

split decision In boxing, a bout in which two of the three judges favor one fighter, who is declared the winner.

steeplechase In track and field, a race in which runners negotiate a series of walls and water-filled trenches. The men's 3,000-meter steeplechase has 28 walls and seven water jumps.

stolen base In baseball, when a runner advances to the next base without a hit, putout, force out, fielder's choice, error, balk, passed ball, or wild pitch. The runner usually starts for the next base when the pitcher begins his windup and gets a stolen base if the catcher fails to throw him out.

strike In baseball, a pitch that is over the plate and not swung at, or a pitch that is swung at and missed or fouled off.

stroke play In golf, a tournament in which the winner has the fewest number of strokes. Also known as medal play.

sudden death A game or match decided in overtime as soon as one player or team scores.

super lightweight In boxing, a division with a 140-pound limit. Also known as junior welterweight.

super middleweight In boxing, a division with a 168-pound limit.

super welterweight In boxing, a division with a 154-pound limit. Also known as junior middleweight.

superspeedway A racetrack that is a mile or more in distance.

swingman In basketball, a player who can play guard and forward.

technical knockout In boxing, a fight stopped by the referee because one fighter is injured, unwilling to continue, or unable to continue in the referee's judgment.

T-formation In football, first used by the Chicago Bears, who had the quarterback directly behind the center and a fullback four or five yards behind the quarterback, flanked by two halfbacks. The key to the formation was one of the halfbacks going in motion, laterally and behind the line of scrimmage, before the snap.

three-point shot In basketball, a field goal made from beyond an arc 23 feet from the basket in the NBA, and 19 feet, 9 inches from the basket in high school and college.

Top Fuel In drag racing, the quickest-accelerating of all dragsters. They are powered by supercharged, custom-built 500-cubic inch engines mounted behind the driver.

topspin   In tennis, an overspin put on the ball by brushing the ball from low to high. Topspin allows the ball to be hit very hard and high over the net and still keep it in the court.

touchdown   In football, when a team crosses the opponent's goal line with the ball. It is worth six points.

Tour de France   Cycling's most prestigious event; held annually, it is contested over four weeks and runs throughout France, sometimes passing into neighboring countries. The race is run in stages. The cyclist with the lowest combined time after all the stages is the winner. The 2000 Tour de France was made up of 20 stages and covered 2,276 miles.

Triple Crown   In baseball, a batter who leads the league in batting average, home runs, and runs batted in; in horse racing, winning the Kentucky Derby, Preakness, and Belmont Stakes in the same year.

triple play   In baseball, when three players of the batting team are put out on the same play as a result of continuous action by the defense.

triple-double   In basketball, when a player records double digits in three statistical categories, such as points, rebounds, and assists.

turnover   Losing possession of the ball or the puck during play.

two-minute drill   In football, several plays called in the huddle to save time near the end of a half or the end of a game.

two-point conversion   In football, running a play from scrimmage, starting at the two-yard line, following a touchdown.

United States Golf Association (USGA)   The governing body of golf in the United States and Mexico.

United States Tennis Association (USTA)   The governing body of tennis in the United States.

uppercut   In boxing, a punch thrown from the waist or below the waist.

Vezina Trophy   Given to the principal goaltender(s) on the team that gives up the fewest goals during the regular season.

volley   In tennis, to hit the ball before it touches the ground. The stroke is usually executed at the net.

welterweight   In boxing, a division with a 147-pound limit.

wild card   Playoff berths that go nondivision winners in the NFL and Major League Baseball.

Winston Cup   A series of more than 30 races, with points awarded for each race. Drivers earn points for where they finish and laps led. The race winner, for example, earns 175 points. The points accumulate throughout the season. The driver with the most points at season's end is the Winston Cup champion.

Women's World Cup   A soccer competition between countries, held every four years and started in 1991.

World Cup   A men's soccer competition between countries, held every four years and started in 1930.

World Hockey Association   Debuted in the 1972–73 season to compete with the National Hockey League. The WHA began with 12 teams and lasted seven seasons, disbanding in 1979.

zone defense   In basketball, a defense where players cover an area of the court, as opposed to a particular man.

Champions

Welcome to the Champions appendix, where you'll find the winners of the World Series, Super Bowl, NBA Finals, and Stanley Cup. Also included are champions from NASCAR, Indy car, and Formula One racing; players of the year in men's and women's golf; and the No. 1 ranked player each year in men's and women's tennis.

Major League Baseball World Series Champions

Note: National League teams listed in capital letters.

1903 Boston Red Sox

1904 Not held

1905 NEW YORK GIANTS

1906 Chicago White Sox

1907 CHICAGO CUBS

1908 CHICAGO CUBS

1909 PITTSBURGH PIRATES

1910 Philadelphia A's

1911 Philadelphia A's

1912 Boston Red Sox

1913 Philadelphia A's

1914 BOSTON BRAVES

1915 Boston Red Sox

1916 Boston Red Sox

1917 Chicago White Sox

1918 Boston Red Sox

1919 CINCINNATI REDS

1920 Cleveland Indians

1921 NEW YORK GIANTS

1922 NEW YORK GIANTS

1923 New York Yankees

1924 Washington Senators

1925 PITTSBURGH PIRATES

1926 ST. LOUIS CARDINALS

1927 New York Yankees

1928 New York Yankees

1929 Philadelphia A's

1930 Philadelphia A's

1931 ST. LOUIS CARDINALS

1932 New York Yankees

1933 NEW YORK GIANTS

1934 ST. LOUIS CARDINALS

1935 Detroit Tigers

1936 New York Yankees

1937 New York Yankees

1938 New York Yankees

1939 New York Yankees

1940 CINCINNATI REDS

1941 New York Yankees

1942 ST. LOUIS CARDINALS

1943 New York Yankees

1944 ST. LOUIS CARDINALS

1945 Detroit Tigers

1946 ST. LOUIS CARDINALS

1947 New York Yankees

1948 Cleveland Indians

1949 New York Yankees

1950 New York Yankees

1951 New York Yankees

1952 New York Yankees

1953 New York Yankees

1954 NEW YORK GIANTS

1955 BROOKLYN DODGERS

1956 New York Yankees

1957 MILWAUKEE BRAVES

1958 New York Yankees

1959 LOS ANGELES DODGERS

1960 PITTSBURGH PIRATES

1961 New York Yankees

1962 New York Yankees

1963 LOS ANGELES DODGERS

1964 ST. LOUIS CARDINALS

1965 LOS ANGELES DODGERS

1966 Baltimore Orioles

1967 ST. LOUIS CARDINALS

1968 Detroit Tigers

1969 NEW YORK METS

1970 Baltimore Orioles

1971 PITTSBURGH PIRATES

1972 Oakland A's

1973 Oakland A's

1974 Oakland A's

1975 CINCINNATI REDS

1976 CINCINNATI REDS

1977 New York Yankees

1978 New York Yankees

1979 PITTSBURGH PIRATES

1980 PHILADELPHIA PHILLIES

1981 LOS ANGELES DODGERS

1982 ST. LOUIS CARDINALS

1983 Baltimore Orioles

1984 Detroit Tigers

1985 Kansas City Royals

1986 NEW YORK METS

1987 Minnesota Twins

1988 LOS ANGELES DODGERS

1989 Oakland A's

1990 CINCINNATI REDS

1991 Minnesota Twins

1992 Toronto Blue Jays

1993 Toronto Blue Jays

1994 Not held (players' strike)

1995 ATLANTA BRAVES

1996 New York Yankees

1997 FLORIDA MARLINS

1998 New York Yankees

1999 New York Yankees

2000 New York Yankees

National Football League Champions

Note: The first Super Bowl was held in 1967, following the 1966 season.

1933 Chicago Bears

1934 New York Giants

1935 Detroit Tigers

1936 Green Bay Packers

1937 Washington Redskins

1938 New York Giants

1939 Green Bay Packers

1940 Chicago Bears

1941 Chicago Bears

1942 Washington Redskins

1943 Chicago Bears

1944 Green Bay Packers

1945 Cleveland Rams

1946 Chicago Bears

1947 Chicago Cardinals

1948 Philadelphia Eagles

1949 Philadelphia Eagles

1950 Cleveland Browns

1951 Los Angeles Rams

1952 Detroit Lions

1953 Detroit Lions

1954 Cleveland Browns

1955 Cleveland Browns

1956 New York Giants

1957 Detroit Lions

1958 Baltimore Colts

1959 Baltimore Colts

1960 Philadelphia Eagles

1961 Green Bay Packers

1962 Green Bay Packers

1963 Chicago Bears

1964 Cleveland Browns

1965 Green Bay Packers

1966 Green Bay Packers (Super Bowl I)

1967 Green Bay Packers (Super Bowl II)

1968 New York Jets (Super Bowl III)

1969 Kansas City Chiefs (Super Bowl IV)

1970 Baltimore Colts (Super Bowl V)

1971 Dallas Cowboys (Super Bowl VI)

1972 Miami Dolphins (Super Bowl VII)

1973 Miami Dolphins (Super Bowl VIII)

1974 Pittsburgh Steelers (Super Bowl IX)

1975 Pittsburgh Steelers (Super Bowl X)

1976 Oakland Raiders (Super Bowl XI)

1977 Dallas Cowboys (Super Bowl XII)

1978 Pittsburgh Steelers (Super Bowl XIII)

1979 Pittsburgh Steelers (Super Bowl XIV)

1980 Oakland Raiders (Super Bowl XV)

1981 San Francisco 49ers (Super Bowl XVI)

1982 Washington Redskins (Super Bowl XVII)

1983 Oakland Raiders (Super Bowl XVIII)

1984 San Francisco 49ers (Super Bowl XIX)

1985 Chicago Bears (Super Bowl XX)

1986 New York Giants (Super Bowl XXI)

1987 Washington Redskins (Super Bowl XXII)

1988 San Francisco 49ers (Super Bowl XXIII)

311

1989 San Francisco 49ers (Super Bowl XXIV)

1990 New York Giants (Super Bowl XXV)

1991 Washington Redskins (Super Bowl XXVI)

1992 Dallas Cowboys (Super Bowl XXVII)

1993 Dallas Cowboys (Super Bowl XXVIII)

1994 San Francisco 49ers (Super Bowl XXIX)

1995 Dallas Cowboys (Super Bowl XXX)

1996 Green Bay Packers (Super Bowl XXXI)

1997 Denver Broncos (Super Bowl XXXII)

1998 Denver Broncos (Super Bowl XXXIII)

1999 St. Louis Rams (Super Bowl XXXIV)

2000 Baltimore Ravens (Super Bowl XXXV)

National Basketball Association Champions

1947 Philadelphia Warriors	1962 Boston Celtics
1947 Baltimore Bullets	1963 Boston Celtics
1948 Minneapolis Lakers	1964 Boston Celtics
1949 Minneapolis Lakers	1965 Boston Celtics
1950 Rochester Royals	1966 Philadelphia 76ers
1951 Minneapolis Lakers	1967 Boston Celtics
1952 Minneapolis Lakers	1968 Boston Celtics
1953 Minneapolis Lakers	1969 New York Knicks
1954 Syracuse Nationals	1970 Milwaukee Bucks
1955 Philadelphia Warriors	1971 Los Angeles Lakers
1956 Boston Celtics	1972 New York Knicks
1957 St. Louis Hawks	1973 Boston Celtics
1958 Boston Celtics	1974 Golden State Warriors
1959 Boston Celtics	1975 Boston Celtics
1960 Boston Celtics	1976 Portland Trail Blazers
1961 Boston Celtics	1977 Washington Bullets

1978 Seattle SuperSonics	1990 Chicago Bulls
1979 Los Angeles Lakers	1991 Chicago Bulls
1980 Boston Celtics	1992 Chicago Bulls
1981 Los Angeles Lakers	1993 Houston Rockets
1982 Philadelphia 76ers	1994 Houston Rockets
1983 Boston Celtics	1995 Chicago Bulls
1984 Los Angeles Lakers	1996 Chicago Bulls
1985 Boston Celtics	1997 Chicago Bulls
1986 Los Angeles Lakers	1998 San Antonio Spurs
1987 Los Angeles Lakers	1999 Los Angeles Lakers
1988 Detroit Pistons	2000 Los Angeles Lakers
1989 Detroit Pistons	2001 Los Angeles Lakers

National Hockey League Stanley Cup Champions

1927 Ottawa Senators	1943 Detroit Red Wings
1928 New York Rangers	1944 Montreal Canadiens
1929 Boston Bruins	1945 Toronto Maple Leafs
1930 Montreal Canadiens	1946 Montreal Canadiens
1931 Montreal Canadiens	1947 Toronto Maple Leafs
1932 Toronto Maple Leafs	1948 Toronto Maple Leafs
1933 New York Rangers	1949 Toronto Maple Leafs
1934 Chicago Blackhawks	1950 Detroit Red Wings
1935 Montreal Maroons	1951 Toronto Maple Leafs
1936 Detroit Red Wings	1952 Detroit Red Wings
1937 Detroit Red Wings	1953 Montreal Canadiens
1938 Chicago Blackhawks	1954 Detroit Red Wings
1939 Boston Bruins	1955 Detroit Red Wings
1940 New York Rangers	1956 Montreal Canadiens
1941 Boston Bruins	1957 Montreal Canadiens
1942 Toronto Maple Leafs	1958 Montreal Canadiens

1959 Montreal Canadiens	1981 New York Islanders
1960 Montreal Canadiens	1982 New York Islanders
1961 Chicago Blackhawks	1983 New York Islanders
1962 Toronto Maple Leafs	1984 Edmonton Oilers
1963 Toronto Maple Leafs	1985 Edmonton Oilers
1964 Toronto Maple Leafs	1986 Montreal Canadiens
1965 Montreal Canadiens	1987 Edmonton Oilers
1966 Montreal Canadiens	1988 Edmonton Oilers
1967 Toronto Maple Leafs	1989 Calgary Flames
1968 Montreal Canadiens	1990 Edmonton Oilers
1969 Montreal Canadiens	1991 Pittsburgh Penguins
1970 Boston Bruins	1992 Pittsburgh Penguins
1971 Montreal Canadiens	1993 Montreal Canadiens
1972 Boston Bruins	1994 New York Rangers
1973 Montreal Canadiens	1995 New Jersey Devils
1974 Philadelphia Flyers	1996 Colorado Avalanche
1975 Philadelphia Flyers	1997 Detroit Red Wings
1976 Montreal Canadiens	1998 Detroit Red Wings
1977 Montreal Canadiens	1999 Dallas Stars
1978 Montreal Canadiens	2000 New Jersey Devils
1979 Montreal Canadiens	2001 Colorado Avalanche
1980 New York Islanders	

Auto Racing

NASCAR: Winston Cup Champions

From 1949–70, referred to as Grand National champion.

1949 Red Byron	1952 Tim Flock
1950 Bill Rexford	1953 Herb Thomas
1951 Herb Thomas	1954 Lee Petty

1955 Tim Flock	1978 Cale Yarborough
1956 Buck Baker	1979 Richard Petty
1957 Buck Baker	1980 Dale Earnhardt
1958 Lee Petty	1981 Darrell Waltrip
1959 Lee Petty	1982 Darrell Waltrip
1960 Rex White	1983 Bobby Allison
1961 Ned Jarrett	1984 Terry Labonte
1962 Joe Weatherly	1985 Darrell Waltrip
1963 Joe Weatherly	1986 Dale Earnhardt
1964 Richard Petty	1987 Dale Earnhardt
1965 Ned Jarrett	1988 Bill Elliott
1966 David Pearson	1989 Rusty Wallace
1967 Richard Petty	1990 Dale Earnhardt
1968 David Pearson	1991 Dale Earnhardt
1969 David Pearson	1992 Alan Kulwicki
1970 Bobby Isaac	1993 Dale Earnhardt
1971 Richard Petty	1994 Dale Earnhardt
1972 Richard Petty	1995 Jeff Gordon
1973 Benny Parsons	1996 Terry Labonte
1974 Richard Petty	1997 Jeff Gordon
1975 Richard Petty	1998 Jeff Gordon
1976 Cale Yarborough	1999 Dale Jarrett
1977 Cale Yarborough	2000 Bobby Labonte

Indy Car: CART

Known as AAA from 1909–55, USAC from 1956–78.

1909 George Robertson	1913 Earl Cooper
1910 Ray Harroun	1914 Ralph DePalma
1911 Ralph Mulford	1915 Earl Cooper
1912 Ralph DePalma	1916 Dario Resta

1917 Earl Cooper

1918 Ralph Mulford

1919 Howard Wilcox

1920 Tommy Milton

1921 Tommy Milton

1922 Jimmy Murphy

1923 Eddie Hearne

1924 Jimmy Murphy

1925 Peter DePaolo

1926 Harry Hartz

1927 Peter DePaolo

1928 Louie Meyer

1929 Louie Meyer

1930 Billy Arnold

1931 Louis Schneider

1932 Bob Carey

1933 Louie Meyer

1934 Bill Cummings

1935 Kelly Petillo

1936 Mauri Rose

1937 Wilbur Shaw

1938 Floyd Roberts

1939 Wilbur Shaw

1940 Rex Mays

1941 Rex Mays

1942–1945 No racing

1946 Ted Horn

1947 Ted Horn

1948 Ted Horn

1949 Johnnie Parsons

1950 Henry Banks

1951 Tony Bettenhausen

1952 Chuck Stevenson

1953 Sam Hanks

1954 Jimmy Bryan

1955 Bob Sweikert

1956 Jimmy Bryan

1957 Jimmy Bryan

1958 Tony Bettenhausen

1959 Rodger Ward

1960 A.J. Foyt

1961 A.J. Foyt

1962 Rodger Ward

1963 A.J. Foyt

1964 A.J. Foyt

1965 Mario Andretti

1966 Mario Andretti

1967 A.J.Foyt

1968 Bobby Unser

1969 Mario Andretti

1970 Al Unser

1971 Joe Leonard

1972 Joe Leonard

1973 Roger McCluskey

1974 Bobby Unser

1975 A.J. Foyt

1976 Gordon Johncock

1977 Tom Sneva

1978 A.J. Foyt

1979 Rick Mears

1980 Johnny Rutherford

1981 Rick Mears

1982 Rick Mears

1983 Al Unser

1984 Mario Andretti

1985 Al Unser

1986 Bobby Rahal

1987 Bobby Rahal

1988 Danny Sullivan

1989 Emerson Fittipaldi

1990 Al Unser Jr.

1991 Michael Andretti

1992 Bobby Rahal

1993 Nigel Mansell

1994 Al Unser Jr.

1995 Jacques Villeneuve

1996 Jimmy Vasser

1997 Alex Zanardi

1998 Alex Zanardi

1999 Juan Montoya

2000 Gil de Ferran

Indy Racing League

1996 Buzz Calkins, Scott Sharp

1997 Tony Stewart

1998 Kenny Brack

1999 Greg Ray

2000 Buddy Lazier

Formula One: World Championship of Drivers

1950 Guiseppe Farina

1951 Juan-Manuel Fangio

1952 Alberto Ascari

1953 Alberto Ascari

1954 Juan-Manuel Fangio

1955 Juan-Manuel Fangio

1956 Juan-Manuel Fangio

1957 Juan-Manuel Fangio

1958 Mike Hawthorn

1959 Jack Brabham

1960 Jack Brabham

1961 Phil Hill

1962 Phil Hill

1963 Jim Clark

1964 John Surtees

1965 Jim Clark

1966 Jack Brabham

1967 Denis Hulme

1968 Graham Hill

1969 Jackie Stewart

1970 Jochen Rindt

1971 Jackie Stewart

1972 Emerson Fittipaldi

1973 Jackie Stewart

1974 Emerson Fittipaldi

1975 Niki Lauda

1976 James Hunt

1977 Niki Lauda

1978 Mario Andretti

1979 Jody Scheckter

1980 Alan Jones

1981 Nelson Piquet

1982 Keke Rosberg

1983 Nelson Piquet

1984 Niki Lauda

1985 Alain Prost

1986 Alain Prost

1987 Nelson Piquet

1988 Ayrton Senna

1989 Alain Prost

1990 Ayrton Senna

1991 Ayrton Senna

1992 Nigel Mansell

1993 Alain Prost

1994 Michael Schumacher

1995 Michael Schumacher

1996 Damon Hill

1997 Jacques Villeneuve

1998 Mika Hakkinen

1999 Mika Hakkinen

2000 Michael Schumacher

Golf

PGA of America Player of the Year

1948 Ben Hogan

1949 Sam Snead

1950 Ben Hogan

1951 Ben Hogan

1952 Julius Boros

1953 Ben Hogan

1954 Ed Furgol

1955 Doug Ford

1956 Jack Burke

1957 Dick Mayer

1958 Dow Finsterwald

1959 Art Wall

1960 Arnold Palmer

1961 Jerry Barber

1962 Arnold Palmer

1963 Julius Boros

1964 Ken Venturi

1965 Dave Marr

1966 Billy Casper

1967 Jack Nicklaus

1968 No award

1969 Orville Moody

1970 Billy Casper

1971 Lee Trevino

1972 Jack Nicklaus

1973 Jack Nicklaus

1974 Johnny Miller

1975 Jack Nicklaus

1976 Jack Nicklaus

1977 Tom Watson

1978 Tom Watson

1979 Tom Watson

1980 Tom Watson

1981 Bill Rogers

1982 Tom Watson

1983 Hal Sutton

1984 Tom Watson

1985 Lanny Wadkins

1986 Bob Tway

1987 Paul Azinger

1988 Curtis Strange

1989 Tom Kite

1990 Nick Faldo

1991 Corey Pavin

1992 Fred Couples

1993 Nick Price

1994 Nick Price

1995 Greg Norman

1996 Tom Lehman

1997 Tiger Woods

1998 Mark O'Meara

1999 Tiger Woods

2000 Tiger Woods

LPGA Player of the Year

1966 Kathy Whitworth

1967 Kathy Whitworth

1968 Kathy Whitworth

1969 Kathy Whitworth

1970 Sandra Haynie

1971 Kathy Whitworth

1972 Kathy Whitworth

1973 Kathy Whitworth

1974 JoAnne Carner

1975 Sandra Palmer

1976 Judy Rankin

1977 Judy Rankin

1978 Nancy Lopez

1979 Nancy Lopez

1980 Beth Daniel

1981 JoAnne Carner

1982 JoAnne Carner

1983 Patty Sheehan

1984 Betsy King

1985 Nancy Lopez

1986 Pat Bradley

1987 Ayako Okamoto

1988 Nancy Lopez

1989 Betsy King

1990 Beth Daniel

1991 Pat Bradley

1992 Dottie Mochrie

1993 Betsy King

1994 Beth Daniel

1995 Annika Sorenstam

1996 Laura Davies

1997 Annika Sorenstam

1998 Annika Sorenstam

1999 Karrie Webb

2000 Karrie Webb

Tennis

Players ranked No. 1 since 1968, the start of the Open era.

Men

1968 Rod Laver

1969 Rod Laver

1970 John Newcombe

1971 John Newcombe

1972 Stan Smith

1973 Ilie Nastase

1974 Jimmy Connors

1975 Jimmy Connors

1976 Jimmy Connors

1977 Jimmy Connors

1978 Jimmy Connors

1979 Bjorn Borg

1980 Bjorn Borg

1981 John McEnroe

1982 John McEnroe

1983 John McEnroe

1984 John McEnroe

1985 Ivan Lendl

1986 Ivan Lendl

1987 Ivan Lendl

1988 Mats Wilander

1989 Ivan Lendl

1990 Stefan Edberg

1991 Stefan Edberg

1992 Jim Courier

1993 Pete Sampras

1994 Pete Sampras

1995 Pete Sampras

1996 Pete Sampras

1997 Pete Sampras

1998 Pete Sampras

1999 Andre Agassi

2000 Gustavo Kuerten

Women

1968 Billie Jean King	1985 Martina Navratilova
1969 Margaret Court	1986 Martina Navratilova
1970 Margaret Court	1987 Steffi Graf
1971 Evonne Goolagong	1988 Steffi Graf
1972 Billie Jean King	1989 Steffi Graf
1973 Margaret Court	1990 Steffi Graf
1974 Billie Jean King	1991 Monica Seles
1975 Chris Evert	1992 Monica Seles
1976 Chris Evert	1993 Steffi Graf
1977 Chris Evert	1994 Steffi Graf
1978 Martina Navratilova	1995 Steffi Graf
1979 Martina Navratilova	1996 Steffi Graf
1980 Chris Evert	1997 Martina Hingis
1981 Chris Evert	1998 Lindsay Davenport
1982 Martina Navratilova	1999 Martina Hingis
1983 Martina Navratilova	2000 Martina Hingis
1984 Martina Navratilova	

Hall of Famers

National Baseball Hall of Fame and Museum, Cooperstown, N.Y.

Catchers	Year Inducted	Catchers	Year Inducted
Bench, Johnny	1989	Ewing, Buck	1939
Berra, Yogi	1972	Ferrell, Rick	1984
Bresnahan, Roger	1945	Fisk, Carlton	2000
Campanella, Roy	1969	Hartnett, Gabby	1955
Cochrane, Mickey	1947	Lombardi, Ernie	1986
Dickey, Bill	1954	Schalk, Ray	1955

First Basemen	Year Inducted	First Basemen	Year Inducted
Anson, Cap	1939	Greenberg, Hank	1956
Beckley, Jake	1971	Kelly, George	1973
Bottomley, Jim	1974	Killebrew, Harmon	1984
Brouthers, Dan	1945	McCovey, Willie	1986
Cepeda, Orlando	1999	Mize, Johnny	1981
Chance, Frank	1946	Perez, Tony	2000
Connor, Roger	1976	Sisler, George	1939
Foxx, Jimmie	1951	Terry, Bill	1954
Gehrig, Lou	1939		

Second Basemen	Year Inducted	Second Basemen	Year Inducted
Carew, Rod	1991	Hornsby, Rogers	1942
Collins, Eddie	1939	Lajoie, Nap	1937
Doerr, Bobby	1986	Lazzeri, Tony	1991
Evers, Johnny	1946	Mazeroski, Bill	2001
Fox, Nellie	1997	McPhee, Bid	2000
Frisch, Frankie	1947	Morgan, Joe	1990
Gehringer, Charlie	1949	Robinson, Jackie	1962
Herman, Billy	1975	Schoendienst, Red	1989

Shortstops	Year Inducted	Shortstops	Year Inducted
Aparicio, Luis	1984	Reese, Pee Wee	1984
Appling, Luke	1964	Rizzuto, Phil	1994
Bancroft, Dave	1971	Sewell, Joe	1977
Banks, Ernie	1977	Tinker, Joe	1946
Boudreau, Lou	1970	Vaughan, Arky	1985
Cronin, Joe	1956	Wagner, Honus	1936
Davis, George	1998	Wallace, Bobby	1953
Jackson, Travis	1982	Ward, Monte	1964
Jennings, Hugh	1945	Yount, Robin	1999
Maranville, Rabbit	1954		

Third Basemen	Year Inducted	Third Basemen	Year Inducted
Baker, Frank	1955	Mathews, Eddie	1978
Brett, George	1999	Robinson, Brooks	1983
Collins, Jimmy	1945	Schmidt, Mike	1995
Kell, George	1983	Traynor, Pie	1948
Lindstrom, Fred	1976		

Left Fielders	Year Inducted	Left Fielders	Year Inducted
Brock, Lou	1985	Musial, Stan	1969
Burkett, Jesse	1946	O'Rourke, Jim	1945
Clarke, Fred	1945	Simmons, Al	1953
Delahanty, Ed	1945	Stargell, Willie	1988
Goslin, Goose	1968	Wheat, Zack	1959
Hafey, Chick	1971	Williams, Billy	1987
Kelley, Joe	1971	Williams, Ted	1966
Kiner, Ralph	1975	Winfield, Dave	2001
Manush, Heinie	1964	Yastrzemski, Carl	1989
Medwick, Joe	1968		

Center Fielders	Year Inducted	Center Fielders	Year Inducted
Ashburn, Richie	1995	Mantle, Mickey	1974
Averill, Earl	1975	Mays, Willie	1979
Carey, Max	1961	Puckett, Kirby	2001
Cobb, Ty	1936	Roush, Edd	1962
Combs, Earle	1970	Snider, Duke	1980
DiMaggio, Joe	1955	Speaker, Tris	1937
Doby, Larry	1998	Waner, Lloyd	1967
Duffy, Hugh	1945	Wilson, Hack	1979
Hamilton, Billy	1961		

Right Fielders	Year Inducted	Right Fielders	Year Inducted
Aaron, Hank	1982	Klein, Chuck	1980
Clemente, Roberto	1973	McCarthy, Tommy	1946
Crawford, Sam	1957	Ott, Mel	1951
Cuyler, Kiki	1968	Rice, Sam	1963
Flick, Elmer	1963	Robinson, Frank	1982
Heilmann, Harry	1952	Ruth, Babe	1936
Hooper, Harry	1971	Slaughter, Enos	1985
Jackson, Reggie	1993	Thompson, Sam	1974
Kaline, Al	1980	Waner, Paul	1952
Keeler, Willie	1939	Youngs, Ross	1972
Kelly, King	1945		

Pitchers	Year Inducted	Pitchers	Year Inducted
Alexander, Grover	1938	Lyons, Ted	1955
Bender, Chief	1953	Marichal, Juan	1983
Brown, Mordecai	1949	Marquard, Rube	1971
Bunning, Jim	1996	Mathewson, Christy	1936
Carlton, Steve	1994	McGinnity, Joe	1946
Chesbro, Jack	1946	Niekro, Phil	1997
Clarkson, John	1963	Newhouser, Hal	1992
Coveleski, Stan	1969	Nichols, Kid	1949
Dean, Dizzy	1953	Palmer, Jim	1990
Drysdale, Don	1984	Pennock, Herb	1948
Faber, Red	1964	Perry, Gaylord	1991
Feller, Bob	1962	Plank, Eddie	1946
Fingers, Rollie	1992	Radbourne, Old Hoss	1939
Ford, Whitey	1974	Rixey, Eppa	1963
Galvin, Pud	1965	Roberts, Robin	1976
Gibson, Bob	1981	Ruffing, Red	1967
Gomez, Lefty	1972	Rusie, Amos	1977
Grimes, Burleigh	1964	Ryan, Nolan	1999
Grove, Lefty	1947	Seaver, Tom	1992
Haines, Jess	1970	Spahn, Warren	1973
Hoyt, Waite	1969	Sutton, Don	1998
Hubbell, Carl	1947	Vance, Dazzy	1955
Hunter, Catfish	1987	Waddell, Rube	1946
Jenkins, Ferguson	1991	Walsh, Ed	1946
Johnson, Walter	1936	Welch, Mickey	1973
Joss, Addie	1978	Wilhelm, Hoyt	1985
Keefe, Tim	1964	Willis, Vic	1995
Koufax, Sandy	1972	Wynn, Early	1972
Lemon, Bob	1976	Young, Cy	1937

Managers	Year Inducted	Managers	Year Inducted
Alston, Walter	1983	Mack, Connie	1937
Anderson, Sparky	2000	McCarthy, Joe	1957
Durocher, Leo	1994	McGraw, John	1937
Hanlon, Ned	1996	McKechnie, Bill	1962
Harris, Bucky	1975	Robinson, Wilbert	1945
Huggins, Miller	1964	Selee, Frank	1999
Lasorda, Tommy	1997	Stengel, Casey	1966
Lopez, Al	1977	Weaver, Earl	1996

Umpires	Year Inducted	Umpires	Year Inducted
Barlick, Al	1989	Evans, Billy	1973
Chylak, Nestor	1999	Hubbard, Cal	1976
Conlan, Jocko	1974	Klem, Bill	1953
Connolly, Tom	1953	McGowan, Bill	1992

From Negro Leagues	Year Inducted	From Negro Leagues	Year Inducted
Bell, Cool Papa (OF)	1974	Johnson, Judy (3B)	1975
Charleston, Oscar (1B-OF)	1976	Leonard, Buck (1B)	1972
Dandridge, Ray (3B)	1987	Lloyd, Pop (SS)	1977
Day, Leon (P-OF-2B)	1995	Paige, Satchel (P)	1971
Dihigo, Martin (P-OF)	1977	Rogan, Wilber (P)	1998
Foster, Rube (P-MGR)	1981	Smith, Hilton (P)	2001
Foster, Willie (P)	1996	Stearnes, Turkey (CF)	2000
Gibson, Josh (c)	1972	Wells, Willie (SS)	1997
Irvin, Monte (OF)	1973	Williams, Joe (P)	1999

Pioneers and Executives	Year Inducted	Pioneers and Executives	Year Inducted
Barrow, Ed	1953	Johnson, Ban	1937
Bulkeley, Morgan	1937	Landis, Kenesaw	1944
Cartwright, Alexander	1938	MacPhail, Larry	1978
Chadwick, Henry	1938	MacPhail, Lee	1998
Chandler, Happy	1982	Rickey, Branch	1967
Comiskey, Charles	1939	Spalding, Al	1939
Cummings, Candy	1939	Veeck, Bill	1991
Frick, Ford	1970	Weiss, George	1971
Giles, Warren	1979	Wright, George	1937
Griffith, Clark	1946	Wright, Harry	1953
Harridge, Will	1972	Yawkey, Tom	1980
Hulbert, William	1995		

Naismith Memorial Basketball Hall of Fame, Springfield, Mass.

Men	Year Inducted	Men	Year Inducted
Abdul-Jabbar, Kareem	1995	Goodrich, Gail	1996
Archibald, Nate	1991	Greer, Hal	1981
Arizin, Paul	1977	Gruenig, Robert	1963
Barlow, Thomas (Babe)	1980	Hagan, Cliff	1977
Barry, Rick	1987	Hanson, Victor	1960
Baylor, Elgin	1976	Havlicek, John	1983
Beckman, John	1972	Hawkins, Connie	1992
Bellamy, Walt	1993	Hayes, Elvin	1990
Belov, Sergei	1992	Haynes, Marques	1998
Bing, Dave	1990	Heinsohn, Tom	1986
Bird, Larry	1998	Holman, Nat	1964
Borgmann, Benny	1961	Houbregs, Bob	1987
Bradley, Bill	1982	Howell, Bailey	1997
Brennan, Joe	1974	Hyatt, Chuck	1959
Cervi, Al	1984	Issel, Dan	1993
Chamberlain, Wilt	1978	Jeannette, Buddy	1994
Cooper, Charles (Tarzan)	1976	Johnson, Bill (Skinny)	1976
Cosic, Kresimir	1996	Johnston, Neil	1990
Cousy, Bob	1970	Jones, K.C.	1989
Cowens, Dave	1991	Jones, Sam	1983
Cunningham, Billy	1986	Krause, Edward (Moose)	1975
Davies, Bob	1969	Kurland, Bob	1961
DeBernardi, Forrest	1961	Lanier, Bob	1992
DeBusschere, Dave	1982	Lapchick, Joe	1966
Dehnert, Dutch	1968	Lovellette, Clyde	1988
Endacott, Paul	1971	Lucas, Jerry	1979
English, Alex	1997	Luisetti, Hank	1959
Erving, Julius (Dr. J)	1993	Macauley, Ed	1960
Foster, Bud	1964	Malone, Moses	2001
Frazier, Wilt	1987	Maravich, Pete	1987
Friedman, Marty	1971	Martin, Slater	1981
Fulks, Joe	1977	McAdoo, Bob	2000
Gale, Laddie	1976	McCracken, Branch	1980
Gallatin, Harry	1991	McCracken, Jack	1962
Gates, William (Pop)	1989	McDermott, Bobby	1988
Gervin, George	1996	McGuire, Dick	1993
Gola, Tom	1975	McHale, Kevin	1999

Men	Year Inducted	Men	Year Inducted
Mikan, George	1959	Schommer, John	1959
Mikkelsen, Vern	1995	Sedran, Barney	1962
Monroe, Earl	1990	Sharman, Bill	1975
Murphy, Calvin	1993	Steinmetz, Christian	1961
Murphy, Charles (Stretch)	1960	Thompson, David	1996
Page, Harlan (Pat)	1962	Thompson, John (Cat)	1962
Pettit, Bob	1970	Thurmond, Nate	1984
Phillip, Andy	1961	Twyman, Jack	1982
Pollard, Jim	1977	Unseld, Wes	1988
Ramsey, Frank	1981	Vandivier, Robert (Fuzzy)	1974
Reed, Willis	1981	Wachter, Ed	1961
Risen, Arnie	1998	Walton, Bill	1993
Robertson, Oscar	1979	Wanzer, Bobby	1987
Roosma, John	1961	West, Jerry	1979
Russell, Bill	1974	Wilkens, Lenny	1989
Russell, John (Honey)	1964	Wooden, John	1960
Schayes, Dolph	1972	Yardley, George	1996
Schmidt, Ernest J.	1973		

Women	Year Inducted	Women	Year Inducted
Blazejowski, Carol	1994	Lieberman-Cline, Nancy	1996
Crawford, Joan	1997	Meyers, Ann	1993
Curry, Denise	1997	Miller, Cheryl	1995
Donovan, Anne	1995	Semenova, Juliana	1993
Harris, Lucy	1992	White, Nera	1992

Teams	Year Inducted
Buffalo Germans	1961
First Team	1959
New York Renaissance	1963
Original Celtics	1959

Referees	Year Inducted	Referees	Year Inducted
Enright, Jim	1978	Nucatola, John	1977
Hepbron, George	1960	Quigley, Ernest (Quig)	1961
Hoyt, George	1961	Shirley, J. Dallas	1979
Kennedy, Pat	1959	Strom, Earl	1995
Leith, Lloyd	1982	Tobey, Dave	1961
Mihalik, Red	1986	Walsh, David	1961

Coaches	Year Inducted	Coaches	Year Inducted
Allen, Forrest (Phog)	1959	Keogan, George	1961
Anderson, Harold (Andy)	1984	Knight, Bob	1991
Auerbach, Red	1968	Krzyzewski, Mike	2001
Barry, Sam	1978	Kundla, John	1995
Blood, Ernest (Prof)	1960	Lambert, Ward (Piggy)	1960
Cann, Howard	1967	Litwack, Harry	1975
Carlson, Henry (Doc)	1959	Loeffler, Ken	1964
Carnesecca, Lou	1992	Lonborg, Dutch	1972
Carnevale, Ben	1969	McCutchan, Arad	1980
Carril, Pete	1997	McGuire, Al	1992
Case, Everett	1981	McGuire, Frank	1976
Chaney, John	2001	Meanwell, Walter (Doc)	1959
Conradt, Judy	1998	Meyer, Ray	1978
Crum, Denny	1994	Miller, Ralph	1988
Daly, Chuck	1994	Moore, Billie	1999
Dean, Everett	1966	Nikolic, Aleksandar	1998
Diaz-Miguel, Antonio	1997	Ramsay, Jack	1992
Diddle, Ed	1971	Rubini, Cesare	1994
Drake, Bruce	1972	Rupp, Adolph	1968
Gaines, Clarence (Bighouse)	1981	Sachs, Leonard	1961
Gardner, Jack	1983	Shelton, Everett	1979
Gill, Amory (Slats)	1967	Smith, Dean	1982
Gomelsky, Aleksandr	1995	Summitt, Pat	2000
Hannum, Alex	1998	Taylor, Fred	1985
Harshman, Marv	1984	Thompson, John	1999
Haskins, Don	1997	Wade, Margaret	1984
Hickey, Eddie	1978	Watts, Stan	1985
Hobson, Howard (Hobby)	1965	Wilkens, Lenny	1998
Holzman, Red	1986	Wooden, John	1972
Iba, Hank	1968	Wooten, Morgan	2000
Julian, Alvin (Doggie)	1967	Woolpert, Phil	1992
Keaney, Frank	1960		

Contributors	Year Inducted	Contributors	Year Inducted
Abbott, Senda Berenson	1984	Duer, Al	1981
Bee, Clair	1967	Embry, Wayne	1999
Biasone, Danny	2000	Fagen, Clifford B.	1983
Brown, Walter A.	1965	Fisher, Harry	1973
Bunn, John	1964	Fleisher, Larry	1991
Douglas, Bob	1971	Gottlieb, Eddie	1971

329

Contributors	Year Inducted	Contributors	Year Inducted
Gulick, Luther	1959	Olsen, Harold G	1959
Harrison, Les	1979	Podoloff, Maurice	1973
Hepp, Ferenc	1980	Porter, Henry (HV)	1960
Hickox, Ed	1959	Reid, William A.	1963
Hinkle, Tony	1965	Ripley, Elmer	1972
Irish, Ned	1964	St. John, Lynn W.	1962
Jones, R. William	1964	Saperstein, Abe	1970
Kennedy, Walter	1980	Schabinger, Arthur	1961
Liston, Emil (Liz)	1974	Stagg, Amos Alonzo	1959
McLendon, John	1978	Stankovic, Boris	1991
Mokray, Bill	1965	Steitz, Ed	1983
Morgan, Ralph	1959	Taylor, Chuck	1968
Morgenweck, Frank (Pop)	1962	Teague, Bertha	1984
Naismith, James	1959	Tower, Oswald	1959
Newell, Pete	1978	Trester, Arthur (Al)	1961
Newton, Charles	2000	Wells, Cliff	1971
O'Brien, John J. (Jack)	1961	Wilke, Lou	1982
O'Brien, Larry	1991	Zollner, Fred	1999

International Boxing Hall of Fame, Canastota, N.Y.

Boxers (Modern Era)	Year Inducted	Boxers (Modern Era)	Year Inducted
Ali, Muhammad	1990	Chandler, Jeff	2000
Angott, Sammy	1998	Charles, Ezzard	1990
Arguello, Alexis	1992	Conn, Billy	1990
Armstrong, Henry	1990	Elorde, Gabriel (Flash)	1993
Basilio, Carmen	1990	Foster, Bob	1990
Benitez, Wilfredo	1996	Frazier, Joe	1990
Benvenuti, Nino	1992	Fullmer, Gene	1991
Berg, Jackie (Kid)	1994	Galaxy, Khaosai	1999
Bivins, Jimmy	1999	Gavilan, Kid	1990
Brown, Joe	1996	Giardello, Joey	1993
Buchanan, Ken	2000	Gomez, Wilfredo	1995
Burley, Charley	1992	Graham, Billy	1992
Canto, Miguel	1998	Graziano, Rocky	1991
Carter, Jimmy	2000	Griffith, Emile	1990
Cerdan, Marcel	1991	Hagler, Marvelous Marvin	1993
Cervantes, Antonio	1998	Harada, Masahiko (Fighting)	1995

Boxers (Modern Era)	Year Inducted	Boxers (Modern Era)	Year Inducted
Jack, Beau	1991	Patterson, Floyd	1991
Jenkins, Lew	1999	Pedroza, Eusebio	1999
Jofre, Edre	1992	Pep, Willie	1990
Johnson, Harold	1993	Perez, Pascual	1995
LaMotta, Jake	1990	Pryor, Aaron	1996
Leonard, Sugar Ray	1997	Robinson, Sugar Ray	1990
Liston, Sonny	1991	Rodriguez, Luis	1997
Louis, Joe	1990	Saddler, Sandy	1990
Marciano, Rocky	1990	Saldivar, Vicente	1999
Maxim, Joey	1994	Sanchez, Salvador	1991
Montgomery, Bob	1995	Schmeling, Max	1992
Monzon, Carlos	1990	Spinks, Michael	1994
Moore, Archie	1990	Tiger, Dick	1991
Muhammad, Matthew Saad	1998	Torres, Jose	1997
Napoles, Jose	1990	Walcott, Jersey Joe	1990
Norton, Ken	1992	Williams, Ike	1990
Olivares, Ruben	1991	Wright, Chalky	1997
Olson, Carl	2000	Zale, Tony	1991
Oritz, Carlos	1991	Zarate, Carlos	1994
Ortiz, Manuel	1996	Zivic, Fritzie	1993

Boxers (Old-Timers)	Year Inducted	Boxers (Old-Timers)	Year Inducted
Ambers, Lou	1992	Dixon, George	1990
Attell, Abe	1990	Driscoll, Jim	1990
Baer, Max	1995	Dundee, Johnny	1991
Barry, Jimmy	2000	Fitzsimmons, Bob	1990
Britton, Jack	1990	Flowers, Theodore (Tiger)	1993
Brown, Panama Al	1992	Gans, Joe	1990
Burns, Tommy	1996	Genaro, Frankie	1998
Canzoneri, Tony	1990	Gibbons, Mike	1992
Carpentier, Georges	1991	Gibbons, Tommy	1993
Chocolate, Kid	1991	Greb, Harry	1990
Choynski, Joe	1998	Griffo, Young	1991
Corbett, James J.	1990	Herman, Pete	1997
Coulon, Johnny	1999	Jackson, Peter	1990
Darcy, Les	1993	Jeanette, Joe	1997
Delaney, Jack	1996	Jeffries, James J.	1990
Dempsey, Jack	1990	Johnson, Jack	1990
Dillon, Jack	1995	Ketchel, Stanley	1990

Boxers (Old-Timers)	Year Inducted	Boxers (Old-Timers)	Year Inducted
Kilbane, Johnny	1995	O'Brien, Philadelphia Jack	1994
LaBarba, Fidel	1996	Petrolle, Bille	2000
Langford, Sam	1990	Rosenbloom, Maxie	1993
Lavigne, George (Kid)	1998	Ross, Barney	1990
Leonard, Benny	1990	Ryan, Tommy	1991
Levinsky, Battling	2000	Sharkey, Jack	1994
Lewis, John Henry	1994	Steele, Freddie	1999
Lewis, Ted (Kid)	1992	Stribling, Young	1996
Loughran, Tommy	1991	Tendler, Lew	1999
Lynch, Benny	1998	Tunney, Gene	1990
Mandell, Sammy	1998	Villa, Pancho	1994
McAuliffe, Jack	1995	Walcott, Joe (Barbados)	1991
McCoy, Charles (Kid)	1991	Walker, Mickey	1990
McFarland, Packey	1992	Welsh, Freddie	1997
McGovern, Terry	1990	Wilde, Jimmy	1990
McLarnin, Jimmy	1991	Williams, Kid	1996
McVey, Sam	1999	Wills, Harry	1992
Miller, Freddie	1997	Wolgast, Ad	2000
Nelson, Battling	1992		

Pioneers	Year Inducted	Pioneers	Year Inducted
Belcher, Jem	1992	Mace, Jem	1990
Brain, Ben	1994	Mendoza, Daniel	1990
Broughton, Jack	1990	Molineaux, Tom	1997
Burke, James (Deaf)	1992	Morrissey, John	1996
Bribb, Tom	1991	Pearce, Henry	1993
Chambers, Arthur	2000	Richmond, Bill	1999
Donovan, Prof. Mike	1998	Sam, Dutch	1997
Duffy, Paddy	1994	Sayers, Tom	1990
Figg, James	1992	Spring, Tom	1992
Jackson, Gentleman John	1992	Sullivan, John L.	1990
Johnson, Tom	1995	Thompson, William	1991
King, Tom	1992	Ward, Jem	1995
Langham, Nat	1992		

Non-Participants	Year Inducted	Non-Participants	Year Inducted
Andrews, Thomas S.	1992	Ballarati, Giuseppe	1999
Arcel, Ray	1991	Blackburn, Jack	1992
Arum, Bob	1999	Brady, William A.	1998

Non-Participants	Year Inducted	Non-Participants	Year Inducted
Brenner, Teddy	1993	Johnston, Jimmy	1999
Chambers, John Graham	1990	Kearns, Jack (Doc)	1990
Clancy, Gil	1993	King, Don	1997
Coffroth, James W.	1991	Lectoure, Tito	2000
D'Amato Cus	1995	Liebling, A.J.	1992
Dickson, Jeff	2000	Lonsdale, Lord	1990
Donovan, Arthur	1993	Markson, Harry	1992
Duff, Mickey	1999	Mercante, Arthur	1995
Dundee, Angelo	1992	Morgan, Dan	2000
Dundee, Chris	1994	Muldoon, William	1996
Dunphy, Don	1998	Odd, Gilbert	1995
Duva, Lou	1998	O'Rourke, Tom	1999
Egan, Pierce	1991	Parker, Dan	1996
Fleischer, Nat	1990	Parnassus, George	1991
Fox, Richard K.	1997	Queensberry, Marquis of	1990
Futch, Eddie	1994	Rickard, Tex	1990
Goldman, Charley	1992	Rudd, Irving	1999
Goldstein, Ruby	1994	Siler, George	1995
Goodman, Murray	1999	Solomons, Jack	1995
Humphreys, Joe	1997	Steward, Emanuel	1996
Jacobs, Jimmy	1993	Taub, Herman	1998
Jacobs, Mike	1990	Walker, James J. (Jimmy)	1992

Pro Football Hall of Fame, Canton, Ohio

Quarterbacks	Year Inducted	Quarterbacks	Year Inducted
Baugh, Sammy	1963	Jurgensen, Sonny	1983
Blanda, George (also PK)	1981	Luckman, Sid	1965
Bradshaw, Terry	1989	Montana, Joe	2000
Clark, Dutch	1963	Namath, Joe	1985
Conzelman, Jimmy	1964	Parker, Clarence (Ace)	1972
Dawson, Len	1987	Starr, Bart	1977
Driscoll, Paddy	1965	Staubach, Roger	1985
Fouts, Dan	1993	Tarkenton, Fran	1986
Graham, Otto	1965	Tittle, Y.A.	1971
Griese, Bob	1990	Unitas, Johnny	1979
Herber, Arnie	1966	Van Brocklin, Norm	1971
Layne, Bobby	1967	Waterfield, Bob	1965

Running Backs	Year Inducted	Running Backs	Year Inducted
Battles, Cliff	1968	McAfee, George	1966
Brown, Jim	1971	McElhenny, Hugh	1970
Campbell, Earl	1991	McNally, Johnny (Blood)	1963
Canadeo, Tony	1974	Moore, Lenny	1975
Csonka, Larry	1987	Motley, Marion	1968
Dickerson, Eric	1999	Nagurski, Bronko	1963
Dorsett, Tony	1994	Nevers, Ernie	1963
Dudley, Bill	1966	Payton, Walter	1993
Gifford, Frank	1977	Perry, Joe	1969
Grange, Red	1963	Riggins, John	1992
Guyon, Joe	1966	Sayers, Gale	1977
Harris, Franco	1990	Simpson, O.J.	1985
Hinkle, Clarke	1964	Strong, Ken	1967
Hornung, Paul	1986	Taylor, Jim	1976
Johnson, John Henry	1987	Thorpe, Jim	1963
Kelly, Leroy	1994	Trippi, Charley	1968
Leemans, Tuffy	1978	Van Buren, Steve	1965
Matson, Ollie	1972	Walker, Doak	1986

Ends and Wide Receivers	Year Inducted	Ends and Wide Receivers	Year Inducted
Alworth, Lance	1978	Mackey, John	1992
Badgro, Red	1981	Maynard, Don	1987
Berry, Raymond	1973	McDonald, Tommy	1998
Biletnikoff, Fred	1988	Millner, Wayne	1968
Chamberlin, Guy	1965	Mitchell, Bobby	1983
Ditka, Mike	1988	Newsome, Ozzie	1999
Fears, Tom	1970	Pihos, Pete	1970
Hewitt, Bill	1971	Smith, Jackie	1994
Hirsch, Elroy (Crazylegs)	1968	Swann, Lynn	2001
Hutson, Don	1963	Taylor, Charley	1984
Joiner, Charlie	1996	Warfield, Paul	1983
Largent, Steve	1995	Winslow, Kellen	1996
Lavelli, Dante	1975		

Linemen (pre–World War II)	Year Inducted	Linemen (pre–World War II)	Year Inducted
Edwards, Turk (T)	1969	Hein, Mel (c)	1963
Fortmann, Dan (G)	1985	Henry, Pete (T)	1963
Healey, Ed (T)	1964	Hubbard, Cal (T)	1963

Linemen (pre–World War II)	Year Inducted	Linemen (pre–World War II)	Year Inducted
Kiesling, Walt (G)	1966	Stydahar, Joe (T)	1967
Kinard, Bruiser (T)	1971	Trafton, George (c)	1964
Lyman, Link (T)	1964	Turner, Bulldog (c)	1966
Michalske, Mike (G)	1964	Wojciechowicz, Alex (c)	1968
Musso, George (T-G)	1982		

Offensive Linemen	Year Inducted	Offensive Linemen	Year Inducted
Bednarik, Chuck (C-LB)	1967	Munchak, Mike (G)	2001
Brown, Roosevelt (T)	1975	Munoz, Anthony (T)	1998
Dierdorf, Dan (T)	1996	Otto, Jim (c)	1980
Gatski, Frank (c)	1985	Parker, Jim (G)	1973
Gregg, Forrestt (T-G)	1977	Ringo, Jim (c)	1981
Groza, Lou (T-PK)	1974	St. Clair, Bob (T)	1990
Hannah, John (G)	1991	Shaw, Billy (G)	1999
Jones, Stan (T-G-DT)	1991	Shell, Art (T)	1989
Langer, Jim (c)	1987	Slater, Jackie	2001
Little, Larry (G)	1993	Stephenson, Dwight (c)	1998
Mack, Tom (G)	1999	Upshaw, Gene (G)	1987
McCormack, Mike (T)	1984	Webster, Mike (c)	1997

Defensive Linemen	Year Inducted	Defensive Linemen	Year Inducted
Atkins, Doug	1982	Marchetti, Gino	1972
Buchanan, Buck	1990	Nomellini, Leo	1969
Creekmur, Lou	1996	Olsen, Merlin	1982
Davis, Willie	1981	Page, Alan	1988
Donovan, Art	1968	Robustelli, Andy	1971
Ford, Len	1976	Selmon, Lee Roy	1995
Greene, Jon	1987	Stautner, Ernie	1969
Jones, Deacon	1980	Weinmeister, Arnie	1984
Jordan, Henry	1995	White, Randy	1994
Lilly, Bob	1980	Willis, Bill	1977
Long, Howie	2000	Youngblood, Jack	2001

Linebackers	Year Inducted	Linebackers	Year Inducted
Bell, Bobby	1983	George, Bill	1974
Buoniconti, Nick	2001	Ham, Jack	1988
Butkus, Dick	1979	Hendricks, Ted	1990
Connor, George (DT-OT)	1975	Huff, Sam	1982

Linebackers	Year Inducted	Linebackers	Year Inducted
Lambert, Jack	1990	Singletary, Mike	1998
Lanier, Willie	1986	Taylor, Lawrence	1999
Nitschke, Ray	1978	Wilcox, Dave	2000
Schmidt, Joe	1973		

Defensive Backs	Year Inducted	Defensive Backs	Year Inducted
Adderley, Herb	1980	Krause, Paul	1998
Barney, Lem	1992	Lane, Dick (Night Train)	1974
Blount, Mel	1989	Lary, Yale	1979
Brown, Willie	1984	Lott, Ronnie	2000
Christiansen, Jack	1970	Renfro, Mel	1996
Haynes, Mike	1997	Tunnell, Emlen	1967
Houston, Ken	1986	Wilson, Larry	1978
Johnson, Jimmy	1994	Wood, Willie	1989

Placekickers	Year Inducted
Stenerud, Jan	1991

Coaches	Year Inducted	Coaches	Year Inducted
Brown, Paul	1967	Landry, Tom	1990
Ewbank, Weeb	1978	Levy, Marv	2001
Flaherty, Ray	1976	Lombardi, Vince	1971
Gibbs, Joe	1996	Neale, Earle (Greasy)	1969
Gillman, Sid	1983	Noll, Chuck	1993
Grant, Bud	1994	Owen, Steve	1966
Halas, George	1963	Shula, Don	1997
Lambeau, Curly	1963	Walsh, Bill	1993

Contributors	Year Inducted	Contributors	Year Inducted
Bell, Bert	1963	Mara, Wellington,	1997
Bidwill, Charles	1967	Marshall, George	1963
Carr, Joe	1963	Ray, Hugh (Shorty)	1966
Davis, Al	1992	Reeves, Dan	1967
Finks, Jim	1995	Rooney, Art	1964
Halas, George	1963	Rooney, Dan	2000
Hunt, Lamar	1972	Rozelle, Pete	1985
Mara, Tim	1963	Schramm, Tex	1991

World Golf Hall of Fame, Jacksonville, Fla.

Men	Year Inducted	Men	Year Inducted
Anderson, Willie	1975	Locke, Bobby	1977
Armour, Tommy	1976	Mangrum, Lloyd	1999
Ball, John Jr.	1977	Middlecoff, Cary	1986
Ballesteros, Seve	1999	Miller, Johnny	1998
Barnes, Jim	1989	Morris, Tom Jr.	1975
Boros, Julius	1982	Morris, Tom Sr.	1976
Braid, James	1976	Nelson, Byron	1974
Burke, Jack Jr.	2000	Nicklaus, Jack	1974
Casper, Billy	1978	Norman, Greg	2001
Cooper, Lighthorse Harry	1992	Ouimet, Francis	1974
Cotton, Thomas	1980	Palmer, Arnold	1974
Demaret, Jimmy	1983	Player, Gary	1974
De Vicenzo, Roberto	1989	Runyan, Paul	1990
Evans, Chick	1975	Sarazen, Gene	1974
Faldo, Nick	1999	Smith, Horton	1990
Floyd, Ray	1989	Snead, Sam	1974
Guldahl, Ralph	1981	Stewart, Payne	2001
Hagen, Walter	1974	Taylor, John H.	1975
Hilton, Harold	1978	Thomson, Peter	1988
Hogan, Ben	1974	Travers, Jerry	1976
Irwin, Hale	1992	Travis, Walter	1979
Jones, Bobby	1974	Trevino, Lee	1981
Little, Lawson	1980	Vardon, Harry	1974
Littler, Gene	1990	Watson, Tom	1988

Women	Year Inducted	Women	Year Inducted
Alcott, Amy	1999	Lopez, Nancy	1989
Berg, Patty	1974	Mann, Carol	1977
Bradley, Pat	1991	Rankin, Judy	2000
Caponi, Donna	2001	Rawls, Betsy	1987
Carner, JoAnne	1985	Sheehan, Patty	1993
Daniel, Beth	2000	Suggs, Louise	1979
Haynie, Sandra	1977	Vare, Glenna Collett	1975
Howe, Dorothy C.H.	1978	Wethered, Joyce	1975
Inkster, Juli	2000	Whitworth, Kathy	1982
Jameson, Betty	1951	Wright, Mickey	1976
King, Betsy	1995	Zaharias, Babe Didrikson	1974

Contributors	Year Inducted	Contributors	Year Inducted
Campbell, William	1990	Jones, Robert Trent	1987
Corcoran, Fred	1975	Roberts, Clifford	1978
Crosby, Bing	1978	Rodriguez, Chi Chi	1992
Dey, Joe	1975	Ross, Donald	1977
Graffis, Herb	1977	Shore, Dinah	1994
Harlow, Robert	1988	Tufts, Richard	1992
Hope, Bob	1983		

Hockey Hall of Fame, Toronto, Ontario, Canada

Forwards	Year Inducted	Forwards	Year Inducted
Abel, Sid	1969	Cournoyer, Yvan	1982
Adams, Jack	1959	Cowley, Bill	1968
Apps, Syl	1961	Crawford, Rusty	1962
Armstrong, George	1975	Darragh, Jack	1962
Bailey, Ace	1975	Davidson, Scotty	1950
Bain, Dan	1945	Day, Hap	1961
Baker, Hobey	1945	Delvecchio, Alex	1977
Barber, Bill	1990	Denneny, Cy	1959
Barry, Marty	1965	Dionne, Marcel	1992
Bathgate, Andy	1978	Drillon, Gordie	1975
Bauer, Bobby	1996	Drinkwater, Graham	1950
Beliveau, Jean	1972	Dumart, Woody	1992
Bentley, Doug	1964	Dunderdale, Tommy	1974
Bentley, Max	1966	Dye, Babe	1970
Blake, Toe	1966	Esposito, Phil	1984
Bossy, Mike	1991	Farrell, Arthur	1965
Boucher, Frank	1958	Foyston, Frank	1958
Bowie, Dubbie	1945	Frederickson, Frank	1958
Broadbent, Punch	1962	Gainey, Bob	1992
Bucyk, John (Chief)	1981	Gardner, Jimmy	1962
Burch, Billy	1974	Gartner, Mike	2001
Clarke, Bobby	1987	Geoffrion, Bernie	1972
Colville, Neil	1967	Gerard, Eddie	1945
Conacher, Charlie	1961	Gilbert, Rod	1982
Conacher, Roy	1998	Gilmour, Billy	1962
Cook, Bill	1952	Goulet, Michel	1998
Cook, Bun	1995	Gretzky, Wayne	1999

Forwards	Year Inducted	Forwards	Year Inducted
Griffis, Si	1950	Olmstead, Bert	1985
Hawerchuk, Dale	2001	Patrick, Lynn	1980
Hay, George	1958	Perreault, Gilbert	1990
Hextall, Bryan	1969	Phillips, Tom	1945
Hooper, Tom	1962	Primeau, Joe	1963
Howe, Gordie	1972	Pulford, Bob	1991
Howe, Syd	1965	Rankin, Frank	1961
Hull, Bobby	1983	Ratelle, Jean	1985
Hyland, Harry	1962	Richard, Henri	1979
Irvin, Dick	1958	Richard, Maurice (Rocket)	1961
Jackson, Busher	1971	Richardson, George	1950
Joliat, Aurel	1947	Roberts, Gordie	1971
Keats, Duke	1958	Russel, Blair	1965
Kennedy, Ted (Teeder)	1966	Russell, Ernie	1965
Keon, Dave	1986	Ruttan, Jack	1962
Kurri, Jari	2001	Savard, Denis	2000
Lach, Elmer	1966	Scanlan, Fred	1965
Lafleur, Guy	1988	Schmidt, Milt	1961
Lalonde, Newsy	1950	Schriner, Sweeney	1962
Laprade, Edgar	1993	Seibert, Oliver	1961
Lemaire, Jacques	1984	Sittler, Darryl	1989
Lemieux, Mario	1997	Smith, Alf	1962
Lewis, Herbie	1989	Smith, Clint	1991
Lindsay, Ted	1966	Smith, Hooley	1972
MacKay, Mickey	1952	Smith, Tommy	1973
Mahovlich, Frank	1981	Stanley, Barney	1962
Malone, Joe	1950	Stastny, Peter	1998
Marshall, Jack	1965	Stewart, Nels	1962
Maxwell, Fred	1962	Stuart, Bruce	1961
McDonald, Lanny	1992	Taylor, Fred (Cyclone)	1947
McGee, Frank	1945	Trihey, Harry	1950
McGimsie, Billy	1962	Trottier, Bryan	1997
Mikita, Stan	1983	Ullman, Norm	1982
Moore, Dickie	1974	Walker, Jack	1960
Morenz, Howie	1945	Walsh, Marty	1962
Mosienko, Bill	1965	Watson, Harry	1994
Mullen, Joe	2000	Watson, Harry (Moose)	1962
Nighbor, Frank	1947	Weiland, Cooney	1971
Noble, Reg	1962	Westwick, Harry (Rat)	1962
O'Connor, Buddy	1988	Whitcroft, Fred	1962
Oliver, Harry	1967		

339

Goaltenders	Year Inducted	Goaltenders	Year Inducted
Benedict, Clint	1965	Hutton, J.B. (Bouse)	1962
Bower, Johnny	1976	Lehman, Hughie	1958
Brimsek, Frankie	1966	LeSueur, Percy	1961
Broda, Turk	1967	Lumley, Harry	1980
Cheevers, Gerry	1985	Moran, Paddy	1958
Connell, Alex	1958	Parent, Bernie	1984
Dryden, Ken	1983	Plante, Jacques	1978
Durnan, Bill	1964	Rayner, Chuck	1973
Esposito, Tony	1988	Sawchuk, Terry	1971
Gardiner, Chuck	1945	Smith, Billy	1993
Giacomin, Eddie	1987	Thompson, Tiny	1959
Hainsworth, George	1961	Tretiak, Vladislav	1989
Hall, Glenn	1975	Vezina, Georges	1945
Hern, Riley	1962	Worsley, Gump	1980
Holmes, Hap	1972	Worters, Roy	1969

Defensemen	Year Inducted	Defensemen	Year Inducted
Boivin, Leo	1986	Horton, Tim	1977
Boon, Dickie	1952	Howell, Harry	1979
Bouchard, Butch	1966	Johnson, Ching	1958
Boucher, George	1960	Johnson, Ernie	1952
Cameron, Harry	1962	Johnson, Tom	1970
Clancy, King	1958	Kelly, Red	1969
Clapper, Dit	1947	Laperriere, Jacques	1987
Cleghorn, Sprague	1958	Lapointe, Guy	1993
Conacher, Lionel	1994	Laviolette, Jack	1962
Coulter, Art	1974	Mantha, Sylvio	1960
Dutton, Red	1958	McNamara, George	1958
Fetisov, Viacheslav	2001	Orr, Bobby	1979
Flaman, Fernie	1990	Park, Brad	1988
Gadsby, Bill	1970	Patrick, Lester	1947
Gardiner, Herb	1958	Pilote, Pierre	1975
Goheen, F.X. (Moose)	1952	Pitre, Didier	1962
Goodfellow, Ebbie	1963	Potvin, Denis	1991
Grant, Mike	1950	Pratt, Babe	1966
Green, Wilf (Shorty)	1962	Pronovost, Marcel	1978
Hall, Joe	1961	Pulford, Harvey	1945
Harvey, Doug	1973	Quackenbush, Bill	1976
Horner, Red	1965	Reardon, Kenny	1966

Defensemen	Year Inducted	Defensemen	Year Inducted
Robinson, Larry	1995	Simpson, Joe	1962
Ross, Art	1945	Stanley, Allan	1981
Salming, Borje	1996	Stewart, Jack	1964
Savard, Serge	1986	Stuart, Hod	1945
Seibert, Earl	1963	Wilson, Gordon (Phat)	1962
Shore, Eddie	1947		

Referees and Linesmen	Year Inducted	Referees and Linesmen	Year Inducted
Armstrong, Neil	1991	Ion, Mickey	1961
Ashley, John	1981	Pavelich, Matt	1987
Chadwick, Bill	1964	Rodden, Mike	1962
D'Amico, John	1993	Smeaton, J. Cooper	1961
Elliott, Chaucer	1961	Storey, Red	1967
Hayes, George	1988	Udvari, Frank	1973
Hewitson, Bobby	1963	van Hellemond, Andy	1999

Builders	Year Inducted	Builders	Year Inducted
Adams, Charles	1960	Dudley, George	1958
Adams, Weston W. Sr.	1972	Dunn, James	1968
Ahearn, Frank	1962	Francis, Emile	1982
Ahearne, J.F. (Bunny)	1977	Gibson, Jack	1976
Allan, Sir Montagu	1945	Gorman, Tommy	1963
Allen, Keith	1992	Griffiths, Frank A.	1993
Arbour, Al	1996	Hanley, Bill	1986
Ballard, Harold	1977	Hay, Charles	1984
Bauer, Fr. David	1989	Hendy, Jim	1968
Bickell, J.P.	1978	Hewitt, Foster	1965
Bowman, Scotty	1991	Hewitt, W.A.	1945
Brown, George	1961	Hume, Fred	1962
Brown, Walter	1962	Imlach, Punch	1984
Buckland, Frank	1975	Ivan, Tommy	1964
Butterfield, Jack	1980	Jennings, Bill	1975
Calder, Frank	1945	Johnson, Bob	1992
Campbell, Angus	1964	Juckes, Gordon	1979
Campbell, Clarence	1966	Kilpatrick, John	1960
Cattarinich, Joseph	1977	Knox, Seymour III	1993
Dandurand, Leo	1963	Leader, Al	1969
Dilio, Frank	1964	LeBel, Bob	1970

341

Builders	Year Inducted	Builders	Year Inducted
Lockhart, Tom	1965	Raymond, Donat	1958
Loicq, Paul	1961	Robertson, John Ross	1945
Mariucci, John	1985	Robinson, Claude	1945
Mathers, Frank	1992	Ross, Philip	1976
McLaughlin, Frederic	1963	Sather, Glen	1997
Milford, Jake	1984	Sebetzki, Gunther	1995
Molson, Hartland	1973	Selke, Frank	1960
Morrison, Ian (Scotty)	1999	Sinden, Harry	1983
Murray, Athol (Pere)	1998	Smith, Frank	1962
Nelson, Francis	1945	Smythe, Conn	1958
Norris, Bruce	1969	Snider, Ed	1988
Norris, James D.	1962	Stanley, Lord of Preston	1945
Norris, James Sr.	1958	Sutherland, James	1945
Northey, William	1945	Tarasov, Anatoli	1974
O'Brien, J.A.	1962	Torrey, Bill	1995
O'Neill, Brian	1994	Turner, Lloyd	1958
Page, Fred	1993	Tutt, William Thayer	1978
Patrick, Frank	1958	Voss, Carl	1974
Pickard, Allan	1958	Waghorne, Fred	1961
Pilous, Rudy	1985	Wirtz, Arthur	1971
Poile, Bud	1990	Wirtz, Bill	1976
Pollock, Sam	1978	Ziegler, John	1987

International Motorsports Hall of Fame, Talladega, Ala.

Drivers	Year Inducted	Drivers	Year Inducted
Allison, Bobby	1993	Clark, Jim	1990
Allison, Davey	1998	DePalma, Ralph	1991
Andretti, Mario	2000	Donahue, Mark	1990
Ascari, Alberto	1992	Evans, Richie	1996
Baker, Buck	1990	Fangio, Juan Manuel	1990
Bettenhausen, Tony	1991	Foyt, A.J.	2000
Bonnett, Neil	2001	Flock, Tim	1991
Brabham, Jack	1990	Gregg, Peter	1992
Campbell, Sir Malcolm	1990	Gurney, Dan	1990
Caracciola, Rudolph	1998	Haley, Donald	1996

Drivers	Year Inducted	Drivers	Year Inducted
Hill, Graham	1990	Piquet, Nelson	2000
Hill, Phil	1991	Prost, Alain	1999
Holbert, Al	1993	Prudhomme, Don	2000
Isaac, Bobby	1996	Roberts, Fireball	1990
Jarrett, Ned	1991	Roberts, Kenny	1992
Johncock, Gordon	1999	Rose, Mauri	1994
Johnson, Junior	1990	Rutherford, Johnny	1996
Jones, Parnelli	1990	Scott, Wendell	1999
Lauda, Niki	1993	Senna, Ayrton	2000
Lorenzen, Fred	1991	Shaw, Wilbur	1991
Lund, Tiny	1994	Smith, Louise	1999
Mays, Rex	1993	Stewart, Jackie	1990
McLaren, Bruce	1991	Surtees, John	1996
Meyer, Louis	1992	Thomas, Herb	1994
Moss, Stirling	1990	Turner, Curtis	1992
Nuvolari, Tazio	1998	Unser, Al Sr.	1998
Oldfield, Barney	1990	Vukovich, Bill	1991
Parsons, Benny	1994	Ward, Rodger	1992
Pearson, David	1993	Weatherly, Joe	1994
Petty, Lee	1990	Yarborough, Cale	1993

Contributors	Year Inducted	Contributors	Year Inducted
Bignotti, George	1993	Marcum, John	1994
Breedlove, Craig	2000	Matthews, Banjo	1998
Champman, Colin	1994	Moody, Ralph	1994
Chevrolet, Louis	1992	Parks, Wally	1992
Ferrari, Enzo	1994	Penske, Roger	1998
Ford, Henry	1993	Porsche, Ferdinand	1996
France, Bill Sr.	1990	Rickenbacker, Eddie	1992
Granatelli, Andy	1992	Shelby, Carroll	1991
Hulman, Tony	1990	Thompson, Mickey	1990
Hyde, Harry	1999	Yunick, Smokey	1990

International Tennis Hall of Fame, Newport, R.I.

Men	Year Inducted	Men	Year Inducted
Adee, George	1964	Hoad, Lew	1980
Alexander, Fred	1961	Hovey, Fred	1974
Allison, Wilmer	1963	Hunt, Joe	1966
Alonso, Manuel	1977	Hunter, Frank	1961
Anderson, Mal	2000	Johnston, Bill	1958
Ashe, Arthur	1985	Jones, Perry	1970
Behr, Karl	1969	Kelleher, Robert	2000
Borg, Bjorn	1987	Kodes, Jan	1990
Borotra, Jean	1976	Kramer, Jack	1968
Bromwich, John	1984	Lacoste, Rene	1976
Brookes, Norman	1977	Larned, William	1956
Brugnon, Jacques	1976	Larsen, Art	1969
Budge, Don	1964	Laver, Rod	1981
Campbell, Oliver	1955	Lendl, Ivan	2001
Chace, Malcolm	1961	Lott, George	1964
Clark, Clarence	1983	Mako, Gene	1973
Clark, Joseph	1955	McEnroe, John	1999
Clothier, William	1956	McGregor, Ken	1999
Cochet, Henri	1976	McKinley, Chuck	1986
Connors, Jimmy	1998	McLoughlin, Maurice	1957
Cooper, Ashley	1991	McMillan, Frew	1992
Crawford, Jack	1979	McNeill, Don	1965
David, Herman	1998	Mulloy, Gardnar	1972
Doeg, John	1962	Murray, Lindley	1958
Doherty, Lawrence	1980	Myrick, Julian	1963
Doherty, Reginald	1980	Nastase, Ilie	1991
Drobny, Jaroslav	1983	Newcombe, John	1986
Dwight, James	1955	Nielsen, Arthur	1971
Emerson, Roy	1982	Olmedo, Alex	1987
Etchebaster, Pierre	1978	Osuna, Rafael	1979
Falkenburg, Bob	1974	Parker, Frank	1966
Fraser, Neale	1984	Patterson, Gerald	1989
Garland, Chuck	1969	Patty, Budge	1977
Gonzales, Pancho	1968	Perry, Fred	1975
Grant, Bryan (Bitsy)	1972	Pettitt, Tom	1982
Griffin, Clarence	1970	Pietrangeli, Nicola	1986
Hackett, Harold	1961	Quist, Adrian	1984
Hewitt, Bob	1992	Ralston, Dennis	1987

Men	Year Inducted	Men	Year Inducted
Renshaw, Ernest	1983	Stolle, Fred	1985
Renshaw, William	1983	Talbert, Bill	1967
Richards, Vincent	1961	Tilden, Bill	1959
Riggs, Bobby	1967	Trabert, Tony	1970
Roche, Tony	1986	Van Ryn, John	1963
Rose, Murray	2000	Vilas, Guillermo	1991
Rosewall, Ken	1980	Vines, Ellsworth	1962
Santana, Manuel	1984	von Cramm, Gottfried	1977
Savitt, Dick	1976	Ward, Holcombe	1956
Schroeder, Ted	1966	Washburn, Watson	1965
Sears, Richard	1955	Whitman, Malcolm	1955
Sedgman, Frank	1979	Wilding, Anthony	1978
Segura, Pancho	1984	Williams, Richard 2nd	1957
Seixas, Vic	1971	Wood, Sidney	1964
Shields, Frank	1964	Wrenn, Robert	1955
Slocum, Henry	1955	Wright, Beals	1956
Smith, Stan	1987		

Women	Year Inducted	Women	Year Inducted
Atkinson, Juliette	1974	Hard, Darlene	1973
Austin, Bunny	1997	Hart, Doris	1969
Austin, Tracy	1992	Haydon Jones, Ann	1985
Barger-Wallach, Maud	1958	Heldman, Gladys	1979
Betz Addie, Pauline	1965	Hotchkiss Wightman, Hazel	1957
Bjurstedt Mallory, Molla	1958	Jacobs, Helen Hull	1962
Bowrey, Lesley Turner	1997	King, Billie Jean	1987
Brough Clapp, Louise	1967	Lenglen, Suzanne	1978
Browne, Mary	1957	Mandlikova, Hana	1994
Bueno, Mario	1978	Marble, Alice	1964
Cahill, Mabel	1976	McKane Godfree, Kitty	1978
Casals, Rosie	1996	Moore, Elisabeth	1971
Connolly Brinker, Maureen	1968	Mortimer Barrett, Angela	1993
Dod, Charlotte (Lottie)	1983	Navratilova, Martina	2000
Douglass Chambers, Dorothy	1981	Nuthall Shoemaker, Betty	1977
Evert, Chris	1995	Osborne duPont, Margaret	1967
Fry Irvin, Shirley	1970	Palfrey Danzig, Sarah	1963
Gibson, Althea	1971	Roosevelt, Ellen	1975
Goolagong Cawley, Evonne	1988	Round Little, Dorothy	1986
Hansell, Ellen	1965	Ryan, Elizabeth	1972

345

Women	Year Inducted	Women	Year Inducted
Sears, Eleanora	1968	Wade, Virginia	1989
Smith Court, Margaret	1979	Wagner, Marie	1969
Sutton Bundy, May	1956	Wills Moody Roark, Helen	1959
Townsend Toulmin, Bertha	1974		

Contributors	Year Inducted	Contributors	Year Inducted
Baker, Lawrence Sr.	1975	Laney, Al	1979
Chatrier, Philippe	1992	Martin, Alastair	1973
Collins, Bud	1994	Martin, William M.	1982
Cullman, Joseph F. 3rd	1990	Maskell, Dan	1996
Danzig, Allison	1968	Outerbridge, Mary	1981
Davis, Dwight	1956	Pell, Theodore	1966
Gray, David	1985	Tingay, Lance	1982
Gustaf, V (King of Sweden)	1980	Tinling, Ted	1986
Hester, W.E. (Slew)	1981	Van Alen, James	1965
Hopman, Harry	1978	Wingfield, Walter Clopton	1997
Hunt, Lamar	1993		

Additional Resources

General

Best of a Century. www.members.tripod.com.

Brown, Gerry and Michael Morrison eds. *The 2001 ESPN Information Please Sports Almanac.* (New York: Hyperion Books, 2000).

CBS Sportsline. www.cbssportsline.com.

CNN/SI, *Sports Illustrated for Women.* www.sportsillustrated.cnn.com.

First Base Sports. www.firstbasesports.com.

Hickok, Ralph. *A Who's Who of Sports Champions: Their Stories & Records.* (Boston: Houghton Mifflin Co., 1995).

International Amateur Athletic Association. www.iaaf.org.

Johnson, Anne Janette. *Great Women in Sports.* (Detroit: Visible Ink Press, 1996).

Latino Legends in Sports. www.latinosportslegends.com.

MacCambridge, Michael, ed. *ESPN SportsCentury.* (New York: Hyperion, 1999).

Meserle, Mike. *Sports Illustrated's 20th Century Sports: Images of Greatness.* (Kingston, N.Y.: Total/Sports Illustrated, 1999).

Murray, Tom ed. *Sport Magazine: All-Time All-Stars.* New York: Athenium Press, 1977.

Sports Illustrated 2001 Sports Almanac. (New York: Time, Inc., 2000).

Sugar, Bert Randolph. *The 100 Greatest Athletes of All Time: A Sports Editor's Personal Ranking.* (New York: Citadel Press, 1995).

Auto Racing

CART. www.cart.com.

Championship Auto Racing Teams, Inc. *FedEx Championship Series Media Guide 2001.* (Troy, Mich.: Championship Auto Racing Teams, Inc., 2001).

Grand Prix Hall of Fame. www.ddavid.com.

Hunter, Don and Al Pearce. *The Illustrated History of Stock Car Racing.* (Osceola, Wis.: MBI Publishing Co., Osceola, 1998).

International Motorsports Hall of Fame. www.motorsportshalloffame.com.

Motorsports Hall of Fame. www.mshf.com.

NASCAR Winston Cup Series Media Guide 2001. (Winston-Salem, N.C.: Sports Marketing Enterprises, 2001).

The Official NASCAR Preview and Press Guide 2001. (Charlotte, N.C.: UMI Publications, Inc., 2001).

NHRA. nhra.com.

NHRA Winston Drag Racing 2001 Media Guide. (Winston-Salem, N.C.: Sports Marketing Enterprises, 2001).

Schwartz, Larry. "Mario Andretti synonymous with racing." www.espn.com/sportscentury.

Shirley Muldowney. www.shirleymuldowney.com.

Baseball

Baseball Online Library. www.sportsline.com.

Berra, Yogi. *The Yogi Book.* (New York: Workman Publishing, 1998.

Bucek, Jeanine et al., ed. *The Baseball Encyclopedia: Tenth Edition.* (New York: McMillan, 1996.)

Major League Baseball. www.majorleaguebaseball.com.

National Baseball Hall of Fame. www.baseballhalloffame.org.

Schell, Michael J. *Baseball's All-Time Best Hitters.* (Princeton, N.J.: Princeton University Press, 1999).

Shouler, Ken. *The Real 100 Best Baseball Players of All Time.* (Lenexa, Kan.: Addax Publishing Group, 1998).

The Sporting News Baseball Register, 2001 edition. (St. Louis: The Sporting News, 2001).

Smith, Ron. *The Sporting News Selects Baseball's Greatest Players.* (St. Louis: The Sporting News, 1998).

The Sporting News Baseball. www.thesportingnews.com.

The Sporting News Baseball Register, 2001 edition. (St. Louis: The Sporting News, 2001).

Total Baseball. www.totalbaseball.com.

Vecsey, George. *McGuire and Sosa: Baseball's Greatest Home Run Story.* (London: Carlton Books, 1998).

Basketball

Bjarkman, Peter C. *The Biographical History of Basketball,* (Lincolnwood, Ill.: Masters Press, 1998).

National Basketball Association. www.nba.com.

Schare, Alex. *The Naismith Memorial Basketball Hall of Fame's 100 Greatest Basketball Players of All Time.* (New York: Pocket Books, 1997).

The Sporting News Official NBA Guide, 2000-2001 edition. (St. Louis: The Sporting News, 2000).

The Sporting News Official NBA Register, 2000-2001 edition. (St. Louis: The Sporting News, 2000).

USA Basketball. www.usabasketball.com.

WNBA. www.wnba.com.

Boxing

The Cyber Boxing Zone. cyberboxingzone.com.

Delacourt, Christian. *Boxing.* (New York: Universe Publishing, 1997).

Evander Holyfield. ipcress.com.

HBO Boxing: Greats. hbo.com/boxing.

International Boxing Hall of Fame. www.ibhof.com.

Roberts, James B., and Alexander G. Skutt. *The Boxing Register: International Boxing Hall of Fame Official Record Book.* (Ithaca, N.Y.: McBooks Press 1999).

Cycling

Cycling News. www.cyclingnews.com.

Lance Armstrong On-line! www.lancearmstrong.com.

The Legendary Greg Lemond. gl.nidus.net.

Figure Skating

The U.S. Figure Skating Association. *The Official Book of Figure Skating,* New York: Simon & Schuster, 1998.

Football

NFL Players Inc. www.sportsline.com.

Pro Football Hall of Fame. www.profootballhof.com.

Schwartz, Larry. "Galloping Ghost scared opponents." www.espn.com/sportscentury.

Smith, Ron. *The Sporting News Selects Football's 100 Greatest Players: A Celebration of the 20th Century's Best.* (St. Louis: The Sporting News, 1999).

Golf

Barkow, Al, and David Barrett. *"Golf Greats: 100 Legends of the Game."* (Lincolnwood, Ill.: Publications International, Ltd., 1998).

Golf Europe. www.golfeurope.com.

Golf Online. www.golfonline.com.

Golfer Profiles. www.library.thinkquest.org.

Jack Nicklaus: Facts and Figures. (North Palm Beach, Fla.: Golden Bear International, Inc., 1998).

LPGA Tour Media Guide 2001. (Daytona Beach, Fla.: LPGA Tour, 2001).

The Official Tiger Woods Web site. www.sportsline.com.

PGA European Tour. www.europetour.com.

PGA Tour. www.pgatour.com.

PGA Tour Media Guide 2001. (Ponte Vedra, Fla.: PGA Tour Creative Services, 2001.)

Senior PGA Tour Media Guide 2001. (Ponte Vedra, Fla.: PGA Tour Creative Services, 2001).

U.S. Golf Association 2001 Championships Media Guide. (Far Hills, N.J.: The United States Golf Association, 2001.)

Gymnastics

USA Gymnastics. www.usa-gymnastics.org.

Hockey

National Hockey League. www.nhl.com.

Olympics Competition

Leder, Jane. *Grace & Glory: A Century of Women in the Olympics*. (Chicago: Triumph Books, 1996).

USA Track and Field. www.usatf.org.

United States Olympic Committee. www.usoc.org.

Wallechinsky, David. *Sports Illustrated Presents The Complete Book of the Summer Olympics*. (Boston: Little, Brown and Company, 1996).

Winter Olympics—CBS Sportsline. www.poll.sportsline.com.

Soccer

Radnedge, Keir. *The World Encyclopedia of Soccer: The Definitive Illustrated History*. (SevenOaks, 2000).

SoccerTimes.com. www.soccertimes.com.

Women's Soccer World Online. www.womensoccer.com.

Tennis

Association of Tennis Professionals. www.atptour.com.

Ashe Jr., Arthur R. *Hard Road to Glory*. (New York: Amistad Press, 1993).

Collins, Bud and Zander Hollander eds. *Bud Collins' Tennis Encyclopedia, third edition*. (Detroit: Visible Ink Press, 1997).

International Tennis Hall of Fame. www.tennisfame.com.

Johnson, Salvatore. *The Official U.S. Open Almanac*. (Dallas: Taylor Publishing Co., 1995).

Thoroughbred Racing

Jockeys Guild Online. www.jockeyguild.com.

National Thoroughbred Racing Association. www.ntra.com.

Index

S

Y–Z